I0834179

THE

Librarian's Manual;

A

Treatiſe on Bibliography,

COMPRISING A

SELECT AND DESCRIPTIVE LIST

OF

BIBLIOGRAPHICAL WORKS;

TO WHICH ARE ADDED,

Sketches of Publick Libraries.

Illuſtrated with Engravings.

By REUBEN A. GUILD, A. M.

Librarian of Brown Univerſity, Providence, R. I.

"Non minima Pars eſt Eruditionis bonos nôſſe Libros."

NEW YORK:

CHARLES B. NORTON,

AGENT FOR LIBRARIES.

MDCCCLVIII.

Edition, 500. 10 Copies on large Paper.

TO

PROFESSOR CHARLES C. JEWETT,

THE

Accomplished Bibliographer and Scholar,

THIS WORK

IS RESPECTFULLY DEDICATED,

AS A

TOKEN OF LONG CONTINUED FRIENDSHIP,

AND

IN GRATEFUL ACKNOWLEDGMENT OF VALUED

ACADEMICK AND PROFESSIONAL INSTRUCTION.

"If you are troubled with a Pride of Accuracy, and would have it completely taken out of you, print a Catalogue."—*Stevens.*

PREFACE.

THE following Work has been undertaken with a View, aſide from perſonal Conſiderations, to the Improvement of our publick Libraries.

The First Part conſiſts of a deſcriptive Liſt of four hundred and ninety-five ſeparate Works, compriſing nineteen hundred and ſixteen Volumes of ſuch bibliographical Books as are conſidered to be of the firſt Importance for a *Library Apparatus*. The Liſt could eaſily have been extended, had it been thought deſirable to make it general and complete, rather than ſelect, including ſuch only as are regarded as indiſpenſable to the Knowledge of Books, and to the efficient Growth and Management of a publick Library.

The Second Part contains hiſtorical Sketches of fourteen of the largeſt Publick Libraries in this Country and in Europe. Eſpecial Attention has been given to the Character and general Arrangements of the Libraries defcribed, and to detailed Accounts of the Buildings appropriated to their Ufe. The largeft Space has been given to the Britifh Mufeum, the Library of which is generally acknowledged to be the beft managed one of its Kind in the World. Appended to this Account is an Article compiled from the *North Britifh Review*, giving Details refpecting the daily Adminiftration of this noble Collection, from which valuable Suggeftions may be derived for the Management of fmaller Libraries, whether publick or private.

The fpecial Acknowledgments of the Author are hereby made to Mr. John H. Hickcox, Affiftant Librarian of the New York State Library at Albany, for his generous Affiftance in revifing and enlarging the Author's Account of faid Library; grateful Acknowledgments are alfo made to the following Gentlemen, for recent Information in regard to other Libraries, viz: John L. Sibley, A. M. of Cambridge, Mafs.; Wm. F. Poole, A. M. of Bofton; Prof. Charles C. Jewett, of Roxbury; Prof. George P. Fifher, of New Haven; Jofeph G. Cogfwell, LL. D. of New York; Lloyd P. Smith, Efq. of Philadelphia; and Prof. Wm. E. Jillfon, of Wafhington.

The Work has many Errours both of Omiſſion and Commiſſion; theſe, however, a Work of this Character muſt always have to a greater or leſs Extent. Conſtituting as it does a Manual of Information, or rather the SOURCES of Information upon the moſt important Points connected with the Increaſe and Management of Libraries, and with Books in general, it is hereby ſubmitted to the Publick, with the confident Hope that it may prove acceptable and uſeful.

Brown Univerſity, May 4, 1858.

LIST OF ENGRAVINGS.

LIBRARY EDIFICES.

CONTENTS.

PART FIRST.

BIBLIOGRAPHY.

PART SECOND.

LIBRARIES.

PART FIRST.

BIBLIOGRAPHY.

"In eſtimating the Importance of the Study of Bibliography, we muſt conſider how much it would promote the Progreſs of Learning, by ſhowing what has been attempted and accompliſhed, and what yet remains to be achieved; how much by rebuking the Raſhneſs which ruſhes into Authorſhip, ignorant of what others have written, adding to the Maſs of Books without adding to the Sum of Knowledge; how much, by giving Confidence to the earneſt Student, who fears no Labour, ſo that it bring him to the Height at which he aims — the Summit of Learning in the Branch to which he devotes himſelf."—*Jewett.*

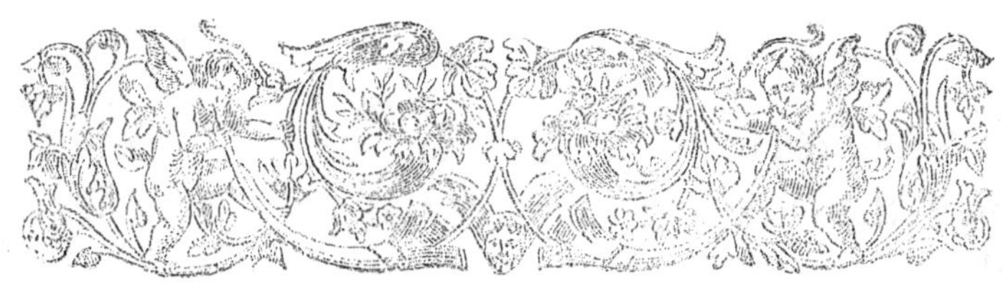

BIBLIOGRAPHY.

BIBLIOGRAPHY, from Βιβλιον, a Book, and γραφω, I deſcribe, ſignifies literally the Deſcription of Books. Among the Greeks, the Term Βιβλιογραφια ſignified only the Writing or Tranſcription of Books; and a Bibliographer with them was merely a Writer of Books, in the Senſe of a Copyiſt. The French Term *Bibliographie* was long uſed to ſignify only an Acquaintance with ancient Writings, and with the Art of deciphering them. In its modern and more extended Senſe, Bibliography may be defined to be the SCIENCE OR KNOWLEDGE OF BOOKS, in regard to the Materials of which they are compoſed, — their different Degrees of Rarity, Curioſity, reputed or real Value, — the

Subjects discussed by their respective Authours,— and the Rank which they ought to hold in the Classification of a Library. It is therefore divided into two Branches, the first of which has Reference to the *Contents* of Books, and may be termed, for Want of a better Phrase, INTELLECTUAL Bibliography; the second treats of their external Character, the History of particular Copies, Editions, &c. and may be termed MATERIAL Bibliography. The Object of the first Kind is to acquaint literary Men with the most important Books in every Department of Study, either by Means of CLASSED CATALOGUES simply, or by similar or alphabetical Catalogues, accompanied by critical and bibliographical Remarks.

This Species of Knowledge has been cultivated most thoroughly and successfully in Italy, Germany, and France, to which Countries, and especially to the latter, we are indebted for the most popular and useful Treatises in Bibliography. This is undoubtedly owing in a great Measure to the free Access which is allowed the Publick to all their large Libraries, the great Number of fine private Collections, and the Familiarity of their Scholars and literary Men with Books of all Ages and Countries. The Researches of BARBIER and BRUNET,

Ebert and Ersch, Tiraboschi and Gamba, will ever be held in grateful Remembrance by all Lovers of Learning.

In Great Britain Bibliography as a Science has received leſs Attention than upon the Continent, although valuable Works have been produced by Horne and Lowndes, Dibdin and Watt, which will compare favourably with thoſe of their European Contemporaries. In this Country the Science has been very naturally neglected. Owing however to the general Diffuſion of Knowledge and Wealth, and the rapid Formation and Increaſe of Libraries of every Deſcription, it is now receiving increaſed Attention; and the Importance of its Claims as a *practical* Science are ſucceſsfully urged upon the Publick by our leading literary and educational Men. Already we have Bibliographers, ſuch as Cogswell, and Ticknor, and Jewett, whoſe profeſſional Attainments are known and appreciated even in the older Countries.

It is the Fault of many of the Votaries of this Science, eſpecially in France, that they have exaggerated the Value of their favourite Purſuit, far beyond that Rank to which it is fairly entitled in the Scale of human Knowledge; and Peignot, Achard, and others (whoſe Writings are noticed in the Courſe of this Treatiſe) have repreſented it as one of the moſt extenſive, and even univerſal of all Sciences. Nothing certainly can be more abſurd than to view it in this Light, merely becauſe it treats of Books, and becauſe Books are the Vehicles of all Sorts of Knowledge. Yet this is the only Foundation to be diſcovered for theſe extravagant Repreſentations, that tend, as in all other Caſes of exaggerated Pretenſion, to bring Ridicule upon a Subject, which, were its Nature and Objects correctly defined, could not fail to appear highly important and uſeful.

Conformably to what has now been ſtated, it is the Province of the Bibliographer to be acquainted with the Materials of which Books are compoſed, their different Forms or Sizes, the Number of Pages, the typographical Character, the Number and Deſcription of the Plates, the Completeneſs, the Correctneſs, and all the other external Peculiarities or Diſtinctions of an Edition. He knows not only the beſt Treatiſes that have been written on any particular Topick, and their comparative Value, but alſo the various Editions of Books, and the important Reſpects in which one Edition differs from another; when and from what Cauſe Omiſſions have been made, Deficiencies ſupplied, Errours corrected, and Additions ſubjoined. When Books have been publiſhed either anonymouſly or pſeudonymouſly, he indicates the real Name of the concealed Authour; and, with regard to the Rarity of Books, he is acquainted with all the Cauſes which have contributed to render them ſcarce. Finally, as a Library deſtitute of Arrangement is a "Chaos, and not a Coſmos," he diſpoſes the Books which it compriſes, in ſuch an Order, as will preſent an agreeable Appearance to the Eye; and, in compiling a Catalogue, he aſſigns to them that Place which they ought to hold in the Syſtem of Claſſification adopted for arranging a Library.

Such are the legitimate Duties of the Bibliographer, evidently requiring a Variety and Extent of Knowledge, ſeldom if ever poſſeſſed by a ſingle Individual. Hence different Writers have diſcuſſed particular Topicks of Bibliography; and from their united Labours can be collected the multifarious Information requiſite to conſtitute ſuch a Bibliographer as has been deſcribed. A Collection of all the Works of this Kind extant, including General and Special Bibliography, Literary Hiſtory, and a certain Claſs of Periodicals and Univerſal Biography, would, it has been eſtimated, exceed twenty thouſand Volumes. Indeed NAMUR in his

Bibliographie, publiſhed in 1838, gives a Liſt of upwards of ten thouſand *ſeparate Works.* We propoſe in the further Progreſs of this Treatiſe, to give a SELECT LIST of the beſt Sources of Information, ſo far as we are acquainted, upon the moſt important Branches of Bibliography, arranging them in alphabetical Order under their appropriate Heads, and adding ſuch Deſcriptions and explanatory Remarks, as may ſeem beſt calculated to render the whole a uſeful Manual or Guide for Inquirers in this Department of Knowledge.

DESCRIPTIVE LIST.

I. Books containing Lifts of Bibliographical Works.

COGSWELL (J. G.). Alphabetical Index to the Aftor Library, or Catalogue, with fhort Titles, of the Books now collected and of the propofed Acceffions, as fubmitted to the Truftees of the Library for their Approval. Jan. 1851. 8°. New York, 1851,

Compiled by the Superintendent to ferve as a Guide in collecting Books for the Aftor Library. Prefixed is a claffed Lift of Works upon Bibliography occupying 30 Pages. The Department of Bibliography in the Aftor Library, has been founded by Dr. Cogfwell, and continued at his Expenfe. It is far more complete than any Collection of the Kind in the Country. The Lift gives fhort Titles merely, without Dates.

NAMUR (M. P.). Bibliographie Paléographico-Diplomatico-Bibliologique Générale, ou Répertoire Syftématique, &c. 2 Vols. 8°. Liége. 1838.

Giving the Titles of 10,236 feparate Works relating to Paleography or Writing, Diplomaticks or Manufcripts, the Hiftory of Printing and the Book Trade, Bibliography, the Hiftory of Libraries, Notices of Periodicals, &c. No Work extant contains ſo complete a Liſt of this Claſs of Books. The Titles however are frequently inaccurate, and the Deſcriptions are few and exceedingly meagre. The ſyſtematick and alphabetical Indexes at the End of each Volume greatly enhance the Value of the Work.

PEIGNOT (Gabriel). Répertoire Bibliographique Univerſel; contenant la Notice raiſonné des Bibliographies ſpéciales, &c. &c. 8°. Paris. 1812.

Peignot is one of the ableſt of French Bibliographers, and by his various Writings, has contributed moſt eſſentially to the Illuſtration of the Study of Bibliography. This elaborate Work, not only gives an inſtructive Account of ſpecial Bibliographies publiſhed in his Day, but alſo an Account of a great Number of other Works upon Bibliography in its various Branches, Literary Hiſtory, &c.

See alſo BOHN'S *General Catalogue*, Vol. I. 8°. Lond. 1847, pp. 409–441; HORNE'S *Introduction to the Study of Bibliography*, Vol. II. pp. 403–742; BRUNET'S *Manuel du Libraire*, Vol. V.; and PETZHOLDT'S *Anzeiger für Bibliographie und Bibliothekwiſſenſchaft*, a very important bibliographical Periodical, commenced in 1840, and publiſhed monthly at Dreſden, making annually an octavo Volume. A complete Liſt of all the bibliographical Works which have been publiſhed in any Language down to the preſent Time, with full deſcriptive Notes in Engliſh, would do much towards the more general Cultivation of the Science among us. The Preparation of ſuch a Liſt was commenced by Prof. C. C. JEWETT, while Librarian of the Smithſonian Inſtitution at Waſhington. No one is better qualified than he for an Undertaking of this Character, and it is earnestly hoped that his present multifarious and important Duties may not interfere with its ultimate and successful Accomplishment. In the Number of the *Anzeiger* for May, 1857, Dr. PETZHOLDT announces a Work which he has in Preparation, entitled *Bibliotheca Bibliographica, Bibliographisches Handbuch für Deutschland.* This is intended to be a Work like PEIGNOT'S or NAMUR'S, continued to the latest Dates, and enriched with critical and bibliographical Notes. It will undoubtedly be executed well and promptly.

II. Elementary Bibliographies.

UNDER this Head, we design to point out a few of those Works more particularly worthy of Notice, which treat generally of all Matters appertaining to Bibliography. It is a Matter of Regret that no Book presenting a well-written, judicious, and comprehensive Digest of these Matters, has been recently published. The following, however, contain much curious and useful Information.

ACHARD (C. F.). Cours Elémentaire de Bibliographie. 3 Vols. 8o. Marseille. 1806–7.

The most useful Part of this Work, is the Collection of the different Systems recommended by De Bure, Peignot, Barbier, and others, for the Classifying of Books. We learn from the Introduction, that M. FRANCIS DE NEUFCHÂTEAU, when Minister of the Interiour, ordered the Librarians of all the Departments to deliver Lectures on Bibliography; but that the Plan failed, theſe Librarians having been found incapable of prelecting upon their Vocation.

BOULARD (M. S.). Traité Elémentaire de Bibliographie. 8°. Paris. 1806.

This Work diſcuſſes the Qualifications of Bibliographers, the principal Works of which a Library ought to conſiſt, the Rarity and Depreciation of Books, the Choice of Books and Editions, the Invention of Printing, the Formation of a Library, Manuſcripts, &c. &c.

DENIS (Michael). Einleitung in die Bücherkunde. 2d Ed. 2 Vols. 4. Wien. 1795-6.

This Work, although like every other of Denis greatly eſteemed in Europe, has never been tranſlated from the German. It embodies the Subſtance of a Courſe of academical Lectures delivered by the Authour upon the Hiſtory of Literature, as well as upon the Subſtances, Forms and Claſſification of Books.

DENIS (F.) and PINCON (P.). Nouveau Manuel de Bibliographie Univerſelle. 8°. Paris. 1857.

One of the *Manuels Roret.*

DIBDIN (T. F.). Bibliographical Decameron; or Ten Days' pleaſant Diſcourſe upon Illuminated Manuſcripts, and Subjects connected with early Engraving, Typography and Bibliography. 3 Vols. Royal 8°. London. 1817.

Elegantly printed, and embelliſhed with many fine Engravings. It is now exceedingly ſcarce, and too dear for ordinary Purchaſers. The Authour was an Enthuſiaſt in this Department of Learning, and his numerous Publications are indiſpenſable to the bibliographical Student.

FORTIA D'URBAN. Nouveau Syſtème Alphabétique de Bibliographie Alphabétique. 12°. Paris. 1822.

HORNE (T. H.). An Introduction to the Study of Bibliography; to which is prefixed a Memoir on the Publick Libraries of the Antients. Illustrated with Engravings. 2 Vols. 8°. London. 1814.

The most useful Book of the Kind that has been published in the English Language, and to which we are greatly indebted in the Preparation of this Work. It comprises a summary Account of the Materials used for Writing in all Ages and Countries, the Origin and Progress of Printing, Remarks on the Forms of Books, different Styles of Binding, the Knowledge of Books, and the Causes of their relative Value and Scarcity, the Principles which should govern in the Arrangement and Classification of a Library, &c. &c. The most extensive Division of the Work is appropriated to a Notice of the principal Writers who have treated on the different Branches of Bibliography. It contains the fullest Account that we have ever seen of Catalogues of Libraries both British and foreign. The Specimens of early Typography, and of the Vignettes and Monograms of the early Printers, are neatly executed. A new Edition of this Work, incorporating the Suggestions and Improvements of a later Period, is greatly needed.

MORTILLARO (Vincenzo). Studio Bibliographico. 2d Ed. 8°. Palermo. 1832.

PEIGNOT (Gabriel). Dictionnaire Raisonné de Bibliologie. (With Supplement). 3 Vols. 8°. Paris. 1802-4.

Containing 1st. An Explanation of Terms relative to Bibliography, Typography, the Languages, Archives, Manuscripts, Medals, Antiquities, &c. 2d. Detailed historical Notices of the principal Libraries, ancient and modern, the different Sects of Philosophers, the most celebrated Printers, and Bibliographers, including a List of their Works. 3d. An Explanation of the different bibliographical Systems, &c. Peignot also published in 1800 an octavo Volume upon the Knowledge of Books, their Forms, Editions, &c. &c., called *Manuel Bibliographique; ou Essai sur les Bibliothèques Anciennes et Modernes, etc.*, which may properly be regarded as an elementary Work.

III. *The Origin and Progreſs of Writing, Manuſcripts and Diplomaticks, Monograms and Autographs, Materials for Writing or Printing, Engraving on Wood, Copper, Stone, &c.*

THE Subjects belonging to this Section have furniſhed Topicks for much elaborate Reſearch, and ſome of them for Speculations and Diſputes not yet brought to any ſatisfactory Concluſion. Our Object in this Work is to indicate the Inquiries which belong to the different Departments of Bibliography, together with ſome of the beſt Guides to Information upon each, leaving the Diſcuſſion of the Topicks themſelves to ſeparate and more extended Articles in their appropriate Places in Encyclopedias like the Britannica, Metropolitan, or New American, now being publiſhed in New York by the Appletons.

1. Writing.

Astle (Thomas). The Origin and Progreſs of Writing, as well hieroglyphick as elementary. Illuſtrated by Engravings. 2d Ed. 4°. London. 1803.

"The completeſt Work on the Subject of Writing extant in this or any other Language."—*Horne*. The Chapters on Tranſcribers and Illuminators, and the Inſtruments, Inks, and other Matters, which they made Uſe of in their Operations, will be found eſpecially intereſting to the Bibliographer. A third Edition has been recently publiſhed in London, by Rowe, in one Volume, royal quarto.

CHAMPOLLION-FIGEAC (J. J.). Précis du Syſtème Hiéroglyphique des Anciens Egyptiens, ou Recherches ſur les Elements premiers de cette Ecriture Sacrée, avec Planches. 2d Ed. Royal 8°. Paris. 1828.

DEARBORN (N. S.). The American Text Book for Letters, with Copious Remarks on the various Letters now in Uſe, together with the moſt Correct Method of producing them with the Pen, Bruſh, Chiſel, or Graver. Oblong 8°. Boſton. 1858.

This is the ſecond Edition of an important Work, giving the various Styles of Letters now in Uſe on plain or ornamental Printing, Engraving, or Sign Painting, ſuch as Block Letters, German Text, Square Text, Open Flower Leaf, Roman Letters, Ornamented or Illuminated Capitals, Writing Print Letters, &c. A large Number of Styles are given, all of them beautifully and accurately deſigned and executed.

FORTIA D' URBAN (Le Marquis de). Eſſai ſur l'Origine de l'Ecriture, ſur ſon Introduction dans la Grèce, et ſon Uſage juſqu'au Temps d'Homère. 8°. Paris. 1832.

FRY (Edmund). Pantographia; containing accurate Copies of all the known Alphabets in the World, together with an Engliſh Explanation of the Force or Power of each Letter. Royal 8° London. 1799.

This highly intereſting Work, ſays Horne, is the Reſult of ſixteen

Years' Refearch; the Specimens of Characters are executed with great Neatnefs.

Silvestre (J. B.). Paléographie Univerfelle. Collection de Fac-Simile d'Ecritures de tous les Peuples, et tous les Temps, etc., et accompagné d' Explications hiftoriques et defcriptives par M. M. Champollion-Figeac et Aimé Champollion Fils. 4 Vols. Folio. Paris. 1839-41.

"Ouvrage capital, exécuté avec le plus grand Luxe."—*Brunet.*

Wailly (M. N. de). Eléments de Paléographie. 2 Vols. Royal 4°. Paris. 1838.

A very handfomely printed Work of 1168 Pages. The fecond Volume contains Plates and a copious general Index.

2. Manuscripts and Diplomaticks.

Delandine (A. F.). Manufcrits de la Bibliothèque de Lyon. Précédés d'un Effai hiftorique fur les Manufcrits en général, avec une Bibliographie fpéciale des Catalogues qui les ont décrits. 3 Vols. 8°. Lyon. 1812.

Ebert (F. A.). Zur Handfchriftenkunde. 2 Vols. 8°. Leipzig. 1825-7.

Humphreys (H. N.). The Illuminated Books of the Middle Ages; an Account of the Development and Progrefs of the Art of Illumination, as a diftinct Branch of Pictorial Ornamentation, &c. Illuftrated by a Series of Examples, of the Size of the Originals, by Owen Jones. Folio. London. 1849.

A fplendid and coftly Work.

LANGLOIS (E. H). Effai fur Calligraphie des Manufcrits du Moyen-Age, et fur les Ornements des premiers Livres d'Heures imprimés. Royal 8°. Rouen. 1841.

MABILLON (Jean). De Re Diplomatica Libri VI; cum Supplemento. 3^d Ed. 2 Vols. Folio. (Fine Plates). Neapoli. 1789.

MONTFAUCON (Dom. Bernard de). Bibliotheca Bibliothecarum Manufcriptorum nova. 2 Vols. Folio. Paris. 1739.

This is a Catalogue of all the Manufcripts of which the Author, one of the moft diftinguifhed Savans of the 18th Century, could obtain any Knowledge, during forty Years of affiduous Refearch in the principal Libraries of Europe. The Manufcripts in the various Libraries are arranged in Claffes feparately. Each Volume has a complete Index.

Nouveau Traité de Diplomatique. Par deux Religieux Bénedictines, de la Cong. de S. Maur. 6 Vols. 4°. Paris. 1750.

The Authors of this highly efteemed work were M. M. Touftain and Taffin. The third Volume contains a moft copious Lift of the Abbreviations occurring in ancient Writings.

VAINES (Dom. De). Dictionnaire Raifonné de Diplomatique. 2 Vols. 8°. Paris. 1774.

The Defign of the learned Author, fays Horne, was to felect and concentrate within the Compafs of two Volumes, the Refearches of all the moft celebrated Writers on the Diplomatick Art. This Object is moft happily accomplifhed; and to thofe who have not the Means of procuring the large and coftly Volumes of Mabillon, Montfaucon, Maffei, and other Writers on the Subject, the Work of M. De Vaines is invaluable. The Plates, thirty-five in Number, faithfully exhibit the various Modes of Writing in different Ages and Nations.

3. Monograms and Autographs.

Brulliot (François). Dictionnaire des Monogrammes, Marques Figurées, Lettres Initials, Noms Abrégés, etc., avec lefquels les Peintres, Deffinateurs, Graveurs, et Sculpteurs ont défigné leurs Noms. 2d Ed. 3 Pts. 4°. Munich. 1832-4.

"Ouvrage très important."—*Brunet.*

Fontaine (P. J.). Des Collections des Autographes et de l'Utilité qu'on peut en retirer. 8°. Paris. 1834.

Fontaine (P. J.). Manuel de l'Auteur des Autographes. 8°. Paris. 1836.

Ifographie des Hommes célèbres, ou Collection de Fac-Simile de Lettres autographes et de Signatures; publiée par MM. Bérard, Châteaugiron, Duchefne, et Frémifot. 4 Vols. Large 4°. Paris. 1843.

Peignot (Gabriel). Recherches hiftoriques et bibliographiques fur les Autographes et fur l'Autographie. 8°. Dijon. 1836.

4. Materials for Writing or Printing.

Koops (Matthias.) Hiftorical Account of the Subftances which have been ufed to defcribe Events and to convey Ideas, from the earlieft Date to the Invention of Paper. 8°. London. 1801.

LE NORMAND (L. S.). Manuel du Fabricant de Papiers, etc. (with Plates). 2 Vols. 12°. Paris. 1834.

PEIGNOT (Gabriel). Eſſai ſur l'Hiſtoire du Parchemin et du Velin. 8°. Paris. 1812.

SAVAGE (William). Treatiſe on the Preparation of Printing Ink of various Colours. 8°. London. 1832.

Publiſhed by Longman at £2 2s.

TAYLOR (Iſaac). Hiſtory of the Tranſmiſſion of Ancient Books to Modern Times; or, a conciſe Account of the Means by which the Genuineneſs and Authenticity of ancient hiſtorical Works are aſcertained. 8°. London. 1827.

The firſt Part of this excellent Work is devoted to the Hiſtory of Manuſcripts, an Account of the Materials of ancient Books, Inſtruments of Writing, Inks, Illuminations, Copyiſts, Writers of the Middle Ages, &c.

WEHRS (G. F.). Von Papier, &c. (with Supplement). 3 Vols. 8°. Halle & Hannover. 1789-90.

5. ENGRAVING ON COPPER, WOOD, STONE, &C.

BARTSCH (Adam de). Le Peintre Graveur. 21 Vols. 8°. Vienne, Degen, et Mechetti. 1803-21.

This Work, ſays Brunet, is certainly the moſt exact of any of the Kind which we have; but it is very incomplete, and the laſt Volumes are of leſs Value than the firſt. Volumes 1-5. Flemiſh and Dutch Schools. 6-11. The German School. 12 and 13. The Italian School. 14 and 15. Marc Antonio, &c. 16-21. The Reſidue of the Italian School.

BRYAN (Michael). A Biographical and Critical Dictionary of Painters and Engravers; with the Ciphers, Monograms, and Marks uſed by each Engraver. A new Edition, reviſed, enlarged and continued to the preſent Time, compriſing above ONE THOUSAND additional Memoirs and large Acceſſions to the Liſts of Pictures and Engravings, alſo new Plates of Ciphers and Monograms. By George Stanley. Royal 8°. London. 1849.

A Book of 963 Pages, embracing without the leaſt Abridgment, as ſtated in the Preface, the whole of the Articles contained in the two quartos publiſhed by Bryan in 1816.

ENGELMANN (M. G.). Traité théorique et pratique de Lithographie. 3ᵈ Ed. 4°. Paris. 1839.

Illuſtrated with a great Number of Plates.

HEINECKEN (M. le Baron). Idée Generale d'une Collection complette d'Eſtampes, avec une Diſſertation ſur l'Origine de la Gravure, et ſur les premiers Livres des Images. 8°. Leipſic. 1771.

The Value and Fidelity of this Work have long been known and duly appreciated by Bibliographers and Amateurs of the fine Arts. A Circumſtance that greatly enhances its Merit is, that the Author actually ſaw every Book of Images, &c. which he has deſcribed. It is illuſtrated with 28 fine Engravings, ſeveral of which are Doubles.

FIELDING (T. H.) The Art of Engraving; being an hiſtorical and diſtinct Account of the various Styles now practiſed, with Inſtructions as to the various Modes of Operation, &c. Royal 8°. London. 1840.

JACKSON (John). A Treatiſe on Wood Engraving, hiſtorical and practical. With upwards of three hundred Illuſtrations, engraved on Wood. Royal 8°. London. 1839.

The third Chapter of this important Work is devoted to an Examination of the Claims of Gutemburg and Coſter to the Honour of the Invention of Typography. The Author ſupports the Claims of the former.

NAGLER (G. K.). Neues Allgemeines Künſtler-Lexicon, oder Nachrichten von dem Leben und den Werken der Maler, Bildhauer, etc. 22 Vols. 8°. München. 1835-52.

A biographical Dictionary, with critical Notices of the Works of Painters, Sculptors, Engravers, Deſigners, Lithographers, etc., being the beſt and moſt extenſive Work of the Kind extant.

OTTLEY (W. Y.). Hiſtory of Engraving upon Copper and Wood, with an Account of Engravers and their Works. 2 Vols. Royal 4°. London. 1816.

Publiſhed at £8 8s.

This magnificent Book is printed uniformly with Dibdin's Ames, and with that forms a grand Series of the Hiſtory of Printing and Engraving. Like Meerman the Author ſupports the Pretenſions of Coſter as the Inventor of Printing.

SINGER (S. W.). Reſearches into the Hiſtory of Playing Cards; with Illuſtrations of the Origin of Printing and Engraving on Wood. 4°. (Numerous Plates). London. 1816.

"The entire Impreſſion of this Work is limited to 250 Copies; ſo that when its intrinſick Worth and intrinſick Beauty be conſidered, the Curious will not fail to ſecure Copies whenever they make their Appearance."—*Dibdin.*

SPOONER (S.). A Biographical and Critical Dictionary of Painters, Engravers, Sculptors and Architects; with the Monograms, Ciphers, &c. Large 8°. New York. 1853. pp. 1150.

IV. The Origin and Progreſs of Printing, Early Printed Books, and Book Binding.

THE Hiſtory of the Origin of this moſt important of all human Inventions is enveloped in Myſtery, the moſt widely oppoſite Opinions upon the Subject being ſtill entertained. Although within twenty Years from its Diſcovery it was ſpread all over Europe, commemorating all other Inventions, and handing down to Poſterity every important Event, it has unfortunately failed to record in deciſive Terms, the Name of its own Inventor. To determine this, as well as the Place where the Diſcovery was made, has given Employment to the Studies and Reſearches of the moſt learned Men in Europe during the laſt two Centuries. We can only in this Connection, point out ſome of the moſt important Publications on the Subject, together with Manuals and Dictionaries of the Art, and ſuch Works as are particularly deſcriptive of early printed Books.

AMES (Joſeph). Typographical Antiquities; being an hiſtorical Account of Printing in England, Scotland and Ireland, from 1471 to 1600. 4°. London. 1749.

A ſecond Edition of this truly valuable Work, enlarged by William Herbert, was publiſhed in 1785-90, in 3 Vols. 4°. Both theſe Editions are now in a great Degree ſuperſeded by the elaborate and ſplendid Edition by the Rev. T. F. Dibdin, greatly enlarged, with copious Notes and appropriate Engravings. 4 Vols. 4°. Lond. 1810-19. Publiſhed at 60 Guineas.

AUDIFFREDI (J. B.). Catalogus Hiſtorico-Criticus Romanarum Editionum Sæculi XV. Alſo, Specimen Hiſtorico-Criticum Editionum Italicarum Sæculi XV. 2 Vols. 4. Romæ. 1783-94.

Dibdin ſpeaks of theſe Productions as of very great Importance to the Bibliographer. Audiffredi appears to have had Acceſs to the firſt Libraries in Italy; and his Care, Accuracy and Reſearch, entitle him to a Superiority over all his Predeceſſors. Both of theſe Works have good Indexes.

BANDINI (A. M.). De Florentina Juntarum Typographia. 2 Vols. 8°. Lucæ. 1791.

It only goes as far as 1550. Peignot commends it as a "profoundly learned Work."

BÉRARD (A. S. L.). Eſſai bibliographique ſur les Editions des Elzévirs. 8°. Paris. 1822.

BERNARD (Aug.). De l'Origine et des Débuts de l'Imprimerie en Europe. 2 Vols. 8°. Paris. 1853.

Paul Trömel in Petzholdt's *Anzeiger*, ſpeaks of this as the moſt important Work yet written on the Origin of the Art of Printing.

Bibbliotheca Smithiana, ſeu Catalogus Librorum D. Joſephi Smithii Angli per Cognomina Authorum diſpoſitus. pp. 913. 4°. Venetiis. 1755.

This valuable Catalogue was compiled by J. B. Paſchal. It contains the PREFACES and EPISTLES of the rareſt and moſt important Works publiſhed before the Year 1500, this Part of the Book occupying 285 Pages; it contains alſo a complete alphabetical Index of Authors.

COTTON (Henry). Typographical Gazetteer. 3d Ed. 8. Oxford. 1852.

A very uſeful Work, being a Dictionary of all the Places where Printing has been practiced, with an Account of the firſt Books printed at each, a Tranſlation into Engliſh of the foreign Names of Towns, &c.

DAUNOU (P. C. F.). Analyze des Opinions diverſes ſur l'Origine de l'Imprimerie. 8°. Paris. 1802.

This is a clear and compendious View of the various Opinions which have been advanced upon the Origin of Printing. The ſame has alſo been publiſhed in the fourth Volume of the Memoirs of the moral and political Claſs of the French Inſtitute.

DIBDIN (T. F.). Bibliotheca Spenceriana; or a Deſcriptive Catalogue of early printed Books, and of many important firſt Editions in the Library of Earl Spencer. 4 Vols. Superroyal 8°. London. 1814-15.

This ſuperb Collection of Books contains upwards of 45,000 Volumes; among them are ſixty-four Editions from the Preſs of Wm. Caxton, the firſt Engliſh Printer, which are reputed to be worth $60,000. The Abundance and Beauty of the Facſimiles and other Embelliſhments, as well as the Fineneſs of the Paper and Printing, render this Catalogue one of the moſt ſplendid bibliographical Works ever publiſhed in any Country. It deſcribes, 1. Books printed from wooden Blocks about the Middle of the fifteenth Century. 2. Early printed Bibles. 3. Liturgical Works. 4. Works of the Fathers. 5. Greek and Latin Claſſicks. 6. Miſcellaneous Literature. The Poſſeſſors of this Work, to complete it, ſhould procure ÆDES ALTHORPIANÆ, 2 Vols. ſuper royal 8°. London, 1822, containing an Account of the Manſion, Books and Pictures at Althorp, the Reſidence of Earl Spencer; and alſo the CASSANO CATALOGUE, ſuper royal 8°. Lond. 1823, forming a Supplement to the two previous Catalogues, and containing a general Index.

DUPONT (Paul). Notice Hiſtorique ſur l'Imprimerie. Large 8°. Paris. 1849.

FALKENSTEIN (Karl). Geſchichte der Buchdruckerkunſt. 4°. Leipzig. 1840.

A very important and beautiful Work, containing Engravings, many of which are coloured.

GRESWELL (W. P.). Annals of Pariſian Typography, containing an Account of the earlieſt Typographical Eſtabliſhments in Paris. 8°. London. 1818.

This has long been regarded as an important Compilation. It is enriched with numerous intereſting Notes relating to the Hiſtory of Literature. It is deſigned principally to ſhow the particular Influence of the Pariſian Gothic Preſs upon the early Engliſh Preſs.

GRESWELL (W. P.). View of the Early Pariſian Greek Preſs, including the Lives of the Stephani. 2 Vols. 8°. Oxford. 1833.

HAIN (Ludovicus). Repertorium Bibliographicum. 4 Vols. 8°. Stutt. et Tubingæ. 1826-38.

A uſeful Repertory, in which, by means of frequent Abbreviations, the Author has endeavoured to bring into a ſmall Compaſs a deſcriptive Account of all the Editions of the 15th Century known to himſelf. The Number of Articles thus given amounts to 16,299. They are regarded by Bibliographers as extremely accurate.

HANSARD (T. C.). Typographia; an hiſtorical Sketch of the Origin and Progreſs of Printing, with practical Directions for conducting every

Department in an Office, with a Defcription of Stereotype and Lithography. Thick royal 8°. London. 1825.

A beautiful Book of 939 Pages, with a good Index.

HANSARD (T. C.). The Hiftory of the Art of Printing, Copperplate Printing, Type Founding and Lithographick Printing. 8°. Edinburgh. 1840.

HODGSON (Thomas). An Effay on the Origin and Progrefs of Stereotype Printing, including a Defcription of the various Proceffes. 8°. Newcaftle. 1820. pp. 178.

An excellent Work. Only 306 Copies printed.

JOHNSON (John). Typographia, or the Printer's Inftructor. 2 Vols. 8°. London. 1824.

LAIRE (F. X.). Index Librorum ab Inventa Typographia ad Annum 1500, cum notis. (With a Supplement.) 3 Vols. 8°. Paris. 1791-2.

A ufeful Work of its Kind. The Defcriptions are clear, the Notes brief and inftructive, and there are four Indexes.

MAITTAIRE (Michael). Annales Typographici ab Artis Inventæ Origine ad Annum 1664, cum Supplemento Michaelis Denifii. 7 Vols. (or 11 when the Parts are bound up feparately). 4°. Hag. Com. et Viennæ. 1719-89.

Volume I. from the Origin of the Art to the Year 1500, was publifhed in 1719. Volume II. 1500-1536, was publifhed in 1722, in 2 Parts. Volume III. 1536-1557, was publifhed in 1726, in 2 Parts, with an Appendix. Volume IV. from the Origin of the Art to 1664, was publifhed in 1733, in 2 Parts. Volume V. containing a general Index, was publiſhed in 1741, in 2 Parts. Complete Copies of theſe Annals, with both Parts of the Index, are rare, eſpecially in this Country. The Supplement by Michel Denis, publiſhed at Vienna in 1789, in 2 Vols. 4°., contains 6311 Articles, deſcribing Works printed in the 15th Century which were unknown to Maittaire.

Though leſs perfect in ſome reſpects than the Annals of Panzer, it is nevertheleſs indiſpenſable in every bibliographical Collection. It does not confine itſelf like that Work to mere Nomenclature, but gives Information reſpecting the Lives of Printers, Publiſhers, Correctors of the Preſs, and literary Men, and ſuggeſts Inquiries reſpecting the Hiſtory of the Art of Printing. The Author was a Native of London, born in 1668, and educated at Weſtminſter School and Oxford Univerſity.

MEERMAN (Gerard). Origines Typographicæ. 2 Vols. 4 . Hag. Com. 1765.

One of the moſt inſtructive Books extant, as to the Progreſs of the Art, and full of learned and acute Inquiries. The Author, who was a diſtinguiſhed Lawyer of Leyden, ſupports with great Ardour the Pretenſions of Harlem as the Birthplace of the Art, and of Lawrence Coſter as its Inventor. Although the Hypotheſis of Meerman in Support of theſe Pretenſions has long ſince been exploded as a Fable, the Work is highly eſteemed and eagerly ſought after by Bibliographers. The Plates (12 in Number) are frequently taken out to illuſtrate other Works.

MEERSCH (P. C. Van der). Recherches ſur la Vie et les Travaux des Imprimeurs Belges et Neerlandais, établis à l'Etranger, et ſur la Part qu'ils ont priſe à la Régénération littéraire de l'Europe du XVe Siècle. Vol. I. 8°. Gand. 1856.

A very important Work.

PANZER (G. W.). Annales Typographici ab Artis Inventæ Origine ad annum 1536. 11 Vols. 4°. Norimbergæ. 1793-1803.

The moſt extenſive Work extant on the Productions of the 15th Century, and ſurpaſſing in bibliographical Accuracy, as well as in Method and Arrangement, all its Predeceſſors. Volumes I-III contain the dated Productions which appeared up to 1500, in the alphabetical Order of their Places of Printing. Volume IV contains the dated Productions which appeared without any Statement of the Place of Printing, or Name of Printer, arranged in chronological Order; alſo the Productions without Place, Date, or Printer, arranged in alphabetical Order, according to the Authors' Names, and a triple Supplement to the former Volumes. Volume V is a general Index to the previous Volumes. Volumes VI-IX embrace the dated and undated Productions from 1501 to 1536 together with Supplements. Volumes X and XI contain general Indexes to Vols. VI-IX, and alſo a Supplement to the entire Work.

PIETERS (M. Chs.). Analyſe des Matériaux les plus utiles, pour des futures Annales de l'Imprimerie des Elzévirs. Large 8°. Gand. 1843.

PIETERS (M. Chs.). Annales de l'Imprimerie Elſevirienne. 8°. Gand et Paris. 1851.

RENOUARD (A. A.). Annales de l'Imprimerie des Alde. 2d Ed. 3 Vols. 8°. Paris. 1825.

RENOUARD (A. A.). Annales de l'Imprimerie des Eſtienne. 2 Pts. in one Volume 8°. Paris. 1837-8.

Theſe Works upon Aldus Manutius, the Inventor of *Italics*, and his Succeſſors, and upon Henry Stephens and his Succeſſors, the celebrated French Printers of the 16th Century, are very important. A 3d Edition of the firſt named Work, containing a Notice of the Juntas, and a Liſt of their Productions up to 1550, was publiſhed in one thick Volume, 8°. Paris. 1834.

SANTANDER (M. de la Serna). An Hiſtorical Eſſay on the Origin of Printing. Tranſlated from the French. 8°. Newcaſtle. Hodgſon. 1819. pp. 93.

Only 214 Copies printed.

SAVAGE (William). Dictionary of the Art of Printing. (Illuſtrated with Diagrams.) Thick 8°. London. 1841.

A new Edition of this capital Work has long been in Preparation by a competent Gentleman of New York.

SOTHEBY (S. L.) Principia Typographica. The Block Books, or xylographick Delineations of Scripture Hiſtory, iſſued in Holland, Flanders and Germany, during the fifteenth Century, exemplified and conſidered in Connexion with the Origin of Printing, &c. &c. 3 Vols. imp. 4o. London. 1857.

Only 250 Copies printed, of which 220 Copies are to be ſold at Auction on Wedneſday the 5th of May, 1858, in London. The Volumes are illuſtrated with above 120 Plates. None will be ſold for leſs than 9 Guineas.

STOWER (Charles). The Printer's Grammar; or Introduction to the Art of Printing. (With Plates.) 8°. London. 1808.

THOMAS (Iſaiah). The Hiſtory of Printing in America; with a Biography of Printers, and an Account of Newſpapers. To which is prefixed a conciſe View of the Diſcovery and Progreſs of the Art in other Parts of the World. 2 Vols. 8°. Worceſter. 1810.

Rare and very important.

TIMPERLEY (C. H). Encyclopedia of Literary and Typographical Anecdote; compiled from Nichols's Literary Anecdotes, and numerous Authorities. Second Edition, comprifing recent Biographies, chiefly of Bookfellers, and a Practical Manual of Printing. Thick royal 8°. Lond. 1842.

WILLETT (Ralph). A Memoir on the Origin of Printing, in a Letter addreffed to John Topham, Efq. 8°. Newcaftle. T. Hodgfon. 1820. pp. 72.

Only 150 Copies printed.

WOLFIUS (J. C.) Monumenta Typographica. 2 thick Vols. 8°. Hamburgi. 1740.

This Collection confifts of Treatifes by various Authors, and alfo of Extracts illuftrative of the Origin and early Hiftory of the Art, fome of which are in Verfe.

BOOK-BINDING.

A few Works illuftrative of the Hiftory and Art of Book-Binding, may very properly be added to this Part of our LIST.

ANETT (J. A.). An Inquiry into the Nature and Form of the Books of the Ancients, with a Hiftory of the Art of Book-Binding, from the Times of the Greeks and Romans to the prefent Day; interfperfed with bibliographical References to Men and Books of all Ages and Countries. Small 8°. London. 1837.

GREVE (E. W.). Hand und Lehrbuch der Buchbinde, &c. 2d Ed. 2 Vols. 8°. Berlin. 1832.

HANNETT (John). Bibliopegia or the Art of Book-Binding. 4th Ed. 12°. London. 1848.

LE NORMAND (L. S.). Manuel du Relieur. 2d Ed. 18°. Paris. 1831.

One of the *Manuels Roret.*

PEIGNOT (Gabriel). Eſſai hiſtorique et archæologique ſur la Relieure des Livres, etc. 8°. Dijon. 1834.

TUCKETT (C. J.). Specimens of ancient and modern Binding. Royal 4°. London. 1846.

WALKER (Edward). The Art of Book-Binding, its Riſe and Progreſs. (Including a deſcriptive Account of the New York Book Bindery of E. Walker & Sons, with a Liſt of Prices annexed.) Thin 8°. New York. 1850.

V. Rare, Anonymous, Pſeudonymous and Prohibited Books.

1. RARE.

ONE of the Objects of Bibliography is to indicate thoſe Books which, to a greater or leſs Degree, come under this Category. With regard to theſe Compilations we may remark, that though in moſt of them the Epithet RARE is ſometimes applied too vaguely and laviſhly, they are neverthelefs as a Clafs extremely ufeful. It is indeed exceedingly difficult to fpeak in all Cafes with Precifion in regard to rare Books, and hence perhaps impoffible to compile a Work of this Kind which fhall not fometimes miflead thofe who confult it. A Diftinction fhould always be made between the Terms RARE and PRECIOUS, which, while at firft they appear to mean the fame Thing, are yet effentially different. A Book may be rare becaufe it is with Difficulty to be procured, and hence highly valued by Amateurs who defire the exclufive Poffeffion of it, regardlefs of Coft. On the other Hand, Books may be precious, and to be obtained only at a high Price, without being rare. Such are the fplendid Collections of architectural Engravings publifhed by Piranefi and others; the Collections called GALLERIES and CABINETS; the great Collections of Works on Antiquities by Græ-vius, Gronovius, Montfaucon, Muratori and others. The following may be noticed as among the principal bibliographical Works under this Head, in addition to Audiffredi, Dibdin, Hain, Laire, Maittaire and Panzer, defcribed under the preceding Head:

BAUER (J. J.). Bibliotheca Librorum rariorum univerfalis. (With three fupplementary Volumes.) 7 Vols. 8°. Norimbergæ. 1770-91.

Arranged alphabetically according to the Authors' Names. It contains fome good Things, fays Peignot, but the Author has been too lavifh of the words, *rarus, rariffimus, pauciffimus, cognitus,* &c.

CLEMENT (David). Bibliothèque Curieufe; ou

Catalogue Raiſonné des Livres rares et difficiles à trouver. 9 Vols. 4°. Göttingen et Leipzig. 1750-60.

This Work is compiled upon a very extenſive Plan, for, though conſiſting of nine quarto Volumes, it comes down no farther than to the Letter H in the alphabetical Arrangement of Names; terminating here in conſequence of the Author's Death. It is beautifully printed and exhibits great Labour and Learning. The following are the different Claſſes mentioned in which Books may be ſaid to be rare. 1. A Book which it is difficult to find in the Country where it is ſought, ought to be called ſimply *rare*. 2. A Book which it is difficult to find in any Country may be called *very rare*. 3. A Book of which there are only 50 or 60 Copies exiſting, or which appears as ſeldom as if there never had been more at any Time than that Number of Copies, ranks as *extremely rare*. 4. When the whole Number of Copies of a Work does not exceed 10, this conſtitutes *exceſſive* rarity, or rarity in the higheſt Degree. This Claſſification of the Degrees of Rareneſs is copied from Clement by all ſubſequent Writers in this Department.

DIBDIN (T. F.). A Bibliographical Antiquarian and Pictureſque Tour in France and Germany. 2d Edition. 3 Vols. ſmall 8°. London. 1829.

Containing a Fund of uſeful Information upon Topography, Manuſcripts, rare and valuable Books, public and private Libraries, Bookſellers, Book-collectors, Autographs, &c. &c. Numerous Illuſtrations. The firſt Edition, of which the ſecond is an Abridgment, was publiſhed in 1821, in 3 Vols. royal 8°. The Expenſes of the Printing and Engraving of this firſt Edition, amounted to upwards of £6000.

DIBDIN (T. F.). A Bibliographical and Pictureſque Tour in the Northern Counties of England and in Scotland. 2 Vols. Royal 8°. London. 1838.

Profuſely embelliſhed, with Accounts of Libraries, Manuſcripts, rare Books, &c. &c. and a general Index.

FOURNIER (F. I.). Nouveau Dictionnaire Portatif de Bibliographie; contenant plus de vingt trois mille Articles de Livres rares, curieux, eftimés et recherchés, &c. 2d Ed. 8°. Paris. 1809.

Preceded by an Effay on Libraries and Bibliography, and followed by Catalogues of the Editions of Bafkerville, Didot, the Aldi, Elzevirs, &c. &c.

GERDES (Daniel). Florigium hiftorico-criticum Librorum rariorum, etc. 8°. Groningæ. 1773.

This is the third Edition of a Work, defigned in Part as a Supplement to the Catalogue of Vogt,

GUICHARD (J. M.). Notice fur le Speculum Humanæ Salvationis. 8°. Paris. 1840.

HARTSHORNE (C. H.). Book Rarities of the Univerfity of Cambridge; illuftrated by original Letters, and Notes biographical, literary and antiquarian. (With Plates). 8°. London. 1820.

HOYOIS (P. J.). Mufée Bibliographique; Collection d'Ouvrages imprimés et Manufcrits, dont le moindre Prix eft de 1000 Francs. 8°. Mons. 1837.

LALANDE (M. L. C.). Curiofités Bibliographiques. 18°. Paris. 1845.

This little Work, although not ftrictly coming under this Head, neverthelefs contains many interefting Particulars in regard to curious and rare Books, including Titles and Frontifpieces, Dedications, Prefaces, Errours, Binding, Prices paid to Authors, Autographs, Liberty of the Prefs, &c.

OSMONT (J. B. L.). Dictionnaire Typographique, Hiftorique, et Critique des Livres rares, finguliers, eſtimés, et recherchés en tous Genres. 2 Vols. 8°. Paris. 1768.

A ſcarce Work; which, though in ſome reſpects ſuperſeded by later bibliographical Dictionaries, may yet be advantageouſly conſulted for Italian Literature.

PEIGNOT (Gabriel). Eſſai de Curioſités Bibliographiques. 8°. Paris. 1804.

Containing a claſſified Notice of the fineſt Works, the Price of which, at the publick Sales, has exceeded 1000 Francs.

PEIGNOT (Gabriel). Variétés, Notices et Raretés Bibliographiques. 8°. Paris. 1822. pp. 147.

Dibdin in his Preface to the Bibliographical Tour in France, juſt deſcribed, complains that this little Work is but the Reflection or Tranſlation of the 9th and 30th Letters of the 1ſt Edition of the ſame.

PEIGNOT (Gabriel). Répertoire de Bibliographies ſpéciales, curieuſes et inſtructives. 8°. Paris. 1810.

Containing, 1. Special Bibliographies in all Languages. 2. Books of which only 100 Copies were printed. 3. Books of which Copies have been printed on colored Paper. 4. Books, the Text of which is engraved. 5. All Books which have been publiſhed under the Name *Ana*, &c.

SANTANDER (M. de la Serna). Dictionnaire Bibliographique choiſi du quinzième Siècle; ou deſcription des Editions les plus rares, &c. 3 Vols. 8°. Bruxelles et Paris. 1805-7.

The firſt Volume contains an elaborate Hiſtory of Printing (ſee Page 28), which Horne has abridged in his Introduction to the Study of Bibliography. Santander deſcribes only the principal Editions of the 15th Century, obſerving that though there are ſuppoſed to have been not leſs than 15,000 publiſhed within that Period, not more than 1500 deſerve the Attention of the Curious.

SCHELHORN (J. G.). Amœnitas Literariæ, quibus variæ Obſervationes, Scripta item quædam Anecdota et varioſa Opuſcula exhibentur. 2d Ed. 14 Vols. 8o. Frankfort et Leipzic. 1725-31.

VALLIÈRE (M. le Duc de la). Catalogue des Livres de la Biliothèque de Vallière. 9 Vols. 8o. Paris. 1783-8.

The firſt Part of this Catalogue, in three Volumes, was compiled by Guillaume de Bure, and is extremely curious. It compriſes Manuſcripts (deſcribed by M. Van Praet), early Editions, Books printed on Vellum and large Paper, Books rare and precious, Books of Engravings, &c. containing in all 5668 Articles, and two Indexes, one of Authors and one of Titles or Subjects.

The ſecond Part, conſiſting of the laſt ſix Volumes, was compiled by Jean Sue Nyon. It contains 27,000 Articles, arranged under general Diviſions, but without an Index. This Part of the Vallière Library, although conſidered of leſs Value than the preceding Portion, contains a fine Collection of French and Italian Poets, and a Collection of Romances, the moſt complete perhaps that ever was formed, together with numerous Works on the Arts, Sciences, Hiſtory, &c. This Part of the Work therefore belongs to general Bibliography. It is of little practical Value for the Want of deſcriptive Notes and an Index.

VAN PRAET (Joſeph). Catalogue des Livres imprimés ſur Vélin, de la Bibliothèque du Roi. (With Supplement.) 6 Vols. Large 8o. Paris. 1822-8.

"L'Importance et la grande Valeur des Livres décrits, l'Exactitude rigoureuſe des Deſcriptions, et les Anecdotes curieuſes qui les accompagnent, donnent de l'Intérêt à cet excellent Catalogue."—*Brunet.*

The Compiler, one of the moſt profound Bibliographers of Europe, has been for many Years at the Head of the Bibliothèque Royale at Paris, a Library ſingularly rich in Books printed on Vellum.

Van Praet (Joſeph). Catalogue des Livres imprimés ſur Vélin qui ſe trouvent dans des Bibliothèques tant publiques que particulières. 4 Vols. Large 8°. Paris. 1824-8.

Vogt (John). Catalogus hiſtorico-criticus Librorum rariorum. 5th Ed. Thick 8°. Norimbergæ. 1793.

An excellent Work, the Plan and Execution of which are characterized by Dibdin as being at once clear and conciſe. Vogt, however, like many other Authors of this Claſs of Books, is ſomewhat prodigal of the Word *rare*.

2. Anonymous and Pseudonymous Books.

Anonymous Books are thoſe which are publiſhed without any Author's Name. *Cryptonymous* Books are thoſe the Names of the Authors of which are concealed under an Anagram or ſimilar Contrivance. *Pſeudonymous* Books are thoſe which bear falſe Names of Authors. The great Number of Works embraced under this Head renders it a very important Branch of bibliographical Inquiry. Of the various Writers who have deſcribed this Claſs of Books, the following are the principal. They are particularly uſeful in regard to the literary Productions of Periods and Countries which have been greatly reſtricted in the Liberty of the Preſs.

Barbier (A. A.). Dictionnaire des Ouvrages Anonymes et Pſeudonymes. 2d Ed. 4 Vols. 8°. Paris. 1822-7.

By far the moſt perfect and valuable of all the numerous Works which have been publiſhed in this Department of Bibliography, being the Reſults of thirty Years of diligent Labour and Reſearch. The Author was private Librarian of the Emperor Napoleon, and afterwards, on the Return of the Bourbons, Superintendent of the private Royal Libraries. He died in 1825. His Dictionary is confined to Works in the Latin and French Languages, but of theſe it notices between twenty-three and twenty-four thouſand.

LANCETTI (V.). Pſeudonimia Ovvero Tavole alfabetiche de' Nomi finti o ſuppoſti degli Scrittori con la Contrappoſizione de' Veri. 8°. Milano. 1836.

MANNE (M. de). Nouveau Recueil d'Ouvrages Anonymes et Pſeudonymes. 8°. Paris. 1834.

Containing 2131 Articles, not limited like Barbier's Dictionary to Works in the French and Latin Languages, and followed by an alphabetical Index of Authors.

PLACCIUS (Vincent). Theatrum Anonymorum et Pſeudonymorum Operum. (Edited by J. A. Fabricius and M. Dreyer, with a Preface by the former.) 2d Ed. Fol. Hamburgi. 1708.

To this ſhould be added a Supplement, or Continuation, by J. C. Mylius, publiſhed in 1740. folio. Hamburg. The original Work and the Supplement together, comprehend between nine and ten thouſand Articles.

QUÉRARD (J. M.). Les Ecrivains Pſeudonymes et autres Myſtificateurs de la Littérature Française pendant les quatre derniers Siècles reſtitués à leurs véritables Noms. 8°. Paris. 1854-5.

One of the lateſt Works upon the Subject.

SCHMIDT (A. G.). Gallerie deutſcher pſeudonymer Schriftſteller, &c. 8°. Grimmæ. 1840.

3. Prohibited.

The following Works upon condemned and prohibited Books, may very appropriately be added to the above Defcriptions of rare and anonymous Books. They conftitute a melancholy Portion of Bibliography, for though the Facts which they collect fometimes amufe by their Folly, they oftener excite Indignation and Pity at the Oppreffions of Power, and the Sufferings of the Learned.

An exact Reprint of the Roman Index Expurgatorius, the only Vatican Index of this Kind ever publifhed; edited, with a Preface, by Richard Gibbings. Thick 12°. Dublin. 1837.

Hannot (J. B.). Index des principaux Livres condamnés et défendus par l'Eglife. 12°. Namur. 1714.

Index Librorum Prohibitorum juxta Examplar Romanum Juffu Sanctiffimi Domini noftri editum Anno 1835; Acceflerunt fuis Locis Nomina eorum qui ufque ad hanc Diem damnati fuere. Poft 8°. Mechliniæ. 1843.

Mendham (Jofeph). Account of the Indexes, both prohibitory and expurgatory, of the Church of Rome. 8°. London. 1826.

Mendham (Jofeph). Index Librorum Prohibitorum a Sixto V.; Ed. J. Mendham. 4°. London. 1835.

PEIGNOT (Gabriel). Dictionnaire Critique et Bibliographique des Principaux Livres condamnés au Feu, ſupprimés ou cenſurés. 2 Vols. 8°. Paris. 1806.

The moſt complete Work in this Department of Bibliography, although it can hardly be ſaid to contain an Enumeration of all the *principal* ſuppreſſed, condemned or cenſured Books, as there are few Engliſh Works noticed. The firſt Volume contains a Liſt of INDICES EXPURGATORII, and alſo of more than thirty Writers who have treated on this Subject.

VI. Claſſification of Books and Management of Libraries, or Library Economy.

NOTWITHSTANDING the almoſt infinite Number of Libraries and Catalogues that exiſt, ſcarcely any two can be found which entirely agree in their Arrangements, or which are catalogued upon the ſame Principles. It is therefore important to point out ſome of the beſt Guides upon theſe Subjects, for the Benefit of the various publick Libraries which are being formed and developed in all Parts of the Land, in order that they may be conducted in accordance with the moſt approved Principles of Library Economy. Before proceeding with our Liſt, we may remark, that Catalogues reſolve themſelves finally into two Claſſes, viz: CLASSIFIED and ALPHABETICAL. The Utility of the former is very great, conſiſting obviouſly in this, that the Books upon any Subject are found at once by referring to the proper Head.

To refer however every Book to its proper Place in the general Syſtem of human Knowledge, would evidently require clearer and more exact Ideas of the Scope and Objects of all the Departments and Branches of which that Syſtem conſiſts, and a more thorough Acquaintance with the Science of Bibliography in all its Details than moſt Perſons poſſeſs. The Difficulties of ſuch a Taſk, and indeed of the whole Subject of cataloguing, are very happily illuſtrated in the Article on Libraries and Catalogues appended to this Work.

A DESCRIPTIVE CATALOGUE, with the Titles placed in alphabetical Order under the Names of Authors, and accompanied by an alphabetical and claſſified Index of Subjects, is in our Judgment by far the moſt practical and uſeful. Such a Catalogue might well be called "the Eye of the Library." It ſhould in moſt Caſes have *ſhort* Titles, and always give in full the CONTENTS of all the COLLECTED WORKS of Authors, and of all Collections of ſingle Works of various Authors, having a common Title. We notice the moſt important Books under this Head, ſome of which might properly be claſſed with ELEMENTARY Bibliographies already deſcribed.

ALBERT (J. F. M.). Récherches ſur les Principes fondamentaux de la Claſſification biblographique. 8°. Paris. 1847.

A very important Work of its Kind.

AMPÈRE (A. M.). Eſſai ſur la Philoſophie des Sciences, ou Expoſition analytique d'une Claſſification naturelle de toutes les Connaiſſances humaines. 2 Pts. 8°. Paris. 1843.

CAMUS (A. G.). Obſervations ſur la Diſtribution et le Claſſement des Livres d'une Bibliothèque. [Mémoires de l'Inſt. National; Litt. et Beaux Arts, Tome I]. 4°. Paris. 1798. pp. 643-76.

CONSTANTIN (L. A.). Bibliothéconomie, ou nouveau Manuel Complet pour l'Arrangement, la Conſervation et l'Adminiſtration des Bibliothèques. 2d Ed. 18°. Paris. 1841.

An excellent little Manual upon Library Economy, which we hope to preſent to the Publick at ſome future Time, in an Engliſh Dreſs, with Additions, &c. It is very full upon Catalogues and the Statiſticks of Libraries. The Author, whoſe real Name was Heſſe, has recently died at Paris.

EBERT (F. A.). Bildung des Bibliothekars. 2d Ed. 8°. Leipzig. 1820.

Few Perſons, it is believed, have ever engaged in the Work of arranging and cataloguing, even a ſmall Library of learned Books, without being painfully impreſſed with the Importance of all the varied Qualifications which Ebert here enumerates, as eſſential for a *German* Librarian.

EXPOSÉ ſuccinct d'un nouveau Syſtème d'Organiſation des Bibliothèques publiques, par un Bibliothécaire. 8°. Montpellier. 1845.

FOISY (F. M.). Eſſai ſur la Conſervation des Bibliothèques publiques. 8°. Paris. 1833.

FORTIA D'URBAN (Le Marquis). Nouveau Syſtème alphabétique de Bibliographie alphabétique. Seconde Edition, précédée de nouvelles Conſiderations ſur l'Orthographe Françaiſe. 12°. Paris. 1822.

The firſt Part includes a general Syſtem of Bibliography. The ſecond Part includes an encyclopedical Table of human Knowledge. A new Edition has been publiſhed containing Part third, and a general Index. This laſt Part relates to Encyclopedias, ſhowing what they are, in what Languages they have been written, &c.

HORNE (T. H.). Outlines for the Claſſification of a Library, ſubmitted to the Truſtees of the Britiſh Muſeum. 4°. London. 1825.

Now very ſcarce.

JEWETT (C. C.). On the Conſtruction of Catalogues of Libraries, and their Publication by Means of ſeparate, ſtereotyped Titles; with Rules and Examples. 2d Ed. 8°. Waſhington. 1853.

Containing an Explanation of the Author's Plan for preparing and ſtereotyping Catalogues, and ſerving as a Manual for Librarians in carrying the ſame into Practice. The thirty-nine Rules embodied in the Work, founded upon thoſe adopted for the Compilation of the Catalogue of the Britiſh Muſeum, have been drawn up with great Care. Modifications and Additions have been made, adapted to the peculiar Character of the Syſtem propoſed. Theſe Modifications can readily be diſcovered and ſet aſide by thoſe who wiſh to uſe the Rules in the Preparation of an ordinary Catalogue. The Work is an indiſpenſable Guide to Librarians and others, enabling them to compile Catalogues upon the beſt and moſt approved Principles, without the Expenſe of uſeleſs Labour. The Author, it is underſtood, is preparing for the Preſs a third and enlarged Edition of this invaluable Manual.

LUDEWIG (Herman). Zur Bibliotheconomie. 8°. Leipzig. 1840.

MOLBECH (Chriſtian). Ueber Bibliothekwiſſenſchaft, oder Einrichtung und Verwaltung öffentlicher Bibliotheken. (2d Ed. from the Daniſh Originals by H. Ratjen). 8°. Leipzig. 1833.

A very learned and comprehenſive Book upon the whole Subject of Library Economy.

Namur (M. P.). Manuel du Bibliothécaire. 8°. Bruxelles. 1834.

Paris (M. P.). De la Néceſſité de commencer, achever et publier le Catalogue des Livres imprimés, etc. Seconde Edition, dans laquelle on a complété le Plan de Claſſification bibliographique, et répondu à quelques Objections. 8°. Paris. 1847. pp. 63.

Peignot (Gabriel). Manuel du Bibliophile, ou Traité du Choix des Livres. 2 Vols. 8°. Dijon. 1823.

A very uſeful Guide for the Book Purchaſer.

Petzholdt und Reichard. Ankündigung von Beiträgen zur Bibliothekſbaukunſt. 2 Vols. 8°. Dreſden. 1844.

Petzholdt (Julius). Katechiſmus der Bibliothekenlehre. Anleitung zur Einrichtung und Verwaltung von Bibliotheken. Mit 16 in den Text gedruckten Abbildungen und 15 Schrifttafeln. 8°. Leipzig. 1856.

This little Work forms the 27th Number of a Series iſſued by J. J. Weber, entitled *Illuſtrirte Katechiſmen.*

REPORT from the Selećt Committee on Publick Libraries; together with Proceedings of the Committee, Minutes of Evidence, and Appendix. Folio. London. 1849.

This Report of the Houſe of Commons, making, with the Index, a Volume of 417 pages, contains the fulleſt and moſt accurate ſtatiſtical Details reſpecting publick Libraries to be found in Print. It embodies the Teſtimony and Opinions of ſome of the moſt eminent Bibliographers in Europe, upon important Points in the Hiſtory and Management of Libraries, as for Example, E. Edwards, formerly of the Britiſh Muſeum, M. Guizot of France, M. Van der Weyer of Belgium, M. Libri of Italy, &c. &c.

REPORT of the Commiſſioners appointed to inquire into the Conſtitution and Government of the Britiſh Muſeum; with Minutes of Evidence. Folio. pp. 823. London. 1850. Alſo Index to Report, &c. Folio. pp. 172. London. 1850.

The principal Subject of Inquiry related to the Preparation and Printing of a Catalogue. On this Point therefore it contains full Information.

RICHTER (Benedict). Kurze Anleitung eine Bibliothek zu ordnen und in der Ordnung zu erhalten. (With 6 Illuſtrations.) 8°. Augſburg. 1836.

SCHMIDT (J. A. F.). Handbuch der Bibliothekwiſſenſchaft. 8°. Weimar. 1840.

Valuable particularly for its Liſts of Books of Reference on Bibliography, Literary Hiſtory, &c.

SCHRETTINGER (M.). Verſuch eines vollſtändigen Lehrbuchs der Bibliothekwiſſenſchaft. 2 Vols. 2d Ed. 8°. München. 1829.

SCHRETTINGER (M.). Handbuch der Bibliothekwiſſenſchaft, beſonders zum Gebrauche der Richt-Bibliothekare. 8°. Wien. 1834.

SHURTLEFF (N. B.). A Decimal Syſtem for the Arrangement and Adminiſtration of Libraries. 4°. Boſton. 1856.

Deſcriptive of a Syſtem which the Writer, as ſtated in the Preface, has introduced into the Publick Library of the City of Boſton, and which hsa been in practical Operation there ſince the Summer of 1852.

VII. Library Edifices, and Hiſtory and Statiſticks of Libraries.

BALBI (Adrien). Eſſai Statiſtique ſur les Bibliothèques de Vienne, comparées aux plus grands Etabliſſemens de ce Genre, &c. 8°. Vienna. 1835.

Next to the elaborate Article by Ebert, in the *Cyclopädie* of Erſch and Gruber, the firſt ſtatiſtical View of exiſting Libraries to be at all relied upon for general Accuracy, Mr. Edwards places this valuable Treatiſe by Balbi. The *Tableaux Statiſtiques ſur les Bibliothèques Anciennes et Modernes*, by the ſame Author, were publiſhed in the Tranſactions of the French Statiſtical Society in 1836.

BAILLY (J. L. A.). Notices hiſtoriques ſur les Bibliothèques Anciennes et Modernes, ſuivies d'un Tableau Comparatif des Produits de la Preſſe de 1812 à 1825, et d'une Liſte des Lois, &c. concernant les Bibliothèques. 8°. Paris. 1828.

BLUME (Friedrich). Iter Italicum. 4 Vols. 8°. Berlin und Halle. 1824-36.

Containing an Account of the Archives, Infcriptions and Libraries in the Sardinian and Auftrian Provinces.

BUCHON (J. A.). Rapports fur la Situation des Bibliothèques publiques en France. 8°. Paris. 1830.

CLARKE (Wm.). Repertorium Bibliographicum; or fome Account of the moft celebrated Britifh Libraries. Large 8°. London. 1819.

Defigned, fays the Advertifement, to affift the Collector in his Purfuit of valuable Editions of rare Books, and containing Selections from the various Libraries, to give the prominent Features of each.

DELESSERT (M. B.). Mémoire fur la Bibliothéque Royale. 4°. Paris. 1835.

DELESSERT (M. B.). Projet d'une Bibliothèque circulaire fur l'Emplacement, etc. 4°. Paris.

FARNUM (Luther). A Glance at Private Libraries. 8°. Bofton. 1855. pp. 79.

The Libraries noticed in this Account are chiefly of Bofton and its Neighbourhood, embracing thofe of Everett, Prefcott, Ticknor, Parker, Sears (now Prefident of Brown Univerfity, Providence), Livermore, the late Daniel Webfter, &c. Mr. Farnum eftimates the Number of Books in private Libraries of one thoufand Volumes and upwards, within ten Miles of the Bofton State Houfe, to equal or exceed three hundred thoufand.

GLAY (Dr. Le). Mémoire fur les Bibliothèques publiques et les principales Bibliothèques particulières du Départment du Nord. 8°. Lille. 1841.

GREPPO (J. G. H.). Notice hiſtorique ſur les Bibliothèques des Hebreux. 8°. Paris. 1835.

HUNTER (Joſeph). Engliſh Monaſtick Libraries. 4°. London. 1831.

JEWETT (C. C.). Notices of the Publick Libraries in the United States of America. 8°. Waſhington. 1851.

Prepared by Prof. Jewett while Librarian of the Smithſonian Inſtitution, and publiſhed under its Auſpices, being the firſt Work of the Kind of any Extent that has ever appeared in this Country. It is remarkable that the moſt complete Account of our Libraries that had been publiſhed previous to this Work, is to be found in the *Serapeum* for 1846, a foreign Periodical. The Number of Libraries deſcribed by Prof. Jewett is 694, containing an aggregate of nearly two and one quarter millions of Books. This Number has now increaſed to more than three millions.

LABORDE (Le Cmte de). De l'Organization des Bibliothèques de Paris. (With Plates.) 2 Vols. Royal 8°. Paris. 1845-46.

Publiſhed in the Form of *Lettres*. Alſo by the ſame, *Etude ſur la Conſtruction des Bibliothèques*, &c. 1846.

LIVERMORE (George). Remarks on Publick Libraries. From *The North American Review* for July, 1850. For private Diſtribution only. 8°. Cambridge. 1850.

Full of practical and important Suggeſtions and deſerving a wide Circulation. The Author is one of our moſt accompliſhed Bibliographers. For an Account of his private Library, which is particularly rich in Works illuſtrative of early Typography, ſee Farnum's *Glance at Private Libraries*, juſt noticed.

NAMUR (M. P.). Hiſtoire des Bibliothèques

Publiques de la Belgique. 3 Vols. 8°. Bruxelles. 1840.

Norton's Literary Almanac for 1852; Norton's Literary Regifter and Book Buyer's Almanac for 1853; Norton's Literary and Educational Regifter for 1854. 12°. New York.

Thefe three little Volumes, which are bound together and fold as *Norton's Literary Regifter*, contain much ufeful Information in regard to American Libraries, Books, and Publifhers. The third Volume (pages 49-94) contains a full and authentic Account of the Proceedings of the Librarian's Convention, which was held in New York City, Sept. 15, 16, and 17, 1853.

Papworth (J. W. & W.). Mufeums, Libraries, and Picture Galleries, with Illuftrations. Royal 8°. London. 1853.

Containing Suggeftions on the Eftablifhment of fuch Inftitutions; on the Formation and Arrangement of Mufeums for provincial Cities and large Towns; on Plans for building and arranging Libraries for publick and private Ufe; Notes on Cataloguing; and Explanations and Examples of the beft Modes for conftructing and lighting Picture Galleries, etc. etc.; with ten Plates, or Illuftrations. The Authors are diftinguifhed Britifh Architects.

Peignot (Gabriel). Manuel Bibliographique, ou Effai fur les Bibliothèques Anciennes et Modernes, &c. 8°. Paris. 1800.

Peignot (Gabriel). Souvenirs rélatifs à quelques Bibliothèques particulières du Temps paffé. 8°. Dijon. 1836.

Petit-Radel (L. C. F). Recherches fur les Bibliothèques anciennes et modernes jufqu' à la

Fondation de la Bibliothèque Mazarine, et ſur les Cauſes qui ont favoriſé l'Accroiſſement du Nombre des Livres. 8°. Paris. 1819.

PETZHOLDT (Julius). Addreſſbuch Deutſcher Bibliotheken. 8°. Halle. 1853.

The 4th and laſt Edition of a Work of the higheſt Authority on the Libraries of Germany.

PREUSKER (Karl). Ueber öffentliche Vereins- und Privat-Bibliotheken. 2 Parts in one Volume. 8°. Leipzig. 1839-40.

SANTA (L. Della). Della Conſtruzione e del Regolamento di una publica univerſale Biblioteca. (With an Illuſtration). Small 4°. Firenze. 1816.

The Author, who died about the Year 1830, was Secretary in the Bibliotheca Magliabecchiana at Florence. His Treatiſe on the Conſtruction of a publick Library, is in high repute.

SIMS (Richard). Handbook to the Library of the Britiſh Muſeum; containing a brief Hiſtory of its Formation, and of the various Collections of which it is compoſed; Deſcriptions of the Catalogues in preſent Uſe; claſſed Liſts of the Manuſcripts, etc.; with ſome Account of the principal Libraries of London. 12°. London. 1854.

This little Manual of 418 Pages, contains a Catalogue of the printed Books of Reference in the Reading Rooms of the Britiſh Muſeum, regarded as "indiſpenſably neceſſary to Students of all Denominations." Such a Catalogue will be found uſeful to thoſe who have in Charge the Selection of Books for our publick Libraries.

"There are tolerably good Hand-books to ſome Departments of the Muſeum, but the Library is only vaguely known to thoſe who have walked through it, or tried to fathom it through its Catalogues. Mr. Sims has undertaken to ſupply this Deficiency, and being officially connected with the Manuſcript Department of the Library, the Taſk has been eaſier for him than it would have been for an outſider. His Purpoſe is two-fold—to give the publick a general Idea of the Contents and Arrangement of the Library, and to furniſh to literary Men and Readers, a ſyſtematized Means of Reference to the Treaſures of the great Collection. The Work is executed with great Pains and conſiderable Judgment, and will be found very uſeful. Altogether the Work, though not very intereſting to the general Public, will be a Boon to the literary Man and the Book-worm."—*Weſtminſter Review, Jan.* 1854.

VOISIN (Aug.). Documents pour ſervir à l'Hiſtoire des Bibliothèques en Belgique, et de leurs principales Curioſités littéraires. 8°. Gand. 1840.

VOISIN (Aug.). Statiſtiques des principales Bibliothèques de l'Europe. 12°. Bruxelles. 1837.

The fulleſt Statiſtics of publick Libraries are to be found in the Report of the Select Committee, deſcribed under the previous Head. The laſt Edition of *Encyclopedia Britannica* contains a capital Article on Britiſh and Foreign Libraries, by Edward Edwards, Eſq. formerly of the Britiſh Muſeum, and now Librarian of the Free Library, Mancheſter. Prefixed are ſome Remarks on library Economy. The whole Article occupies 26 large quarto Pages.

VIII. Oriental and Claſſical Languages.

ADELUNG (Friedrich). Bibliotheca Sanſcrita. Literatur der Sanſkrit Sprache. 2d Edition, enlarged and improved. 8°. St.-Peterſburg. 1837.

Adelung (Friedrich). An Hiſtorical Sketch of Sanſcrit Literature, with copious bibliographical Notices of Sanſcrit Works and Tranſlations; tranſlated from the German, with numerous Additions and Corrections, by D. A. Talboys. 8°. Oxford. 1832.

"One of the moſt reſpectable and uſeful Books which have for a long Time iſſued from the Preſs. It is, in fact, a Vade Mecum, without which the Library of no Oriental Scholar can be eſteemed perfect; poſ-ſeſſing a Claſſification ſo ſyſtematically regular, that all the known Treaſ-ures of this ſacred Tongue are, as it were, at one Glance brought before the Enquirer."—*Aſiatic Journal.*

Bohn (H. G.). General Catalogue. Part Second. Greek and Latin Claſſics, Commentaries and Tranſlations. 8°. London. 1850.

With Prices and occaſional bibliographical Notices.

Brüggemann (L. W.). A View of the Engliſh Editions and Tranſlations of the ancient Greek and Latin Authors, with Remarks. Thick 8°. Stettin. 1797. pp. 850.

Clarke (Adam). Bibliographical Dictionary, with Supplement. 8 Vols. ſmall 8°. London. 1803-6.

Containing an Account of Books in all Departments of Learning, pub-liſhed in the Latin, Greek, Hebrew, Arabick, and other eaſtern Languages. The Supplement, in 2 Volumes, contains, among other Matter, an Account of the Engliſh Tranſlations of the Claſſicks and Eccleſiaſtical Writers, with Liſts of the beſt Arabick and Perſian Authors, Grammars, Lexicons, &c.

Dibdin (T. F.). Introduction to a Knowledge of rare and valuable Editions of the Greek and Roman Claſſicks. 4th Edition, greatly enlarged and corrected. 2 Vols. 8°. London. 1827.

ENGELMANN (Wilhelm). Bibliotheca Scriptorum Claſſicorum et Græcorum et Latinorum. (6th Edition of Enſlin's *Bibliotheca Auctorum Claſſicorum*, enlarged, &c. by Engelmann, with a Supplement.) 8°. Leipzig. 1847-53.

The moſt complete Work of the Kind extant, giving an Account of all the Editions publiſhed in Germany from 1700 to 1853.

ESCHENBURG (J. J.). Manual of Claſſical Literature. from the German, with Additions, by Prof. N. W. Fiſke, of Amherſt College, Maſſachuſetts. 12th Edition, (or Thouſand.) 8°. Philadelphia. 1857.

Uſed as a Text Book in many of our Colleges. It includes a View of Latin and Greek Authors, with Notices of Editions, &c.

FABRICIUS (J. A.). Bibliotheca Græca, ed. Harles. 4th Ed. 12 Vols. 4°. Hamburgi. 1690-1809.

To this ſhould be added an Index publiſhed at Leipzic in 1838, in one quarto Volume. Of this Bibliotheca Dibdin ſays: "All the known Editions of the Greek Claſſicks, with their Illuſtrators, are recorded in this Work, accompanied by bibliographical and critical Remarks. There is nothing in our own or any other Language which can be put in Competition with it."

FABRICIUS (J. A.). Bibliotheca Latina, ed. Erneſti. 3 Vols. 8°. Lipſiæ. 1773-4.

FABRICIUS (J. A.). Bibliotheca Latina Mediæ et Infimæ Ætatis. 6 Vols. 4°. Patavii. 1754.

FRAEHN (C. M.). Indications bibliographiques relatives pour la plupart à la Littérature hiſtorico-géographique des Arabes, des Perſans, et des Turcs. (New Edition.) 8°. St. Peterſburg. 1845.

Fürst (J.). Bibliotheca Judaica Bibliographica. Handbuch der gesammten Jüdischen Literatur, nach alphabetischer Ordnung der Verfasser bearbeitet. 2 Vols. 8°. Leipzig. 1849-51.

Gildemeister (J.). Bibliotheca Sanscrita. 8°. Bonnæ ad Rhenum. 1847.

Hebenstreit (W.). Dictionarium Editionum tum Selectarum tum Optimarum Auctorum Classicorum et Græcorum et Latinorum cum Notis criticis. 12°. Vindobonæ. 1828.

A Manual in high Repute.

Hadji-Khalfa-Mustafa (B. A. K. I.). Lexicon bibliographicum et encyclopædicum. Latine vertit et Commentariis Indicibusque instruxit G. Flügel. 6 Vols. 4°. Leipzig. 1835-52.

A Work on Oriental Bibliography, &c. consisting largely of descriptive Titles.

Herbelot (B. d'). Bibliothèque Orientale, augmentée par Schultens. Best Edition. 4 Vols. 4°. La Haye. 1777-82.

A Treasure of useful Knowledge, which has done much to draw the Attention of Europeans to the Writings of the Asiatics.

Hoffmann (S. F. W.). Bibliographisches Lexicon der gesammten Literatur der Griechen. 2d Ed. 3 Vols. 8°. Leipzig. 1838-45.

A Work of the highest Authority.

Hoffmann (S. F. W.). Handbuch zur Bücherkunde für Lehre und Studium der beiden alten klaſſiſchen und deutſchen Sprache. 8°. Leipzig. 1838.

Very uſeful for Students.

MOSS (J. W.). Manual of Claſſical Bibliography. New Edition. 2 Vols. 8°. London. 1837.

SCHOELL (FRÉD.). Répertoire de la Littérature Ancienne, ou Choix d'Auteurs Claſſiques Grecs et Latins, imprimés en Allemagne et en France. 2 Vols. 8°. Paris. 1808.

SCHWEIGGER (L. F. A.). Handbuch der Klaſſiſchen Bibliographie. 3 Vols. 8°. Leipzig. 1830-4.

The beſt general Book of the Kind extant. Volumes 2 and 3 (Vol. 2 Parts 1 and 2 in Reality), compriſing the principal Part of the Work, are devoted to the Latin Claſſicks.

WOLFIUS (J. C.). Bibliotheca Hebræa. 4 Vols. 4°. Hamburgi. 1715-33.

ZENKER (J. T.). Manuel de Bibliographie Orientale. 8°. Leipzig. 1846.

IX. Bibliography of Modern Nations, or National Bibliographies.

1. AMERICA.

ALLIBONE (S. A.). A Critical Dictionary of Engliſh Literature, and Britiſh and American Authors, living and deceaſed, from the earlieſt Accounts to the Middle of the nineteenth Century.

This Dictionary, now brought down to the Letter N, will probably be publiſhed during the preſent Year. A full Deſcription of it is given under Section XII. The following Extract from a Letter of the veteran Bibliographer, Thos. Hartwell Horne, addreſſed to the Publiſhers, will ſhow the Importance of the Work in Connection with AMERICAN Bibliography.

"Mr. Allibone's Liſt of Authorities conſulted includes, I believe, every Work of any Value. My own Knowledge of American Authors has hitherto been derived chiefly from the beſt Edition of *Allen's American Biography*, and from Mr. Trübner's conciſe but truly valuable *Guide to American Literature*. But henceforth Mr. Allibone's Reſearches will leave nothing to be deſired."

ASHER (G. M.). Bibliographical and Hiſtorical Eſſay on the Dutch Books and Pamphlets relating to New-Netherland, and to the Dutch Weſt-India Company. Small 4°. Amſterdam. 1854. pp. 120. Alſo a Liſt of the Maps and Charts of New-Netherland, and of the Views of New-Amſterdam, by G. M. Aſher; being a Supplement to his Bibliographical Eſſay on New-Netherland. Small 4°. Amſterdam. 1855. pp. 44.

ASPINWALL (Col. J.). Bibliotheca Americæ Septentrionalis; being a choice Collection of Books relating to North America. 8°. Paris. 1820.

BIBLIOGRAPHICAL Catalogue of Books, Tranſlations of the Scriptures, and other Publications in the Indian Tongues of the United States. 8°. Waſhington. 1849.

BIBLIOTHECA Americana; or a Chronological Catalogue of the moſt curious and intereſting Books, Pamphlets, &c. upon North and South America, in Print and Manufcript; with an introductory Difcourfe on the prefent State of Literature in thofe Countries. 4°. London. 1789.

CATALOGUE of Books on the Mafonic Inftitution, in public Libraries of twenty-eight States of the Union, Antimafonic in Arguments and Conclufions. By diftinguifhed literary Gentlemen, Citizens of the United States. With introductory Remarks by a Member of the Suffolk Committee of 1829. 8°. Bofton. 1852. pp. 270.

A Work on Freemafonry rather than a Bibliography. Important in this Connection however, as the Books referred to are all American.

DALRYMPLE (Alexander). Catalogue of Authors who have written on the Rio de la Plata, Paraguay, and Chaco. 4°. London. 1807.

FARIBAULT (G. B.). Catalogue d'Ouvrages fur l'Hiftoire de l'Amérique, et en particulier fur celle du Canada, de la Louifiane, de l'Acadie, et autres Lieux. 8°. Quebec. 1837. pp. 207.

In three Parts. The firft Part contains the Authors who have written on the Subject, arranged alphabetically; the fecond, anonymous Works arranged chronologically; and the third, a Catalogue of Maps, Charts, and Plans. The Number of Works defcribed is 969, and to many of them defcriptive Notes by the Author, or Notes extracted from other Works, are added.

GIRARD (Charles). Bibliographia Americana Hiftorico-Naturalis; or, Bibliography of American Natural Hiftory for 1851. 8°. Wafhington. 1852. pp. 70.

GOWANS (William). A Catalogue of Books on Freemaſonry and kindred Subjects. 12°. New York. 1858. pp. 59.

Giving a Liſt of Maſonick Publications, moſtly American.

KENNETT (White.) Bibliothecæ Americanæ Primordia; an Attempt towards laying the Foundation of an American Library. 4°. London. 1713.

KOHL (J. G.). Deſcriptive Catalogue of thoſe Maps, Charts and Surveys relating to America, mentioned in Vol. III. of Hakluyt's great Work. 8°. Waſhington. 1857.

LUDEWIG (H. E.). The Literature of American Local Hiſtory; a bibliographical Eſſay. 8°. New York. 1846. Privately printed.

LUDEWIG (H. E.). Trübner's Bibliotheca Glottica. The Literature of American Aboriginal Languages by H. E. Ludewig. With Additions and Corrections by Profeſſor W. W. Turner. Edited by N. Trübner. 8°. London. 1857. pp. 283.

The lateſt Work of this eminent German Bibliographer. "The Name of the Author to all thoſe who are acquainted with his former Works, and who know the Thoroughneſs and profound Character of his Inveſtigations, is a ſufficient Guaranty that this Work will be one of ſtandard Authority, and one that will fully anſwer the Demands of the preſent Time."—*Petzholdt's Anzeiger, Jan.* 1858.

MEUSEL's Bibliotheca Hiſtorica. Vols. 3 and 10. See under Section X.

MUNSELL (Joel). The Typographical Miſcellany, 8°. Albany, 1850. pp. 267.

This Book belongs properly to another Section (IV); having been accidentally omitted in its Place, we have introduced it here on account of its Importance in Connection with American Bibliography. It gives many interesting Details respecting American Printers, &c.

NORTON's Literary Register; or, Annual Book List for 1856. 8°. New York. 1856.

A Catalogue of Books published in the United States during the Year 1855, including Reprints, and containing Titles, Number of Pages, Prices, and Names of Publishers, with an Index of Subjects. Prefixed to this Catalogue is a List of the principal Publishers in the United States.

RICH (Obadiah). A Catalogue of Books relating principally to America, arranged under the Years in which they were printed, from 1500 to 1700. 8°. London. 1832. pp. 129.

Containing 486 Articles, being less by 667 than the Number contained in Ternaux's *Bibliothèque*.

RICH (Obadiah). Bibliotheca Americana Nova; or a Catalogue of Books in various Languages, relating to America, printed since the Year 1700. 8°. London. 1835. pp. 423.

RICH (Obadiah). Supplement to the above. 1701-1800. 8°. London. 1841. pp. 424-508.

These two Catalogues (Bibliotheca and Supplement), although they contain 2523 Articles, are far from being complete. A Merchant of Providence, well known to the Amateurs of this Class of Books, has in his own private Collection 3231 early Works upon America, published between the Years 1700 and 1800, of which 1512 are not mentioned by Rich. He has also 1174 Works published *previous* to the Year 1700, of which 509 are not mentioned by Ternaux; thus making 4405 SEPARATE WORKS relating to America and published previous to the Year 1800, of which 2021 were unknown to the eminent American Bibliographers whose Catalogues are described in this LIST.

Rich (Obadiah). Bibliotheca Americana Nova. 1801-1844. (With an alphabetical Index of Authors.) 8°. London. 1846. pp. 412.

All of Rich's Catalogues are important, and eagerly fought for by Book-collectors, efpecially the earlier ones, which have come to be exceedingly fcarce. Copies of the four Volumes above defcribed have recently been fold in New York for $50. They contain the Titles of the Works in full, with Prices in many Inftances, and occafionally bibliographical Notes. Rich's Sale Catalogues of Works relating to America are alfo important. One of thefe was publifhed in 1832; and a fecond in 1837. pp. 40.

Roorbach (O. A.). Bibliotheca Americana; Catalogue of American Publications, including Reprints and original Works, from 1820 to October, 1852, inclufive; together with a Lift of Periodicals publifhed in the United States. Royal 8°. New York. 1852. pp. 663.

Roorbach (O. A.). Supplement to the Bibliotheca Americana, from October, 1852, to May, 1855. Royal 8°. New York, 1855. pp. 227.

Roorbach (O. A.). Addenda to the Bibliotheca Americana; a Catalogue of American Publications from May, 1855, to March, 1858. Royal 8°. New York. 1858.

Thefe Catalogues all give the Year, Size, Style of Binding, Price and Publifhers. The net Price of the *Bibliotheca* is $7; the *Supplement*, $3; and the *Addenda* $3.

Ternaux-Compans (M. H.). Bibliothèque Américaine, ou Catalogue des Ouvrages relatifs à l'Amérique. 8°. Paris. 1837.

This includes only thofe Works publifhed previous to the Year 1700.

It is much more complete than the correſponding Catalogue of Rich, containing 1153 Articles, while the latter, as has been already mentioned, deſcribes only 486 ſeparate Works.

TRÜBNER'S Bibliographical Guide to American Literature; being a claſſified Liſt of Books (with Prices), in all Departments of Literature and Science, publiſhed in the United States of America during the laſt 40 Years. With an Introduction (giving a brief Outline or Sketch of American Literature), Notes, three Appendices, and an Index. 12°. London. 1855. pp. 140.

A very uſeful little Work, ſuggeſting the Need of a more extenſive one upon a ſimilar Plan, by ſome Bibliographer in this Country. Mr. Trübner alſo publiſhed in 1856, a ſmall octavo Pamphlet of 8 Pages, containing a Liſt of the Books on the Military Arts and Sciences printed in the United States.

WARDEN (D. B.). Bibliotheca Americana; being a choice Collection of Books, Maps, Engravings, and Medals relating to North and South America and the Weſt-Indies, including Voyages to the Southern Hemiſphere, Maps, Engravings and Medals. 8°. Paris. 1840. pp. 124.

To this Liſt ſhould be added Duyckinck's valuable *Cyclopædia of American Literature*, 2 Vols. royal 8°. New York, 1856, which, although biographical rather than bibliographical, is intended to exhibit and illuſtrate the Products of the American Pen; Griſwold's *Poets and Poetry of America, with an hiſtorical Introduction*, 8°. Philadelphia, 1855; Griſwold's *Female Poets of America*, 8°.; Griſwold's *Proſe Writers of America*, 8°. The Inquirer under this Head will alſo conſult the *Literary World*, 15 Vols. 4°. New York, 1847-53; *Norton's Literary Gazette*, 3 Vols. ſmall folio, and 1 Vol. 4°. New York, 1851-4; *Norton's Literary Almanac and Regiſter*, for 1852, 1853, 1854; *The Publiſher's Circular*, a weekly Periodical commenced in New York in 1855, and ftill continued; *Portfolio*, 5 Vols. 4°. and 42 Vols. 8°. Philadelphia, 1801-27; *Analectic Magazine*, 16 Vols. 8°. Philadelphia, 1813-20; *North American Review*, *Biblical Repofitory* and *Bibliotheca Sacra*, *Chriftian Examiner*, *Methodift Quarterly*, *Democratic Review*, *Silliman's Journal*, *New York Review*, *Southern Quarterly Review*, and other leading Periodicals of the Day. A good bibliographical Work on American Literature is univerfally regarded as a Defideratum. Mr. Henry Stevens, of Vermont, a graduate of Yale College, has for feveral Years paft refided in London, partly as an American Agent for Books, but more efpecially to avail himfelf of the rich bibliographical Treafures of the Britifh Mufeum, in the Preparation of a moft important Work, to be called *The Bibliographia Americana*. This will contain a bibliographical Account of the Sources of American Hiftory, comprifing a Defcription of Books relating to America prior to the Year 1700, and of all Books printed in America from 1543 to 1700, together with Notices of many of the more important unpublifhed Manufcripts. When the Work is ready for the Prefs, it will be publifhed in two quarto Volumes. Its Importance to the future Hiftorian will be ineftimable. Would that fome patient, labor-loving Bibliographer like Lowndes, Quérard, or Gamba, might *continue* this Work down to the prefent Time, that we might thus, in our National Bibliography, compare favourably with Great Britain, France, and Italy. Mr. Stevens has recently publifhed a Catalogue of fuch Books in the Library of the Britifh Mufeum as relate to America.

2. Great Britain.

Anderson (Chriftopher). The Annals of the Englifh Bible. 2 Vols. 8°. London. 1845.

An excellent Work publifhed by Pickering. The Appendix to the fecond Volume contains a Lift of the various Editions of the New Teftament and the Bible in Englifh, with certain publick Libraries and individual Proprietors in Poffeffion of Copies; ferving as an Index to the preceding Annals or Hiftory.

Beloe (William). Anecdotes of Literature and fcarce Books. 6 Vols. 8°. London. 1807-12.

A Work containing much bibliographical Information, and Extracts from curious Books, moftly Englifh. The Notices are not always to be depended upon.

BOHN (John). A Catalogue of an extenfive Collection of Englifh Books; to which is appended a Selection of valuable foreign Books, and a Specimen of an intended Claffical Catalogue. 8°. London. 1829.

Ufeful as part of a bibliographical Apparatus. The Notes and Defcriptions interfperfed throughout add to its Value.

BRYDGES (S. E.). Cenfura Literaria; containing Titles, Abftracts, and Opinions of old Englifh Books, with original Difquifitions, &c. *Second and beft Edition, rearranged and enlarged, with a general Index.* 10 Vols. 8°. London. 1815.

"A Work juftly held in high Eftimation by all Antiquarians in Literature."—*Lowndes.*

BRYDGES (S. E.). The Britifh Bibliographer. (With Portraits.) 4 Vols. 8°. London. 1810-14.

BRYDGES (S. E.). Reftituta; or Titles, Extracts and Characters of old Books in Englifh Literature revived. 4 Vols. 8°. London. 1814-16.

Many hundred Volumes in old Englifh Literature are here defcribed; fome of the Articles however are unneceffarily prolix.

CATALOGUE of all the Plays ever printed in the Englifh Language. 8°. London. 1726.

CLAVEL (Robert). General Catalogue of Books printed in England, from 1666 to 1680. 3[d] Ed. Folio. London. 1680.

COTTON (Henry). Editions of the Bible and Parts thereof in Engliſh, from 1505 to 1850; with an Appendix containing Specimens of Tranſlations, and Bibliographical Deſcriptions. 2d Ed. 8o. Oxford. 1852.

COTTON (Henry). Rhemes and Doway. An Attempt to ſhow what has been done by Roman Catholics for the Diffuſion of the Holy Scriptures in Engliſh. 8o. Oxford. 1855.

FOSTER (B. F.). The Origin and Progreſs of Book-keeping; compriſing an Account of all the Works on this Subject, publiſhed in the Engliſh Language, from 1543 to 1852, with Remarks, critical and hiſtorical. 8o. London. 1852. pp. 54.

GRIFFITH (A. F.). Bibliotheca Anglo-Poetica; or a deſcriptive Catalogue of a rare and rich Collection of early Engliſh Poetry. Illuſtrated by occaſional Extracts and Remarks, critical and biographical. 8o. London. 1815.

An important Addition to Britiſh Bibliography, comprehending more poetical Works than any other Publication of the Kind. They are deſcribed with unuſual Minuteneſs and Accuracy.

HALLIWELL (J. O.). Shakeſperiana; a Catalogue of the early Editions of Shakeſpeare's Plays, and of the Commentaries and other Publications illuſtrative of his Works. 8o. London. 1841. pp. 46.

Undertaken, as the Author ſtates in the Preface, chiefly with a View of ſupplying the Critick and Student with the Means of aſcertaining at once what Sources are available on any particular Points of Inquiry in Shakeſperian Criticiſm, and affording the latter a Manual of bibliographical Information which is indiſpenſable to the Attainment of any correct Knowledge in that Department of Literature.

HUME (Rev. A.). The Learned Societies and Printing Clubs of the United Kingdom. 2d Edition, with a Supplement by A. I. Evans. Poſt 8°. London. 1853.

An exceedingly uſeful Work, containing an Account of the learned Societies and printing Clubs of England, Scotland, and Ireland, their reſpective Origin, Hiſtory, Objects, and Conſtitution; with full Details reſpecting Memberſhip, Fees, *Liſts of their publiſhed Works*, etc. etc. The Supplement, conſiſting of 72 Pages, brings the Work down from 1847, the Date of its firſt Publication, to 1853.

LONDON Catalogue of Books, with their Sizes, Prices, and Publiſhers; containing the Books publiſhed in LONDON, and thoſe altered in Size or Price, 1800-1827. 8°. London. W. Bent. 1827.

This Catalogue, now well known as the LONDON CATALOGUE, was firſt publiſhed in 1766, and included the Titles of all Books publiſhed in London from the Beginning of the 18th Century. It has been frequently reprinted. 1773, 1779, 1799, 1805, 1811, 1812, 1822, &c.

LONDON Catalogue, 1814-1839. 8°. London. R. Bent. 1839.

LONDON Catalogue, Supplement, 1839-1844. 8°. London. T. Hodgſon. 1844.

All the Catalogues above mentioned are confined to Books publiſhed in LONDON.

LONDON Catalogue of Books publiſhed in GREAT BRITAIN; with their Sizes, Prices, and Publiſhers' Names, 1831-1855. 8°. London. T. Hodgſon. 1855.

The Defect of all the LONDON CATALOGUES is, that they do not give Dates. In this laſt Edition, however, the Dates of Works relating to Voyages and Travels, as well as Statutes, Law Reports, &c. are inſerted.

LONDON Catalogue. Bibliotheca Londinenſis; a claſſified Index to the Literature of Great Britain during thirty Years; arranged from and ſerving as a Key to the LONDON CATALOGUE of Books, 1814-46. 8°. London. T. Hodgſon. 1848.

LOW (Sampſon). The Britiſh Catalogue of Books publiſhed from October 1837 to December 1851; containing Date of Publication, Size, Price, Publiſhers' Names, and Edition. Vol. I. General Alphabet. 8°. London. 1852.

A ſecond Volume is announced, which will be a complete Index to the firſt, ſyſtematically arranged, ſo as to afford eaſy Reference to all Works upon any given Subject. Low's Catalogue is more uſeful to Bibliographers generally than the London Catalogue, inaſmuch as it gives EDITIONS and DATES.

LOWNDES (W. T.). The Bibliographer's Manual of Engliſh Literature. 4 Vols. 8°. London. 1834.

The only GENERAL bibliographical Work of the Kind, with the Exception of Watt's *Bibliotheca Britannica*, ever publiſhed in England. It contains Notices of upwards of *fifty thouſand* diſtinct Books, publiſhed in Great Britain and Ireland, from the Invention of Printing to 1834. To theſe Notices are annexed, 1. A conciſe Account of the Merits of the Work, taken from Reviews, and Writers of eſtabliſhed Reputation. 2. Its peculiar *bibliographical* Character. 3. Collations of the Contents of the rarer and more important Articles, including a Liſt of the Plates. 4. References to the Number in the Catalogues of celebrated Sales, ſpecifying the Price for which the Work was ſold. The Manual is now out of Print and ſcarce, Copies having been ſold at Auction in New York for $50, at £7 7s. in London, and at private Sale ſtill higher. A new Edition is announced by Bohn, the firſt Volume of which has already appeared. Poſt 8°. London. 1858.

MACRAY (W. D.). A Manual of Britiſh Hiſtorians to the Year 1600; containing a chronological Account of the early Chroniclers and monkiſh Writers, their printed Works and unpubliſhed MSS. 8°. London. 1845.

MALONE (Edmond). Catalogue of early Engliſh Poetry, collected and now preſerved in the Bodleian Library. Folio. Oxford. 1836.

MARTIN (John). Bibliographical Catalogue of Books privately printed in England. 2 Vols. Imp. 8°. London. 1834.

MICHEL (Franciſque). Bibliothèque Anglo-Saxonne. 8°. Paris and London. 1837.

The Introduction conſiſts of a Letter to the Author of 63 Pages, from J. M. Kemble.

MOULE (Thomas). Bibliotheca Heraldica Magnæ Brittanniæ. An Analytical Catalogue of Books on Genealogy, Heraldry, Nobility, Knighthood and Ceremonies. Royal 8°. London. 1822.

An accurate and valuable Work, ſays Lowndes, conſiſting of pp. xxiii and 668, with a Portrait of Camden.

NICHOLS (John). Literary Anecdotes of the Eighteenth Century, compriſing Memoirs of W.

Bowyer, Printer, &c. 9 Vols. Illuſtrations of the Literary Hiſtory of the Eighteenth Century, 7 Vols. Together 16 Vols. 8°. London. 1812-48.

Not ſtrictly an Engliſh bibliographical Work, but too important in this Connection to be omitted. It is too dear for ordinary Purchaſers.

Nicolson (William). Engliſh, Scotch, and Iriſh Hiſtorical Libraries, giving a ſhort View and Character of moſt of our Hiſtorians, with an Account of our Records, Law Books, Coins, &c. Royal 4°. London. 1776.

Publisher's Circular, and General Record of Britiſh and Foreign Literature; containing a complete Alphabetical Liſt of all New Works publiſhed in Great Britain, and of every Work of Intereſt publiſhed abroad. Alſo Advertiſements connected with Literature and the Fine Arts; to which is annexed, a complete alphabetical Catalogue of New Books and new Editions, including Pamphlets, ſingle Sermons, &c. with the Sizes, Prices, Dates of Publication, and Publiſhers' Names. 1837-57. Vols. 1-20. 8°. London. S. Low & Son. 1837-57.

Reid (John). Bibliotheca Scoto-Celtica; or an Account of all the Books which have been printed in the Gælic Language; with bibliographical and biographical Notices. 8°. London. 1832.

Rimbault (E. F.). Catalogue of Muſical and Poetical Works publiſhed in England in the 16th and 17th Centuries, under the Titles of Madrigals, &c. 8°. London. 1847.

Ritson. (Joſeph). Bibliographia Poetica; a Catalogue of Engliſh Poets of the 12th, 13th, 14th, 15th and 16th Centuries, with a ſhort Account of their Works. Crown 8°. London. 1802.

Savage (James). The Librarian; being an Account of ſcarce, valuable and uſeful Engliſh Books, Manuſcripts, Libraries, Public Records, &c. 3 Vols. (18 Numbers.) 8°. London. 1808-9.

This is an excellent Work though now ſcarce. It is particularly uſeful in pointing out the Number of Plates which ought to be found in complete Copies of rare and coſtly Books. Number 19, Volume IV, pp. 48, was publiſhed.

Smith (J. R.). A Bibliographical Liſt of all Works Illuſtrating the Provincial Dialects of England. 8°. London. 1846.

Stevens (Henry). Catalogue of my Engliſh Library. Poſt 8°. London. 1853. pp. 118.

This little Book was printed for private Diſtribution. It gives a ſelect Liſt of 5751 Volumes of the beſt Editions of the principal ſtandard Engliſh Authors, with the Contents of each Volume. The Introduction contains ſome important Suggeſtions in regard to Duties on Books.

Thomson (R. D.). Illuſtrations of the Hiſtory of Great Britain. 2 Vols. 12°. Edinburgh. 1828.

The Introduction, Pages 113, is on the Sources of Britiſh Hiſtory.

Upcott (William). A Bibliographical Account of the principal Works relating to Britiſh Topography. 3 Vols. 8°. London. 1818.

A Work of great Value.

WALPOLE (Horace). Catalogue of Royal and Noble Authors of England; enlarged and continued by Park. 5 Vols. 8°. London. 1806.

WRIGHT (Thomas). Biographia Britannica Literaria; or Biography of literary Characters of Great Britain and Ireland, arranged in chronological Order. Anglo-Saxon and Anglo-Norman Periods. (With bibliographical Lifts of Works, &c.) 2 Vols. 8°. London. 1842-6.

WATT (Robert). Bibliotheca Britannica; or a General Index of Britifh and Foreign Literature. 4 Vols. 4°. Edinburgh. 1824.

A Work of immenfe Labour, and of the higheft Utility; for, notwithftanding its Imperfections, it contains a Mafs of the moft valuable Matter, difpofed in fuch a Form as to be of great Affiftance to Perfons defirous of afcertaining what Works have been written on a particular Subject, or by a particular Author. Vols. 1 and 2 contain an alphabetical Catalogue of Authors and their Works. Vols. 3 and 4, a general Index. It was publifhed at £11 11s. in bds. The Author's Death in 1819, was occafioned, it is faid, by his laborious Exertions in compiling this Bibliography.

WILSON (John). Shakfperiana. Cataloge of all the Books, Pamphlets, &c. relating to Shakfpeare; to which are fubjoined an Account of the early quarto Editions of the great Dramatift's Plays and Poems, the Prices at which many Copies have fold in public Sales, with a Lift of principal Editions of his collected Works. Poft 8°. London. 1827. pp. 110.

3. France.

Bibliographie de la France, ou Journal général de l'Imprimerie et de la Librairie et des Cartes géographiques, &c. 47 Vols. 8°. Paris. 1811-58.

This weekly Periodical, which we have deſcribed under Section XIII, is really the firſt of its Kind, ſhowing how the yearly Accumulation of literary Works can be recorded in the moſt authentick Manner. The Numbers conſtitute a Series of 47 octavo Volumes, with carefully prepared Tables or Indexes.

Bossange (Hector). Catalogue de Livres Français, Anglais, Allemands, Eſpagnols, Grecs et Latins, Italiens, Portugais, Orientaux, etc. etc.; Suivi de Prix courants. Royal 8°. Paris. 1845. pp. 984.

Giving the Titles moſtly of French Books with current Prices. They are arranged according to Subjects, with a Diviſion appropriated to each Department of Literature, Science, and Art, and a general Index. The Author has ſince publiſhed five Supplements, containing in addition to Titles of Books, priced Catalogues and Deſcriptions of Church Ornaments, optical, philoſophical, mathematical, aſtronomical and nautical Inſtruments, anatomical Models in Wax, &c. &c. All of Boſſange's Catalogues are indiſpenſable Manuals for the Collector of foreign Books.

Bossange (Hector). Ma Bibliothèque Françaiſe. Poſt 8°. Paris. 1855.

This is an elegantly printed and very uſeful Book of 480 Pages, giving a ſelect Liſt of about 7000 Volumes of the beſt Editions of ſtandard French Authors, to which is added a threefold Index of Subjects, Authors, and Perſons. The peculiar Merit of the Work, aſide from the good Judgment and Skill evinced in the Selections, is, that it is a model Catalogue, giving brief biographical Notices of the Authors, and adding to the Titles of all collected Works, the accurate Contents of each Volume.

BOSSANGE (Hector) & Fils. Bulletin Bibliographique; Liſte des Ouvrages nouveaux publiés en France. *Duodecimo.* Paris.

A ſmall monthly Sheet of eight Pages. It has now entered upon its 29th Year.

DELANDINE (A. F.). Mémoires bibliographiques et littéraires. 8°. Lyons. 1817.

DESESSARTS (N. L. M.). Siècles Littéraires de la France, ou nouveau Dictionnaire hiſtorique, critique, et bibliographique des Ecrivains Français juſqu'à la Fin du XVIIIe Siècle. (With Supplement.) 7 Vols. 8°. Paris. 1800-3.

DICTIONNAIRE biographique et bibliographique des Prédicateurs et Sermonnaires Français, par l'Abbé de la P. 8°. Paris. 1824.

ERSCH (J. S.). La France Littéraire; contenant les Auteurs Français de 1771 à 1796. 5 Vols. 8°. Hambourg. 1797-1806.

GIRAULT DE SAINT-FARGEAU (A.). Bibliographie hiſtorique et typographique de la France, ou Catalogue de tous les Ouvrages imprimés juſqu'au Mois d'Avril 1845. 4°. Paris. 1845.

GIRAULT DE SAINT-FARGEAU (A.). Bibliographie hiſtorique et typographique de la Ville de Paris. 8°. Paris. 1847.

Girault is a diſtinguiſhed French Bibliographer, and the Author of many uſeful Works.

GONAN (P. M.). Bibliographie Hiſtorique de la Ville de Lyon pendant la Revolution Françaiſe. 8°. Lyons. 1845.

JOURNAL général de la Littérature de France, ou Indicateur bibliographique et raiſoné des Livres nouveaux en tous Genres, Eſtampes, Cartes géographiques, etc., qui paraiſſent en France, claſſés par Ordre de matières, 1798-1840. 43 Vols. (With Tables.) 8°. Paris. Treuttel & Würtz.

" Not very exact."—*Brunet.*

LELONG (Le Père J.). Bibliothèque Hiſtorique de la France, contenant le Catalogue des Ouvrages imprimés et Manuſcrits qui traitent de l'Hiſtoire de ce Royaume, avec des Notes critiques et hiſtoriques. (New Edition reviſed and enlarged by M. Fevret de Fontette.) 5 Vols. Folio. Paris. 1768-78.

This is univerſally acknowledged to be the ableſt and moſt laborious Work which ſpecial Bibliography has produced. It is ſcarcely poſſible to find a Volume or a Manuſcript connected with French Hiſtory, not fully deſcribed in ſome one of the 50,000 Articles which make up the Work. The 5th Volume contains Additions and Corrections, and nine Indexes, geographical, chronological, alphabetical, &c., including a Table of anonymous Authors.

QUÉRARD (J. M.). La France Littéraire, ou Dictionnaire bibliographique des Savants, Hiſtoriens ou Gens de Lettres de la France, ainſi que des Littérateurs étrangers qui ont écrit en Français, plus particulièrement pendant les XVIIIe et XIXe Siècles. 10 Vols. 8°. Paris. 1827-39.

L

La France Littéraire is the moſt extenſive and complete Work on national Bibliography extant. It gives an Account, not only of French Authors and their Works in all Departments of Literature, but alſo of others who have written in the French Language during the 18th and 19th Centuries. The Deſcriptions and critical Remarks are very full, and the Prices are generally given. Each Volume averages 650 Pages of double Columns in ſmall, clear Type. Quérard is an indefatigable Bibliographer whoſe Reputation, Boſſange remarks, is as univerſal as well deſerved. He publiſhes at the preſent Time a monthly Periodical called *Le Quérard Journal de Bibliographie et Bibliographie Françaiſe*, which is highly uſeful.

QUÉRARD (J. M.). La Littérature Françaiſe Contemporaine, 1827-49, par Felix Bourquelot. 6 Vols. 8°. Paris. 1842-57.

Commenced by Quérard in Continuation of his great Work, *La France Littéraire*, and completed by Bourquelot.

QUÉRARD (J. M.). Les Ecrivains Pſeudonymes, &c. 8°. Paris. 1854-5.

QUÉRARD (J. M.). Les Supercheries Littéraires dévoilées. Galeries des Auteurs apocryphes, déguiſés, plagiaires, et des Editeurs infidèles de la Littérature Françaiſe pendant les quatre derniers Siècles. 4 Vols. 8°. Paris. 1847-52.

VENTOUILLAC (L. T.). The French Librarian, or Literary Guide, pointing out the beſt Works of the principal Writers of France, in every Branch of Literature, with Criticiſms, perſonal Anecdotes, and bibliographical Notices. 8°. London. 1829.

BRUNET, deſcribed under Section X, although a

general Work, is very rich in the Department of French Bibliography; ſo alſo is the *Biographie Univerſelle*, noticed under Section XII, a Work abſolutely neceſſary to the bibliographical Apparatus of a firſt Claſs Library.

4. Germany.

Asher (Adolphus). A Bibliographical Eſſay on the Scriptores Rerum Germanicarum. 4°. London and Berlin. 1843.

Giving a detailed bibliographical Account of twenty-two Collections of contemporary German Hiſtorians, publiſhed from 1532 to 1841; with a Liſt of all the Authors noticed in theſe Collections, arranged according to the Periods to which their Writings refer, and an alphabetical Liſt of the Editions of each Author incorporated in the *Scriptores Rerum Germanicarum.* The Information contained in this Eſſay is very important, and cannot be found elſewhere, at leaſt in ſo convenient a Form.

Buderus (C. G.). Bibliotheca Scriptorum Rerum Germanicarum. Folio. Jena. 1730.

Bückner (R.). Bibliographiſches Handbuch der deutſchen dramatiſchen Literatur. 4°. Berlin. 1837.

Engelmann (Wilhelm). Bibliotheca Geographica. 2 Vols. 8°. Leipzig. 1858.

A claſſified Catalogue of all the Works on Geography and Travels publiſhed in Germany from the Middle of the 14th Century down to the End of the Year 1856; with Prices and a complete Index.

Engelmann (Wilhelm.). Bibliothek der ſchönen Wiſſenſchaft. (A Liſt of German Romances,

Plays, and Poems, publiſhed from 1730 to 1845, with Prices, &c.) 2 Vols. 8°. Leipzig. 1837-46.

ENGELMANN (Wilhelm). Bibliotheca Philologica. (A Liſt of Greek and Latin Grammars, Dictionaries, &c. publiſhed in Germany, from 1750 to 1852, with Prices, etc. 3d Ed. 8°. Leipzig. 1853. Alſo, Bibliotheca Juridica. 2 Vols. & Supplement. 8°. Leipzig. 1840-9; Bibliotheca Mechanico-Technologica. 8°. Leipzig. 1844; Bibliotheca Scriptorum Claſſicorum. 8°. Leipzig. 1847-53; Bibliotheca Medico-Chirurgica et Anatomico-Phyſiologica. 8°. Leipzig. 1848; Bibliotheca Œconomica. 8°. Leipzig. 1841; Bibliotheca Veterinaria, 8°. Leipzig. 1843; Bibliotheca Zoologica et Paleontologica. 8°. Leipzig; Bibliothek der Forſt und Jagdwiſſenſchaften. 8°. Leipzig, 1843; Bibliothek der Handlungſwiſſenſchaft. 8°. Leipzig, 1846; Bibliothek der neueren Sprachen, 1800-41. 8°. Leipzig. 1842. Total 12 Vols. 8°. Leipzig. 1840-53.

Theſe are all ſeparate Catalogues, with Prices, of the Books on Technology, the Claſſicks, Zoology, the Healing Art, Anatomy, Surgery, &c. which are publiſhed in Germany, and the adjoining States. They are very accurate and valuable.

ERSCH (J. S.). Handbuch der deutſchen Literatur. 2d Ed. 4 Vols. 8°. Leipzig. 1822-45.

A claſſed Catalogue of all the Books publiſhed in Germany from the Middle of the 18th Century, down to the preſent Time, continued by Reſe and Geiſſler, with Tables, &c. One of the very beſt Works on German Bibliography.

Ersch (J. S.). Bibliographiſches Handbuch der philoſophiſchen Literatur der Deutſchen, 1750-1850. 8°. Leipzig. 1850.

Heinsius (Wilhelm). Algemeines Bücher-Lexicon. (With 6 Supplements.) 14 Vols. 4°. Leipzig. 1812-56.

An alphabetical Catalogue of all the Books publiſhed in Germany from 1700 to 1852, with the Sizes, Dates, Prices, and Publiſhers' Names. The original Work, 1700-1810, was publiſhed in 1812, 4 Vols.; the firſt Supplement, 1811-21, was publiſhed in 1817-22, 2 Vols.; the ſecond, 1822-27, was publiſhed in 1829, 1 Vol.; the third, with Corrections by Kayſer, 1828-34, was publiſhed in 1836-8, 2 Vols.; the fourth, by O. A. Schulz, 1835-41, was publiſhed in 1846-9, 2 Vols.; the fifth, 1842-46, was publiſhed in 1848-9, 2 Vols.; the ſixth Supplement, by L. F. A. Schiller, 1847-52, was publiſhed in 1853-6, 1 Vol. Ebert ſpeaks of the firſt Part of this Work as "extremely faulty and uncertain." The Supplements are prepared with more Care, and are far better Specimens of Typography. A ſeventh Supplement, 1852-6, is in Progreſs.

Hinrichs (T. C.). Verzeichniſs der Bücher, Landkarten, &c. (Catalogue of all the Books, Maps, &c. including new Editions, publiſhed in Germany from year to year, with Sizes, Prices, Publiſhers, and claſſified Indexes.) 12°. Leipzig.

Germany takes Precedence of all Countries in the Book trade, and the Book trade takes Precedence of every other. The Number of publiſhing and book ſelling Houſes of every Deſcription in the Kingdoms and States of Germany, and the adjoining Countries where the German Language prevails, is ſomewhat above a thouſand. Leipſic is the great Centre of this Trade, where the ſemi-annual Book Fairs are held at Eaſter and Michaelmas. Theſe Catalogues, commenced in 1797, and now publiſhed by Hinrichs in Leipſic, in common with other Bookſellers, who ſubſtitute their own Names for that of Hinrichs upon the Title Page, are prepared with reference to theſe Fairs, and may therefore be regarded as the univerſal Catalogues of the German Bookſellers from half Year to half Year.

They conſtitute an important Part of German Bibliography. They are commonly ſold as annual Catalogues, two being bound together. In Göttingen alſo are publiſhed by Vandenhoeck & Ruprecht ſemi-annual Catalogues, very accurately and carefully prepared with the following Titles: *Bibliotheca Theologica,* von C. J. F. W. RUPRECHT; *Bibliotheca Philologica,* von L. RUPRECHT; *Bibliotheca Hiſtorico-Naturalis,* von E. A. ZUCHOLD; *Bibliotheca Medico-Chirurgica,* von C. J. F. W. RUPRECHT; *Bibliotheca Hiſtorico-Geographica,* von G. SCHMIDT.

JULIUS (N. H.). Bibliotheca Germano-Glottica. 8°. Hamburgi. 1817.

KAYSER (C. G.). Vollſtändiges Bücher-Lexicon, &c. (With 3 Supplements.) 13 Vols. 4°. Leipzig. 1834-53).

With the Exception of Heinſius, juſt deſcribed, the moſt extenſive Work on German Bibliography extant; being an alphabetical Catalogue of all Books, &c. publiſhed in Germany, in all Departments of Science, Art, and Literature, from 1700 to 1852, with Sizes, Prices, and Publiſhers. It is a better printed Book than that of Heinſius, and more convenient for Uſe, there being fewer Supplements. The firſt ſix Volumes include the Works publiſhed from 1700 to 1832; Volume VII is a ſyſtematick Index to theſe Volumes, prepared by L. Schumann, and publiſhed in 1838; Volumes VIII and IX conſtitute a Supplement, from 1832 to 1841; Volumes X and XI a Supplement, from 1841 to 1847; Volumes XII and XIII a Supplement, from 1847 to 1853, prepared by E. A. Zuchold. It is a Matter of Regret that this, like moſt other Works on German Bibliography, gives ſimply Titles, unaccompanied by critical or bibliographical Notices. Were the German Works in this Reſpect like the national Bibliographies of Lowndes, Quérard, or Gamba, or the general Bibliographies of Ebert and Brunet, they would be far more uſeful.

SCHWAB (Guſtav). Wegweiſer durch die Literatur der Deutſchen. Ein Handbuch für Laien; herauſgegeben von Guſtav Schwab und Karl Klüpfel. 2d Ed. 8°. Leipzig. 1847.

A third Edition of this capital Book on German Bibliography is announced. The Works defcribed are arranged in Claffes, an alphabetical Index of Authors being appended. The Notes are uncommonly full and accurate, and the Prices in all Cafes are given. As a Guide in the Formation of a felect German Library it is an invaluable Manual.

TAYLOR (William.), Hiftoric Survey of German Poetry, interfperfed with various Tranflations. 3 Vols. 8°. London. 1828-30.

Not ftrictly a bibliographical Work, but too important in this Connection to be omitted.

THIMM (F. L. J.). The Literature of Germany, from its earlieft Period to the prefent Time. Edited by W. H. Farn. 12°. London. 1844.

This is an excellent little Manual of 300 Pages, indicating the principal German Authors and their Works, with biographical and critical Notes, and Lifts of German Periodicals, Works upon German Literature, &c.

Germany is efpecially rich in its literary Hiftories, many of which are highly important to the Bibliographer. The *General Bibliographical Dictionary* of Ebert, defcribed under another Head, is invaluable for its Notices of Works in early German Literature.

5. ITALY.

BIBLIOGRAFIA Italiana offia Elenco generale delle Opere, ftampate in Italia, 11 Vols. 8°. Milan. 1835-46.

The firft Number of this monthly Periodical was publifhed in January, 1835. It is ftrictly bibliographical in its Character, giving the Titles, Pages, Prices, Publifhers, &c., with illuftrative Notes, of all Works publifhed in Italy from Month to Month, and of all Italian Books publifhed in other Countries. Thefe monthly Numbers at the End of each Year are bound up into octavo Volumes, to which are appended ufeful Statifticks, and copious alphabetical and claſſified Indexes. A Set of theſe Volumes would be an invaluable Addition to any bibliographical Library. The Work was diſcontinued in 1846.

BIBLIOGRAFIA od Elenco ragionato delle Opere contenute nella Collezione de' Claſſici Italiani. 8°. Milan. 1814.

This gives a detailed Account of all the Italian Writers publiſhed by the Claſſico-typographical Society of Milan, as well as of the principal early Editions.

BIBLIOGRAFIA dei Romanzi e Poemi Cavallereſchi Italiani. 2d Edition. 8°. Milan. 1838.

This excellent Bibliography is the Work of M. D. Gætano de' Conti Melzi, a celebrated Bookſeller of Milan. It was firſt publiſhed in 1828.

BRYDGES (S. E.). Res Literariæ; Bibliographical and Critical. Oct. 1820 to Feb. 1822. 3 Vols. 8°. Naples, 1821. Rome, 1821. Geneva. 1822.

The main Object of theſe Volumes is Italian Literature, and eſpecially Italian Poetry, of which its Notices are very extenſive. Copies are now very rare, only 75 having been printed. Mr. Harrott's Set ſold for £8.

CANTÙ (Ignazio). L' Italia Scientifica Contemporanea. 8°. Milan. 1844.

Being the Biographies of the ſcientifick Men of Italy, with Liſts of their Works.

FONTANINI (Giuſto). Biblioteca dell' Eloquenza Italiana, con le Annotazioni del Signor Apoſtolo Zeno. 2 Vols. 4°. Parma. 1803-4.

The lateſt and beſt Edition of a Work rendered invaluable as one of the chief Sources, or as Ebert expreſſes it, " the chief Source for Italian Bibliography," by the copious Notes of Zeno. The firſt Edition was publiſhed in 1737. An Index to the laſt Edition was publiſhed in a quarto Volume, in 1811.

GAMBA DA BASSANO (Bartolommeo). Delle Novelle Italiane in Profa Bibliografia. 2d Edition. 8o. Firenze. 1835.

A detailed Account of the Works of the Italian Novellifts, arranged according to Centuries, from the 14th to the 19th, inclufive. Appended are the Collections of Novels of various Authors, and an alphabetical Index to the Whole.

GAMBA DA BASSANO (Bartolommeo). Serie dei Tefti di Lingua. 4th Edition, Royal 8o. Venezia. 1839. pp. 820.

This is truly an admirable Work, being to the Italian Bibliographer, what Rich is to the American, Lowndes to the Englifh, Quérard to the French, and Kayfer or Erfch to the German. The Notices are very full and accurate. It is divided into two Parts. The firft contains the beft Editions, ancient and modern, of all the Works cited in the *Vocabolario degli Accademici della Crufca.* In the fecond Part are defcribed the beft Editions of the principal Works publifhed fince the Invention of Printing, either pertaining to the Study of the Language, or forming a Part of Italian Literature. Like the previous Work, this fecond Part is arranged according to Centuries, from the 14th to the 19th inclufive. To the Whole is appended a copious alphabetical Index. Copies of this Work are now very fcarce.

HAYM (N. F.). Biblioteca Italiana ofia Notizia de' Libri rari Italiani. 2 Vols. 4o. Milan. 1771-2.

Beft Edition, well printed, and provided with a general Index. Haym, fays Ebert, can only be ufed with the greateft Precaution, in confequence of his general Inaccuracy. His Biblioteca neverthelefs is an important Part of Italian Bibliography.

POGGIALI (Gaet.). Serie dei Tefti di Lingua ftampati, che fi citano nel Vocabolario della Crufca. 2 Vols. 8o. Livorno. 1813.

In addition to the above defcribed Works on Italian Bibliography, the Student fhould confult the immortal Work of Tirabofchi, and alfo of Ginguene, both of which, though literary Hiſtories, give Accounts of Authors and their Productions. For the lateſt Publications in Italy the beſt Work is perhaps *Archivio Storico Italiano*, a Periodical publiſhed in Florence.

6. Spain, Portugal and Northern Europe.

Adelung (Friedrich). Kritiſch-literäriſche Ueberſicht der Reiſenden in Rußland bis 1700, deren Berichte bekannt ſind, von demſelben. 2 Vols. Large 8°. St. Peterſburg. 1846.

Antonio (Nicolao). Bibliotheca Hiſpana Vetus, ad Annum 1500. Curante F. P. Bayer. 2 Vols. Folio. Matriti. 1788.

Antonio (Nicolao). Bibliotheca Hiſpana Nova, ab Anno 1500, ad Annum 1684. 2 Vols. Folio. Matriti. 1783-8.

Both theſe Works are highly eſteemed for their Style and general Correctneſs. The Vetus is in chronological, the Nova in alphabetical Order, according to the Chriſtian Names of the Authors. Dibdin in his *Library Companion*, ſpeaks of them as the maſter Key to unlock the Treaſures of Spaniſh Literature, adding: "If this Work of Antonio be valuable, it is unluckily rare and dear. I never ſaw but one Copy of it upon large Paper; and that *one* is magnificently bound in red Morocco, in the Library of Francis Freeling, Eſq." This identical Copy, or one preciſely like it, has recently found its way, among other choice literary Treaſures, into the private Library of a Providence Merchant, to whoſe Collection we have already referred under Rich's *Bibliotheca Americana*.

Bentkowskiego (F.). Hiſtorya Literatury Polſkiey. (The Hiſtory of the Poliſh Literature exhibited in a Liſt of Writings made known through the Preſs.) 2 Vols. 8°. Warſzawie, 1814.

BOLETIN Bibliografico Eſpañole Eſtrangero. 12°. Madrid. 1840.

Similar to the *Bibliografia Italiana.* It is a fortnightly Periodical, the firſt Number of which was publiſhed in Auguſt, 1840. At the End of each Year theſe Numbers are bound together, with Indexes appended.

BOUTERWEK (Frederick). Hiſtory of Spaniſh and Portugueſe Literature, tranſlated by Roſs. (With biographical and bibliographical Notices.) 2 Vols. 8°. London. 1823.

BUHLE (J. G.). Verſuch einer kritiſchen Literatur der Ruſſiſchen Geſchichte. Theil I. enthaltend die Literatur der älteren allgemeinen nordiſchen Geſchichte. 8°. Moſkwa. 1810.

The 2d and 3d Volumes of this Work, which were announced, have not yet appeared.

CASIRI (Michaelis). Bibliotheca Arabico-Hiſpana Eſcurialenſis. 2 Vols. Folio. Matriti. 1760-70.

Containing large Extracts in the original Arabick and Latin from the MSS. in the Eſcurial, with an Account of their Ages, and a Life of the Author when known. Gibbon has made great Uſe of it in his fifty-firſt Chapter, and Harris, in his Philological Inquiries, has analyzed the Contents. The Book is a fine Specimen of Typography.

CASTRO (J. R. de). Biblioteca Eſpanola. 2 Vols. Folio. Madrid. 1781-6.

The firſt Volume contains the Spaniſh Rabbins, and the ſecond the Heathen and Chriſtian Writers to the End of the 13th Century.

CINELLI (C. G.). Biblioteca Volante continuato da San Caſſani. 2d Edition. 4 Vols. 4°. Venezia. 1734-47.

LELEWEL (Joach.). Obſervations ſur la Bibliographie Ancienne de la Pologne, avec l'Hiſtoire des Bibliothèques dans ce Pays. (In Poliſh.) 2 Vols. 8°. Wilna. 1823-6.

MACHADO (P. D. B.). Bibliotheca Luſitana Critica et Chronologica. 4 Vols. Folio. Liſbon. 1741-59.

The great Work on Portugueſe Bibliography, "beyond," ſays Dibdin, "all Competition and beyond all Praiſe." The ſeven Indexes in the fourth Volume are regarded as the *ne plus ultra* of Diligence, Exactneſs, and general Utility. It is rare and difficult to find, even in Portugal, and is conſequently very expenſive.

MEMORIAS de Literatura Portugueza, publiadas pela Real Academia das Sciencias de Liſboa. 8 Vols. 4°. Liſboa. 1785-1812.

MEMORIAS de la Real Academia de la Hiſtoria. 7 Vols. 4°. Madrid & Sancha. 1796-1832.

"On remarque dans ce Recueil pluſieurs Mémoires curieux de MM. Martin de Ulloa, Fr. Martinez Marina, Mart. Fern. de Navarrete, Jos. Ant. Conde, etc."—*Brunet.*

NAPIERSKY (C. E.). Verzeichniſs der neu erſchienen Schriften zur Geſchichte Liv-, Eſth- und Kurlands. Für die Jahre 1847-55. 8°. Regia. 1857.

NYERUP (R.). & KRAFT (J. E.). Almindeligt Litteratur-Lexicon fur Denmark, Norge, og Iſland. 2 Vols. 4°. Kjobenh. 1820.

A univerſal literary Lexicon of Denmark, Norway and Iceland, giving an Account of Authors and their Works, with Dates and Particulars of Editions.

OTTO (Friedrich). Hiſtory of Ruſſian Literature, with a Lexicon of Ruſſian Authors. Tranſlated from the German by George Cox. 8°. Oxford. 1839.

The Lexicon occupies three hundred Pages, conſtituting the principal Part of the Work.

RECKE & NAPIERSKY. Algemeines Schriftſteller- und Gelehrten-Lexikon der Provinzen Livland, Eſthland und Kurland. 4 Vols. Thick 8°. Mitau. 1827-32.

An extenſive Account of the Literature of the Baltic Provinces of Ruſſia, including a Portion of Poland and the eaſtern Provinces of Pruſſia.

SALVA (Vicente). Catalogue of Spaniſh and Portugueſe Books, with bibliographical Remarks. 2 Vols. 8°. London. 1826-7.

Very valuable and extremely rare. Contributions to Spaniſh and Portugueſe Bibliography are to be found in the *Repertorio Americano*, a London Journal, publiſhed by Salva.

STUKKENBERG (J. C.). Verſuch eines Quellen-Anzeigers alter und neuer Zeit für das Studium der Geographie, Topographie, Ethnographie und Statiſtik des Ruſſiſchen Reiches. 2 Vols. (With a Supplement). 8°. St. Peterſburg. 1849-52.

TICKNOR (George). The Hiſtory of Spaniſh Literature. (With biographical and bibliographical Notices, and a copious Index.) 3 Vols. 8°. New York. 1849.

Mr. Ticknor has probably the largeſt private Collection of Spaniſh Books out of Spain. His Hiſtory is univerſally eſteemed, having already been tranſlated into ſeveral European Languages.

WARMHOLTZ (C. G.). Bibliotheca Hiſtorica Sueo-Gothica. (Hiſtoric Library of Sweden, or, Indication of Works, both printed and in Manuſcript, relative to the Hiſtory of Sweden, with critical Notices, continued by Aurivillius. *In Swediſh.*) 15 Vols. 8°. Stockholm. 1782-1817.

BOSSANGE, Barthés et Lowell's Catalogue des Livres Français, Italiens, Eſpagnols, Orientaux, &c. is a very uſeful Work for the Bibliography of French, Italian, Spaniſh, Portugueſe and Oriental Books. They are arranged in Claſſes, with Prices, occaſional Notices, and an Index of Authors; the whole forming a Book of 538 Pages. 8°. London. 1843.

X. General Bibliographies.

THE Works which are to be conſidered under this Section and the one following, ſometimes called DICTIONARIES, ſometimes CATALOGUES, and ſometimes BIBLIOTHECÆ, conſtitute the moſt generally uſeful and intereſting Claſs of bibliographical Publications. By ſhowing what has been written in all the various Branches of human Knowledge in every Age and Country, they act as Guides to the Inquiries of the learned; while, by pointing out the Differences of Editions, etc. etc. they conſtitute Manuals of ready Information for the profeſſed Bibliographer.

Works of this Claſs are called GENERAL or SPECIAL,

according as their Object is to indicate Books in all, or in one only of the Departments of Science or Literature. The former only aspire to point out rare, remarkable or important Books; for no Attempt has yet been made, or probably ever will be made, to compile a COMPLETE UNIVERSAL bibliographical Dictionary. On the other Hand, it is the Object of SPECIAL Bibliographies to notice all, or the greater Part, of those Books, that have been published on the Subjects which they embrace; and hence their superior Utility to such as are engaged in the Study or Investigation of any particular Topic. It is by Means of such Works, says Dr. Johnson, that "the Student comes to know what has been written on every Part of Learning; that he avoids the Hazards of encountering Difficulties which have already been cleared; of discussing Questions which have already been decided; and of digging in Mines of Literature which have already been exhausted." (Preface to the *Catologus Bibliothecæ Harleianæ.*)

Thus Bibliography, or a Knowledge of Books, if it may not aspire to be called Learning, may certainly be considered in this Light, as one of Learning's best Helps. The following are some of the most important Works under this Head:

APPLETON'S Library Manual; containing a Catalogue Raisonné of upwards of 12000 of the most important Works in every Department of Knowledge, in all modern Languages. 8°. New York. 1847.

Barbier (A. A.). Nouveau Bibliothèque d'un Homme de Goût, contenant des Jugements tirés de Journaux les plus connus et des Critiques les plus eſtimés, ſur les meilleurs Ouvrages qui ont paru dans tous les Genres, tant en France que chez l'Etranger. 5 Vols. 8°. Paris. 1808-10.

The Name of Deſeſſarts was put upon the title Page of this Edition, becauſe he ſhared with Barbier the Expenſe of publiſhing. He made no literary Contribution whatever to the Work.—*Quérard.* Barbier's Bibliothèque was for a long Time regarded as indiſpenſable to Book-collectors. It is now ſuperſeded by the more recent Dictionaries of Ebert and Brunet.

Bibliotheca Grenvilliana, or Bibliographical Notices of rare and curious Books, forming Part of the Library of the Right Hon. Thos. Grenville. By John Thos. Payne and Henry Foſs. Part I. 2 Vols. 8°. London. 1842.

Bibliotheca Grenvilliana, Part the Second, completing the Catalogue of the Library, bequeathed to the Britiſh Muſeum by the late Right Hon. Thos. Grenville. By John Thos. Payne and Henry Foſs. 8°. London. 1848.

The firſt Part of this elegantly printed Catalogue was made at Mr. Grenville's own Expenſe. The Titles are arranged alphabetically according to the Names of Authors, accompanied by copious bibliographical Notes, and preceded by a good Index and References to the Books and Manuſcripts upon Vellum. The preſent Price of this Catalogue is ſtated by Mr. Sims to be £3 3s. The ſecond Part was made by Order of the Truſtees after the Library had been depoſited in the Muſeum. This can be purchaſed for the Sum of £1 11s. 6d. The three Volumes conſtitute an invaluable Acceſſion to any Collection of Bibliographical Works. The firſt two come more properly under Section V., rare Books.

The Grenville Library, of which the Catalogues, here defcribed are the Inventory, was the Refult of a continued and unwearied Purfuit of nearly fifty Years on the Part of the illuftrious Collector. It was "formed and preferved," fays the Annual Report of Britifh Mufeum for the Year 1847, "with the exquifite Tafte of an accomplifhed Bibliographer, with the Learning of a profound and elegant Scholar, and the fplendid Liberality of a Gentleman in affluent Circumftances, who employed in adding to his Library whatever his generous Heart allowed him to fpare from filently relieving thofe whofe Wants he alone knew." It confifts of 20,240 Volumes, forming about 16,000 Works, the Coft of which is ftated to have been upwards of £54,000.

BOHN (H. G.). A Catalogue of Books. 8°. London. 1841.

Commonly known as Bohn's *Guinea Catalogue*. It contains 2100 Pages, bound in a fuperiour Manner, having been compiled, as the Publifher ftates in his Preface, at an Outlay of upwards of two thoufand Pounds. The Books enumerated are in various Languages, arranged alphabetically according to Claffes as far as practicable, accompanied with Prices and Indexes, and interfperfed throughout with bibliographical and literary Notices. The Catalogue reprefents, it is ftated, the largeft and moft felect Affortment of Books ever before recorded as the Stock of a Bookfeller. It is now being reproduced in three octavo Volumes, two of which have already appeared; the *firft* (mentioned under Section I.), in 1847; and the *fecond* (mentioned under Section VIII.), in 1850. All of thefe Catalogues are invaluable as a Part of the Book-collector's working Apparatus.

BRUNET (J. C.). Manuel du Libraire et de l'Amateur de Livres. 4th Edition. 5 thick Vols. Royal 8°. Paris. 1842-4.

This Manual, the Refults of more than 40 Years of Experience and Refearch, is by far the moft extenfive and ufeful Work of the Kind extant. The original Edition was publifhed in three octavo Volumes in 1810. The firft four Volumes, confift of an alphabetical and defcriptive Catalogue, of upwards of 20,000 of the moft important Works which have been publifhed, in the ancient, and in the principal modern Languages, from the Invention of Printing to the present Time; with the History of the different Editions, the Prices for which they have been sold within the last 60 Years, critical Remarks, etc. etc. In the fifth Volume are classified, in accordance with the bibliographical System generally adopted in France, not only all the Works described in the previous Volumes, but also 12,000 additional ones, thus making 32,000 separate Works, or about 60,000 Volumes, comprised in the Manual. In this last Volume may be found an extensive List of bibliographical Works. No Library of Importance can dispense with Brunet.

De Bure (G. F.). Bibliographie Instructive, ou Traité de la Connoissance des Livres rares et singuliers. 7 Vols. 8°. Paris. 1763-8.

The Books described in this Work which might very properly come under another Head, are arranged, in Subdivisions, under the five grand Classes of *Theology, Jurisprudence, Sciences and Arts, Belles-Lettres,* and *History.* The Names of the Authors in all these Classes are placed alphabetically in the last Volume. De Bure published a Supplement to this Work with the following Title: *Supplément à la Bibliographie Instructive, ou Catalogue des Livres de Louis Jean Gaignat.* 2 Vols. 8°. Paris, 1769. An Index to anonymous Works was also published in 1782, entitled, *Bibliographie Instructive,* Tome dixième. Probably no Publication has contributed so much to make the Study of Bibliography popular, as this elegant and judicious Performance. The Articles which the Author describes amount to upwards of 6000, in regard to which ample Details are given. The Account of the famous American Collections of De Bry for Instance, extends to 120 Pages. De Bure was a Bookseller at Paris, of great Eminence in his Profession, but still more distinguished for extensive Information in all Matters pertaining to Bibliography and literary History. His Works are much consulted at the present Day.

Denis (F.). & Pinçon (P.). Nouveau Manuel de Bibliographie Universelle. Large 8°. Paris. 1857. pp. 718.

Printed on indifferent Paper and in very small Type, three Columns to a Page. It contains an immense Number of Titles of Books of every

Kind arranged in chronological Order according to Subjects, and accompanied by bibliographical and hiſtorical Remarks. An alphabetical Index of Authors would add greatly to its Uſefulneſs. Appended is a detailed Account of the principal *Collections Typographiques* arranged in chronological Order, with a Catalogue of the moſt celebrated private Libraries. We have already mentioned it under Section II. on account of the bibliographical Information which it furniſhes under the appropriate Heads. The following Extract from the Preface will give an Idea of the general Character of the Work:

"Ce Livre n'eſt pas à proprement parler, un Manuel du Bibliophile, il ne s'adreſſe pas excluſivement au Bibliographe de Profeſſion. Avant tout on a voulu qu'il pût fournir un Renſeignement concis, une Réponſe préciſe, non ſur la Beauté d'une Edition, ſur la Rareté d'un Volume, ſur le Prix arbitraire que l'Opinion accorde à certaines Raretés, mais bien ſur la Série d'Ouvrages à conſulter en telle ou telle Occaſion, par l'Homme de Lettres, l'Artiſte ou le Savant."

DIBDIN (T. F.). The Library Companion; or, the Young Man's Guide, and the Old Man's Comfort in the Choice of a Library. Thick 8°. London. 1824.

Containing a Selection of the moſt important Works under the general Heads of Divinity, Hiſtory, Voyages and Travels, Biography, Philology and Belles-Lettres, Poetry, and the Engliſh Drama; with copious bibliographical Notes, Prices, and a general Index, the Whole making a Volume of 912 Pages.

DICTIONNAIRE Bibliographique. 3 Vols. 8°. Paris. 1790.

This Work, generally known under the Name of Cailleau's Dictionary, was compiled according to Barbier, and others, by the Abbé du Clos. It was republiſhed in 1800, with a ſupplementary Volume by M. Brunet. The laſt Half of the third Volume, has a ſeparate Alphabet for anonymous Works.

EBERT (F. A.). A General Bibliographical Dictionary, from the German. 4 Vols. 8°. Oxford. 1837.

The original Edition of this truly valuable Work was publiſhed at Leipſic, with the following Title: *Allgemeines bibliographiſches Lexicon.* 2 Vols. 4°. 1821-30. It is baſed upon the Manual of Brunet, but is ſomewhat different in its Character, and quite as well adapted to the Wants of Scholars. Eſpecial Attention is given to ancient German Literature and the Greek and Latin Claſſicks. The Author was Librarian to the King of Saxony, and hence was able to give his Deſcriptions, as ſtated in his Preface, from careful Compariſon of the Works themſelves, rather than from Manuals. His Dictionary is neceſſary to all who cultivate Bibliography.

GEORGI (J. T.). Allgemeines Europäiſches Bücher-Lexicon. (Univerſal Dictionary of Books printed in Europe from 1500 to 1757, with the Date, Size, Number of Pages, and Price of each.) 8 Vols. Folio, (including three Supplements). Leipzig. 1742-58.

A laborious Work, containing the Titles of more Books, than any other Catalogue or bibliographical Work ever publiſhed. It is ſcarce, but, according to Ebert, of but little Value "on Account of its Faultineſs throughout."

GRÄSSE (J. G. T.). Lehrbuch einer allgemeinen Literärgeſchichte aller bekannten Völker der Welt, von der älteſten bis auf die neueſte Zeit.

This is a general bibliographical Dictionary ſimilar to thoſe of Ebert and Brunet already deſcribed. It is not yet completed. Petzholdt's *Anzeiger* for July, 1857, announces Pages 1329-1536, Vol. III. as having recently been publiſhed at Leipſic. The Author is alſo preparing a new bibliographical Dictionary containing more than a thouſand Articles on rare and precious Books. A Part of Vol. I. pp. 96, has recently been publiſhed at Dreſden, in a quarto Form.

LEBLANC (P.). Catalogue des Livres, Deſſins et Eſtampes, de la Bibliothèque de M. J. B. Huzard. 3 Vols. 8°. Paris. 1842.

Volume I. contains the Titles of Works arranged under the five general Claſſes or Diviſions of Knowledge, as in Renouard and Santander; Volume II. is devoted particularly to Agriculture and Rural Economy; Volume III. is compoſed of Works upon Medicine and the Veterinary Art, Memoirs of Academies and learned Societies, Works upon Bibliography, Biography, &c. Each Volume has a copious Index. Prefixed to the firſt Volume is a biographical Notice of Huzard (who was General Inſpector of the Veterinary Schools of France), by M. L. Bouchard, and a Eulogy pronounced in 1841, before the Royal Academy of Medicine, by M. Pariſet. This Catalogue, ſays Dr. Cogſwell, is of great Value for "economick Bibliography."

MARTIN (L. Aimé). Plan d'une Bibliothèque Univerſelle; Etudes des Livres qui peuvent ſervir à l'Hiſtoire littéraire et philoſophique du Genre humain; ſuivi du Catalogue des Chefs-d'Œuvre de toutes les Langues et des Ouvrages originaux de tous les Peuples. 8°. Paris. 1837.

MEUSEL (J. G.). Bibliotheca Hiſtorica, poſt Struvium et Buderum, nunc digeſta, amplificata, et emendata; accedunt Indices Auctorum et Rerum. 22 Vols. (in 11) 8°. Leipzig. 1782-1804.

An uncommonly careful Reproduction of a Work which firſt appeared at Jena in 1740. It is very extenſive in its Deſign, comprehending both hiſtorical and geographical Works, relating to all Countries and in all Languages. Vols. III. and X. relate to American Bibliography.

NODIER (Charles). Deſcription Raiſonnée d'une jolie Collection de Livres, (moſtly French, Italian and Spaniſh); précédée d'une Introduction par M. G. Dupleſſis, de la Vie de Nodier par M. Francis Wey, et d'une Notice bibliographique ſur ſes Ouvrages. 8°. Paris. 1844. pp. 528.

The copious Notes to this Catalogue render it a deſirable Work for a bibliographical Collection. It contains 1254 Titles, the Descriptions occupying the greater Part of the Volume.

RENOUARD (A. A.). Catalogue de la Bibliothèque d'un Amateur, avec Notes bibliographiques, critiques et littéraires. 4 Vols. 8°. Paris. 1819.

A fine Specimen of Typography. The Works are arranged under the five general Divisions of Theology, Jurisprudence, Sciences and Arts, Belles-Lettres, and History. The fourth Volume contains a separate List of the Books printed in the 15th Century, the Aldine Editions, Books printed upon Vellum, Designs, and a complete Index of Authors. The bibliographical and critical Notes are very full and instructive. The Work is really a Bibliography rather than a Catalogue, and hence finds its appropriate Place in this LIST.

ROLLAND (J. F.). Conseils pour former une Bibliothèque, ou Catalogue de tous les bons Ouvrages qui peuvent entrer dans une Bibliothèque Chrétienne. 3 Vols. 8°. Lyons. 1833-43.

SANTANDER (M. C. de la Serna). Catalogue des Livres de la Bibliothèque de Santander; rédigé et mis en ordre par lui-même; avec des Notes bibliographiques et littéraires. 5 Vols. 8°. Bruxelles. 1803.

The 5th Volume is a Supplement, containing a Memoir upon the Origin of Signatures and Marks in Typography, a Latin Preface printed in 1800, upon the genuine Collection of Canons by St. Isidore of Seville, &c. and five large Engravings representing the paper Marks used in the 15th Century. This superb Collection is composed, as is stated in the Preface, of the best Works in the various Departments of Learning, and is especially rich in rare and costly Books, among which is a very fine Copy of De Bry's Collection of Voyages. The Books are arranged like the Catalogue of Renouard just noticed, under the general Divisions of Theology, Jurisprudence, Sciences and Arts, Belles-Lettres, and History. A copious general Index of Authors in the fourth Volume enhances the Value of the Work. It may well be called, as Dr. Cogfwell expreffes it, "a bibliographical Catalogue with copious Notes." The Paper and Typography are unfortunately not in keeping with the literary Merits of the Work. Santander's Library was fold at Auction in 1809.

XI. Bibliography of particular Sciences and Branches of Literature, or Special Bibliographies.

THE Dictionaries and Catalogues applicable to PARTICULAR Branches of Knowledge, and comprifing Works publifhed on the Subjects difcuffed, would of themfelves conftitute a Library. We can only Notice, in Addition to fuch as have already been confidered under previous Heads, a few of the more important, and with which we are more efpecially familiar.

AGASSIZ (Louis). Bibliographia Zoologiæ et Geologiæ. General Catalogue of all Books, Tracts, and Memoirs on Zoology and Geology. Corrected, enlarged, and edited by H. E. Strickland. 3 Vols. 8°. London. 1848-52.

ATKINSON (James). Medical Bibliography. A and B. 8°. London. 1834.

A very *amufing* as well as inftructive Book, dedicated to all idle Students in Great Britain. "I only wifh to apprize the Reader, that if he choofe to read my Non-fenfe, with his Eyes and Fingers open, he muft be a greater Fool, if poffible than the Author who wrote it."—*Extract from the Preface.*

AYALA (M. d'). Bibliografia Militare Italiana. 8°. Torino. 1854. pp. 450.

BACKER (Auguſtin et Alois de). Bibliothèque des Ecrivains de la Compagnie de Jéſus, ou Notices bibliographiques; 1r de tous les Ouvrages publiés par les Membres de la Compagnie de Jéſus, depuis la Fondation de l'Ordre juſqu'à nos Jours; 2d des Apologies, des Controverſes religeuſes, des Critiques littéraires et ſcientifiques ſuſcitées à leur Sujet. 4 Vols. Royal 8°. Liege. 1833-56.

This elaborate Work is to conſiſt, according to the Preface, of 5 or 6 Volumes of 800 Pages, double Columns. Each Volume is arranged in alphabetical Order and is complete in itſelf.

BASTIAT (F.). Dictionnaire de l'Economie Politique. 2 Vols. 8°. Paris. 1855.

Containing the general Principles of Political Economy, with a Bibliography of the Science, by Baſtiat, Baudrillart, Blaiſe, Blanqui, Block, and many others, publiſhed under the Direction of Coquelin and Guillaumin.

BÉRARD (A. S. L.). Eſſai bibliographique ſur les Editions des Elzevirs les plus précieuſes et les plus recherchées. 8°. Paris. 1822.

Preceded by an Account of the moſt celebrated Printers.

BLAKEY (R.). Angling Literature of all Nations. 12°. London. 1855. pp. 341.

BLANQUI (M.). Hiſtoire de l'Economie Politique en Europe. 2d Edition. 2 Vols. 8°. Paris. 1842.

In the ſecond Volume may be found the Bibliography of the principal Works on Political Economy.

Blaze (C.). Bibliographie Muſicale de la France et de l'Etranger. 8°. Paris. 1822.

A deſcriptive Account of all the Treatiſes and Works on vocal and inſtrumental Muſick publiſhed in Europe down to 1822.

Boucher de la Richarderie (G.). Bibliothèque Univerſelle des Voyages. 6 Vols. 8°. Paris. 1808.

A claſſified Account of all Voyages, ancient and modern, in different Parts of the World, with Extracts from the moſt important, arranged in chronological Order according to the different Countries, and accompanied with a full Index of Names and Authors.

Bridgman (R. W.). Short View of Legal Bibliography, with critical Obſervations on Law Writers. 8°. London. 1807.

Callisen (A. C. P.). Mediciniſches Schriftſteller-Lexicon. 33 Vols. 12°. Copenhagen. 1830-45.

Camus (A. G.). Lettres ſur la Profeſſion d'Avocat; un Recueil de Pièces concernant l'Exercice de cette Profeſſion, et Bibliothèque choiſie des Livres de Droit. 5th Edition. 2 Vols. 8°. Paris. 1832.

An excellent Work on Juriſprudence and its Bibliography, reviſed and enlarged by Dupin. It was firſt publiſhed in 1772 in a ſmall duodecimo Form.

Clarke (A. & J. B. B.). A conciſe View of the Succeſſion of Sacred Literature, in a chronological Arrangement of Authors and their Works, from the Invention of alphabetical Characters to 1445. 2 Vols. 8°. London. 1830-2.

Coggeshall (W. F.). The Newſpaper Record, containing a complete Liſt of Newſpapers, &c. in the United States, Canada and Great Britain; with a Sketch of the Origin of Printing. 8°. Philadelphia. 1856. pp. 194.

Darling (James). Cyclopædia Bibliographica; a Library Manual of Theological and General Literature, and Guide to Books for Authors, Preachers, Students and Literary Men, analytical, bibliographical and biographical. 2 Vols. Imp. 8°. London. 1854.

Cloſely printed Pages, double Columns and ſmall Type. The Work is chiefly theological, compriſing ancient and modern Authors of Note in Theology, Eccleſiaſtical Hiſtory, Moral Philoſophy, and the various Departments connected therewith, including a Selection in moſt Branches of Literature, with ſhort biographical and bibliographical Notices. In collective Works the Contents of each Volume are minutely deſcribed, and in Volumes of Sermons the Texts are given.

Decanver (H. C.). Catalogue of Works in Refutation of Methodiſm, from its Origin in 1729 to the preſent Time. Large Paper. Thin 8°. Philadelphia. 1846.

De Morgan (Auguſtus). Notices of Arithmetical Books and Authors. Poſt 8°. London. 1847.

Dryander (Jonas). Catalogus Bibliothecæ Hiſtorico-Naturalis Joſephi Banks. 5 Vols. 8°. London. 1796-1800.

This, although the Title ſeems to promiſe only the Catalogue of a private Library, is allowed to furniſh the moſt complete and beſt arranged View of Books in Natural Hiſtory ever publiſhed in any Country. The Contents are, Vol. I. General Writers; Vol. II. Zoology; Vol. III.

Botany; Vol. IV. Mineralogy; Vol V. Supplement. The Books described now form a Part of the Britifh Mufeum.

DUPARCG (E. de la Barre). Des Sources Bibliographiques Militaires. 8°. Paris. 1856.

DUPIN (A. M. J. J.). Lettres fur la Profeffion d'Avocat, ou Bibliothèque choifie des Livres de Droit. (See CAMUS, Page 97.)

DUPIN (A. M. J. J.). Manuel du Droit Public Ecclésiaftique Français. 12°. Paris. 1844.

Containing at the End a Chronology of the Popes and Kings of France, and a *Bibliothèque Choifie*, or Lift of the moft important Works upon Ecclefiaftical Hiftory and Canon Law. pp. 466.

DUPIN (A. M. J. J.). Manuel des Etudians en Droit et des jeunes Avocats; Recueil d'Opufcules de Jurifprudence. 12°. Paris. 1851. pp. 876.

Containing bibliographical Notices of the beft Works upon Law; Hiftory of Law, Roman, and French; Aphorifms of Bacon; Biographies of Magiftrates, &c. &c.

DUPLESSIS (C.). Bibliographie Parémiologique, fuivie d'un Appendice. (Bibliography of Proverbs.) 8°. Paris. 1847.

ELLIS (Henry). Catalogue of Books on Angling. 8°. London. 1811.

ELMES (James). General and Bibliographical Dictionary of the Fine Arts. 8°. London. 1826.

FORBES (John). Manual of Select Medical Bibliography. Royal 8°. London. 1835.

GODDÉ (M. J.). Catalogue raifonné d'une Collection de Livres, etc. relatifs aux Arts de Peinture, Sculpture. 8°. Paris. 1850.

GRÄSSE (J. G. T.) Bibliotheca Magica et Pneumatica. 8°. Leipzig. 1843.

HORNE (T. H.). Manual of Biblical Bibliography; comprising a Catalogue methodically arranged, of the principal Editions and Revisions of the Holy Scriptures; together with Notices of the principal Philologers, Critics, &c. 2[d] Edition. 8°. London. 1846.

HOYER (Dr. J. G. von). Literatur der Kriegswissenschaften und Kriegsgeschichte. 12°. Berlin. 1832-40.

A Work of 661 Pages, with a Supplement of 200 Pages, from 1831 to 1840.

LA LANDE (J. de). Bibliographie Astronomique avec l'Histoire de l'Astronomie depuis 1780, jusqu'à 1802. 4°. Paris. 1803. pp. 966.

With a two-fold Index of Authors and Subjects.

LE LONG (Jacobus). Bibliotheca Sacra, seu Syllabus omnium fere Sacræ Scripturæ Editionum ac Versionum, etc. 2 Vols. Folio. Paris. 1723.

The first Edition of this Work was published in 1709. 2 Vols. octavo. It contains an Account of the various Editions of the Scriptures, with full Indexes, &c. being an invaluable Acquisition to the biblical Scholar.

M'CULLOCH (J. R.). The Literature of Political Economy. 8°. London. 1845.

A classified Catalogue of select Publications in the different Departments of Political Economy, with hiſtorical, critical, and biographical Notices, and a very complete double Index of Authors and Works.

MURHARD (F. W. A.). Bibliotheca Mathematica, oder Literatur der Math. Wiſſenſchaft. 5 Vols. 8°. Leipzig. 1797-1805.

Containing the Literature of Arithmetick, Geometry, and Analyſis, Mechanicks, and Opticks.

ORME (William). Bibliotheca Biblica; a ſelect Liſt of Books on Sacred Literature; with Notices, biographical, critical and bibliographical. 8°. Edinburgh. 1824.

Deſigned to furniſh the Means of eaſy Reference to the moſt uſeful Books in the important Department of biblical Literature. It includes a Selection of foreign Works, and a very full Liſt of Britiſh Works, excluding in its Plan, general Theology, ſyſtematick, practical, and polemical Divinity. An arranged Index enhances the Value of the Work. Orme is the Author of Memoirs of John Owen, Life and Times of Richard Baxter, &c.

OETTINGER (E. M.). Bibliographie Biographique Univerſelle. Dictionnaire des Ouvrages relatifs à l'Hiſtoire de la Vie publique et privée des Perſonnages célèbres de tous les Temps et de toutes les Nations, depuis le Commencement du Monde juſqu'à nos Jours. 2 Vols. 4°. Bruxelles. 1854.

PERCHERON (A.). Bibliographie Entomologique, comprenant l'Indication, 1r des Ouvrages entomologiques publiés en France et à l'Etranger depuis les Temps les plus reculés juſqu'à nos Jours; 2d des Monographies et Mémoires contenus dans les Recueils, &c. 2 Vols. 8°. Paris. 1837.

PLOUCQUET (W. G.). Literatura Medica Digeſta. 4 Vols. Royal 4°. Tubingæ. 1808-9.

A moſt comprehenſive bibliographical Catalogue of Medical Literature, ancient and modern.

POGGENDORFF (J. C.). Biographiſch-literäriſches Handwörterbuch zur Geſchichte der exacten Wiſſenſchaften. 8°. Berlin. 1858.

To be complete in one large octavo Volume of about 1200 Pages, the firſt Number of which, extending to the Article *Dirichlet*, has juſt appeared. It is intended as a Manual for thoſe who cultivate the mathematical and inductive Sciences, preſenting the chief Points of Date, Life, and Works of Mathematicians, Aſtronomers, Chemiſts, Mineralogiſts, Geologiſts, &c. of all Times, and of every Nation, with copious References to the Sources whence more detailed Information may be obtained. For the paſt ten Years the Author has been continually employed in the Compilation of this Work, in which Taſk he has been particularly aided by the extenſive literary and ſcientifick Treaſures of the Royal Library of Berlin, and alſo authentick Communications from ſcientifick Men of the preſent Day.

POOLE (W. F.). An Index of Periodical Literature. 8°. New York. 1853.

An exceedingly uſeful Book, publiſhed by C. B. Norton, being a complete Key to the Contents of fifteen hundred Volumes of ſtandard Engliſh and American Periodicals. An important Feature of the Work is that the Names of anonymous Articles are given in Parentheſes, ſo far as they could be aſcertained. Periodicals, as the Author ſtates in the Preface, form a conſiderable Portion of our publick and private Libraries; their Contents, however, are not available, for the Want of a Clue to the Labyrinth of Topicks diſcuſſed in them. This Index furniſhes the deſired Clue. It conſtitutes a handſome octavo Volume of 800 Pages. Publiſhed at $6. The Work is dedicated to Prof. C. C. Jewett, in Token of Appreciation of his Services in behalf of American Libraries and Bibliography.

PRITZEL (G. A.). Thefaurus Literaturæ Botanicæ omnium Gentium inde a Rerum botanicarum Initiis ad noftra ufque Tempora, quindecim millia Operum recenfens. 4°. Lipfiæ. 1851. pp. 547.

A Work of extraordinary Accuracy and Fullnefs of Defcription. It contains an alphabetical Dictionary of Authors and their Works—a fyftematick Arrangement of the fame, and an alphabetical Index of the Names of Editors and other Perfons incidentally mentioned.

ROY (C. H. à). Catalogus Bibliothecæ Medicæ. 5 Vols. 8°. Amfterdam. 1830.

A fyftematick Catalogue of Works in the European Languages on all Branches of Medicine, Anatomy, Pharmacy, &c.

SIMS (Richard). An Index to all the Pedigrees and Arms in the Heraldic Vifitations and other Genealogical Manufcripts in the Britifh Mufeum. 8°. London. 1849.

"A Book in conftant Ufe by Perfons engaged in genealogical or topographical Studies, affording a ready Clue to the Pedigrees and Arms of above 50,000 of the Gentry of England, their Refidences," &c.

SIMS (Richard). A Manual for the Genealogift, Topographer, Antiquary, and Legal Profeffor; confifting of Defcriptions of Public Records; Parochial and other Regifters; Wills; County and Family Hiftories; Heraldic Collections in Public Libraries, etc. Royal 8°. London. 1856.

"Since the Commencement of the Record Reform by the Act of 1838, feveral Books have been publifhed that are more or lefs Ufeful to the Student or the Antiquarian defirous of purfuing his Inquiries among the national Records; but we have feen none fo ufeful as this *Manual* of Mr. Sims. The Extent of his Coup d'œil, indeed, goes beyond what can be termed Records even in the largeft Senfe. In Addition to thofe Documents which the Law allows to be Records and producible in Evidence, or which Reaſon conſiders Records without Reference to their Cuſtody, Mr. Sims refers to a Variety of illuſtrative Documents, Manuſcripts, and publiſhed Works, ſo numerous as to baffle all Attempts at Enumeration. The *Manual* is not ſolely intended for hiſtorical Students or literary Men, but for the limited though practical Uſes of the Lawyer, the Genealogiſt and the like. It is not a mere bibliographical Account of Muniments, the Place of their Depoſit, whether they have been printed, and when, or by whom; it is a Sort of Hiſtory of our publick Muniments, &c. not unfrequently containing Glimpſes of our ſocial Hiſtory, ſo far as it can be exhibited by the Matter itſelf."—*Spectator, Oct.* 4, 1856.

SWAINSON (William). Taxidermy; with the Biography of Zoologiſts, and Notices of their Works. 12°. London. 1840.

Part II. pp. 98-392, compriſes the Bibliography of Zoology; with biographical Sketches of the principal Authors, and an Index.

TERNAUX-COMPANS (H.). Bibliothèque Aſiatique et Africaine; ou Catalogue des Ouvrages qui ont été publiés ſur ces deux Continents juſqu'à ce Jour. 8°. Paris. 1841.

WALCH (J. G.). Bibliotheca Theologica Selecta. 4 Vols. 8°. Jenæ. 1757-65.

A very valuable Work, accompanied by literary Notices and a general Index of Authors, the Works deſcribed being arranged according to Diviſions or Claſſes.

WALCH (J. G.). Bibliotheca Patriſtica litterariis Annotationibus inſtructa. New Edition edited by J. T. L. Danzius. 8°. Jenæ. 1834.

The firſt Edition was publiſhed in 1770.

WEIGEL (R.). Kunſtlager-Catalog. 8°. Leipzig. 1845.

WINER (G. B.). Handbuch der theologischen Literatur hauptsächlich der protestantischen nebst kurzen biographischen Notizen. 3d Ed. (With a Supplement of 175 Pages, from 1839 to 1842.) 3 Vols. 8°. Leipzig. 1838-42.

WITZLEBEN (A. von). Deutschland's Militär Literatur im letzten Jahrzehent und Uebersicht der wichtigsten Karten und Pläne Central Europas. 8°. Berlin. 1850. pp. 247.

WOHL (R. von). Die Geschichte und Literatur der Staatswissenschaft. 2 Vols. 8°. Erlangen. 1855-6.

XII. Biographical Dictionaries.

ONE of the most useful as well as interesting Parts of a bibliographical Collection of Books, are the Catalogues of publick and private Libraries, including the most important sale Catalogues of Booksellers. As the Design of this Work will not admit of any Details relative to such Catalogues, we refer the Inquirer to the second Volume of Horne's Introduction to the Study of Bibliography, pp. 564-758, where he will find a large Number fully described, with brief Notices of their Contents. The following Account of the biographical Dictionaries which are specially useful to the Bibliographer, together with a Notice of the principal Periodicals devoted to Bibliography, must close our SELECT LIST, already extended beyond its original Limits.

ALLEN (William). The American Biographical Dictionary. 3d Ed. Royal 8°. Boston. 1857.

Truly the *American Bibliographical Dictionary*, containing Notices of 6775 American Names. The first Edition was published in 1809, and the second in 1832. The venerable Author is still living.

ALLIBONE (S. A.). A Critical Dictionary of English Literature, and British and American Authors, living and deceased, from the earliest Accounts to the Middle of the nineteenth Century. Containing thirty-one thousand Biographies and literary Notices, with an Index of Subject-matter.

This truly national Work is to be published by Messrs. Childs & Peterson, Philadelphia, in one Volume, super-royal octavo, 1800 Pages, double Columns. About 1300 Pages, including 21,000 Authors, are already stereotyped. The first Part, A-I, pp. 945, will be issued in September of the present Year. The Author has labored incessantly upon it during the past five Years, bringing to the Undertaking vast Diligence and Research, good Taste and Judgment, and a painstaking Love of Detail and Accuracy. When completed it will prove a most welcome Aid to Bibliographers, Scholars and Readers generally. We speak thus from the Testimony of Everett, Irving, Prescott, Bancroft and other eminent American Scholars, and from personal Examination of Proofs, and Portions already stereotyped. The following Characteristicks of the Work are gathered from a PROSPECTUS.

"1. It is a Biographical Dictionary of English and American Authors, comprising both the living and the dead, furnishing those Incidents respecting the Persons who have made themselves famous in the Republick of Letters, which every Reader desires to know, and few know where to find.

"2. It is a bibliographical Manual, giving Information as to the best Editions of Authors, the Circumstances attending their Publication, the Reception which they met with from the Publick, the Influence they have exercised on the publick Mind, and many other interesting Particulars, not one of which the true Lover of Books, and Student of Letters, would ' willingly let die.'

"As a bibliographical Manual, the Index, which forms the ſecond Portion of the Volume, will prove no ſmall Addition to its Value. In this Index, the Subjects of human Knowledge are divided into forty diſtinct Claſſes, and an Alphabet is allotted to each. By this Means, the Reader is enabled to ſee at a Glance who are the principal Writers on all Subjects, from Agriculture, Claſs 1ſt, to Voyages, Claſs 40th.

"It is thought that this Index will contain between 40,000 and 50,000 Names, yet no Author is mentioned whoſe Works are not noticed in the firſt Part of the Dictionary.

"3. It is a critical, as well as a biographical and bibliographical Dictionary. Here the Author has a great Advantage over his Predeceſſors, *without a ſingle Exception*. Makers of Books approaching to the Character of this, are in the Habit of giving their own Opinions, or Opinions adopted as their own, which muſt be baſed upon very partial Knowledge, and one therefore of little Value; or are apt to be tinctured with Prejudice and party Bias, and are therefore entitled to little Confidence. But Mr. Allibone contents himſelf with adducing the Opinions upon various Writers as they come under his Notice, of Critics of great and extended Reputation, who have earned a Claim to be heard with Reſpect, if not in all Caſes with entire Acquieſcence. Theſe invaluable Specimens of Criticiſm are quoted verbatim, and diſtinguiſhed by a ſmaller Type, which adds greatly to the Beauty of the Work."

APPLETON'S Cyclopædia of Biography; embracing a Series of original Memoirs of the moſt diſtinguiſhed Perſons of all Times. Reviſed American Edition, edited by Francis L. Hawks, D. D. LL. D. Royal 8°. New York. 1856. pp. 1058.

A very handſome Reprint of the Engliſh Edition, which was edited by Elihu Rich. The original Memoirs, the Authorſhip of which is indicated by Initials, were written for this Work by Sir Archibald Aliſon, Wm. Baird, Sir David Brewſter, James Bryce, J. H. Burton, Prof. Creaſy, Prof. Eadie, Prof. Ferguſon, Prof. Gordon, James Hedderwick, J. A.

Heraud, Robert Jamieſon, Charles Knight, James Manſon, J. M'-Connechy, Prof. Nichol, Elihu Rich, Prof. Spalding, Prof. Thomſon, R. N. Wornum. The Articles ſupplied in this American Edition are from different Hands, although the Authorſhip is not indicated, as in the Engliſh Original, by Initials. The numerous Illuſtrations of the Birth-places, Monuments, or other Memorials of departed Greatneſs with which the Volume is enlivened, add much to the Value of the Work.

BIOGRAPHIE Univerſelle, ancienne et moderne. Ouvrage entièrement neuf, rédigé par une Société de Gens de Lettres et de Savants. 52 Vols. 8°. Paris. 1811-28.

By univerſal Conſent, the beſt and moſt extenſive Work of the Kind ever produced in any Language. It might properly be called the Biographie et *Bibliographie* Univerſelle, ſo full and accurate are its Notices of the Works of Authors. A Supplement has been commenced which is ſtill in Progreſs. The 83d Volume (numbering from the laſt Volume of the Original Work), was publiſhed in 1855, containing the Names *Stack* to *Teyſſieu*.

"The eminent Names appended to a large Proportion of the Articles contained in the fifty-two Volumes of the BIOGRAPHIE UNIVERSELLE, are Vouchers for the Ability and Erudition it diſplays. I muſt ſpeak reſpectfully of a Work to which I owe ſo much, and without which, probably, I ſhould never have undertaken the preſent."—*Hallam's Lit. Hiſt.*

BLAKE (J. L.). A Biographical Dictionary; compriſing a Summary Account of the moſt diſtinguiſhed Perſons of all Ages, Nations and Profeſſions. New and reviſed Edition. Royal 8°. Philadelphia. 1857. pp. 1366.

Containing about 12,500 different Articles, 2000 of which are of American Biography. The firſt Edition was publiſhed in 1836, of which there have been 12 Iſſues, the laſt one in 1854. The Number of new Articles introduced into this preſent Edition is about 2400. The Author, a Clergyman, and an early Graduate of Brown Univerſity, recently died at his Reſidence in Orange, New Jerſey.

CHALMERS (Alexander). The General Biographical Dictionary. 32 Vols. 8°. London. 1812-17.

Contains Notices of about 9000 Names. The Author, says Lowndes, has taken more than common Pains in giving accurate Lists of the Works of such as were Authors, with the Dates of the best Editions, &c. He inserts, says Hallam, the most insignificant Names, and quotes the most wretched Authorities; nevertheless we cannot deny the Value of his Dictionary.

CHAMBERS (Robert). A Biographical Dictionary of Eminent Scotsmen. 4 Vols. Imp. 8°. Glasgow. 1835.

An expensive Work, embellished with many splendid and authentick Portraits.

GORTON (John). A General Biographical Dictionary. New Edition, with a Supplement, completing the Work to the present Time. 4 Vols. Thick 8°. London. 1851.

Very accurate and useful, bringing an immense Amount of Information within a small Compass.

JÖECHER (C. G.). Allgemeines Gelehrten Lexicon, darinne die Gelehrten aller Stände welche vom Anfange der Welt bis auf jetzige Zeit. 4 Vols. 4°. Leipzig. 1750-51.

JÖECHER (C. G.). Fortsetzung und Ergänzung von J. C. Adelung. 2 Vols. 4°. Leipzig. 1784-87.

JÖECHER (C. G.). Weiter fortgesetz von H. W. Rotermund. 4 Vols. 4°. Bremen. 1810-19.

This is a biographical Dictionary of learned Men and Women, comprifing, in brief Articles, an immenfe Number of Names. The Continuation by the celebrated Adelung, is incomplete, having reached only to the Letter J. It has been ftill further continued by Rotermund. Each of the ten Volumes above defcribed, contains over a thoufand Pages in double Columns.

NOUVELLE Biographie Générale depuis les Temps les plus reculés jufqu'à nos Jours. 8°. Paris. Vols. 1-23. (To " Hennequin.")

This Work, publifhed by Didot under the Direction of Dr. Hoefer, is to be complete in 45 compact Volumes, one Half of which have already appeared. It is one of the lateft Productions of this Kind, and is of fpecial Value as a BIBLIOGRAPHICAL Dictionary, giving the Titles of the various Authors whofe Lives are contained therein, with Dates, Size, Place of Publication, &c. &c.

ROSE (H. J.). A New General Biographical Dictionary. 12. Vols. 8°. London. 1848.

The beft general bibliographical Dictionary extant in Englifh. It contains Notices of 20,700 Names, "the moft remarkable of which are treated at a Length," as ftated in the Preface, "fully commenfurate with their Importance."

SMITH (William). Dictionary of Greek and Roman Biography and Mythology; edited by William Smith, LL. D. Illuftrated by numerous Wood Engravings. 3 Vols. Thick royal 8°. London. 1846-9.

The Contributors to this invaluable Work are among the moft diftinguifhed European Writers and Scholars. It includes the Names of all Perfons of any Importance which occur in the Greek and Roman Writers down to the Year 1453. The bibliographical Notices are very full and accurate. A fecond Edition abridged, in one royal octavo Volume, was publifhed in 1851.

XIII. *Bibliographical Periodicals.*

THE following are the principal Periodicals which are devoted exclufively to Bibliography and Library Economy. Several of them, it will be feen, have a high literary Character, while others are important chiefly for their Lifts and Notices of new Books.

ALLGEMEINE Bibliographie. Monatliches Verzeichnifs der wichtigern neuen Erfcheinungen der deutfchen und aufländifchen Literatur. *Octavo.* Leipzig.

An excellent monthly Periodical commenced in 1856; edited by Paul Trömel. The firft Volume has a full alphabetical Index of 40 Pages, which adds greatly to the Value of the Work as a Source of bibliographical Information upon the moft important Publications of the Day. It embraces Books in all Languages, American and Afiatick, as well as European.

AMERICAN Publifhers' Circular and Literary Gazette. *Quarto.* New York.

A weekly Journal, conducted by Charles R. Rode, under the Direction of the New York Book-Publifhers' Affociation. It contains Extracts from new Books, literary Intelligence, Lifts of Books publifhed from Month to Month, Announcements, Advertifements, &c. being fimilar to the Publifhers' Circular iffued by Sampfon Low & Son, of London. It was commenced in 1855. An American Periodical more ftrictly literary and bibliographical in its Character is a Defideratum. Such a Journal, fomewhat fimilar to the earlier Numbers of Norton's Literary Gazette, containing Accounts of Libraries with Illuftrations, Treatifes upon Bibliography, Titles of new Books publifhed from Month to Month, Contents of Periodicals, critical Notices of new Works like thofe in the *Athenæum*, Notices of Works upon Bibliography like thofe in *Anzeiger* or *Serapeum*, &c. &c.

would undoubtedly be well ſuſtained in the Hands of an enterpriſing Publiſher.

ATHENÆUM Journal of Engliſh and Foreign Literature, Science and Fine Arts. *Quarto.* London.

An important weekly Periodical publiſhed by J. Francis. It was commenced in 1828. The bound Volumes are accompanied by good Indexes, and are regarded as indiſpenſable to the Student in Engliſh Bibliography, although the Work, as its Title indicates, is devoted to Literature, Science, and the Fine Arts. Reviews and critical Notices of New Books, both Engliſh and Foreign, occupy a large Part of each Number. The Athenæum contains numerous Announcements and Advertiſements, moſtly of Book-Publiſhers in London and Vicinity.

BENT'S Monthly Literary Advertiſer, Regiſter of Books, Engravings, &c. Publiſhed on the tenth of each Month. Annual Subſcription, 8s, including the alphabetical Catalogue. *Quarto.* London.

Eſtabliſhed in the Year 1802.

BIBLIOGRAPHIE de la France ; ou Journal général de l'Imprimerie et de la Librarie. *Octavo.* Paris.

" Cette dernière Suite, rédigée par M. Beuchot, eſt remarkable par ſon Exactitude. Malheureuſement on n'y annonce que les Ouvrages qui ont été dépoſés à la Direction de la Librairie."—*Brunet.* It is a weekly Periodical, commenced in 1811. The firſt Series, called *Journal Typographique,* was commenced by Roux in 1797. This Work is noticed in its proper Place, under Section. IX. See Page 71.

BULLETIN du Bibliophile, petite Revue d'anciens Livres, contenant des Notices bibliographiques, philologiques et littéraires, par divers Auteurs, ſous la Direction de Nodier, Paris, Dupleſſis, etc. *Octavo,* Paris,

A monthly Periodical commenced in 1836, and now publiſhed by J. Techener. Its copious bibliographical and literary Notices of rare, curious and important Books have given it great Succeſs, it having reached its twenty-third Year.

BULLETIN du Bibliophile Belge. *Octavo.* Bruxelles.

"Bruſſels is a Place of great Intereſt for Bibliography. Its Contributions to bibliographical Knowledge in the *Bibliophile Belge*, and the *Annuaire de la Bibliothèque Royale*, from the Pen of Baron de Reiffenberg, the learned Conſervateur of the latter, are among the moſt valuable ever made."—*Cogſwell*, 1851.

This Bulletin is at preſent publiſhed by F. Heuſſner, under the Direction of Auguſtus Scheler, Librarian to the King. It was commenced in 1845. The firſt Series, 9 Volumes, has an Index prepared by Scheler, and publiſhed in 1855, in one octavo Volume.

CRONACA. Giornale di Scienze, Lettere, Arti, Economia, Induſtria con Bolletino bibliografico pubblicato da Ignazio Cantù. *Octavo.* Milan.

Commenced in 1855, and publiſhed on the 1ſt and 15th of every Month. Each Number has at the End, a bibliographical Bulletin of Italian Publications for the Uſe of Bookſellers, Librarians, &c.

NEUER Anzeiger für Bibliographie und Bibliothekwiſſenſchaft. Herauſgegeben von Dr. Julius Petzholdt. *Octavo.* Dreſden.

Publiſhed monthly. This highly uſeful Periodical, as its Title indicates, is ſtrictly bibliographical in its Character, containing Notices of Works upon Diplomaticks, Engraving, Printing, Libraries, Library Economy, Catalogues of publick and private Libraries, Auction Sale Catalogues, &c. It was commenced in 1840. The bound Volumes have copious claſſified and alphabetical Indexes. Dr. Petzhold, the Editor, is Librarian to the King of Saxony, and the Author of ſeveral very important Works upon Libraries and Library Economy.

PUBLISHERS' Circular, and General Record of Britiſh and Foreign Literature; containing a complete alphabetical Liſt of all new Works publiſhed in Great Britain, and of every Work of Intereſt publiſhed abroad. *Octavo.* London.

Commenced in 1837. It is publiſhed on the 1ſt and 15th of every Month, by Sampſon Low and Son. For the Title in full, ſee Section IX, Page 68. It is not literary in its Character, conſiſting chiefly of Liſts and Advertiſements. The bound Volumes are deficient in Indexes.

SERAPEUM. Zeitſchrift für die Bibliothekwiſſenſchaft, Handſchriftenkunde und ältere Literatur. *Octavo.* Leipzig.

Publiſhed on the 1ſt and 15th of each Month. It is ſimilar to Petzholdt's *Anzeiger* already deſcribed, except that it devotes more Space to Ancient Literature and the Hiſtory and Statiſticks of Libraries, and contains occaſional Plates or Illuſtrations. The Volume for 1846, contains the fulleſt and moſt correct Account of the Libraries of America, from the Pen of the late Hermann E. Ludewig, then a Reſident of New York, that had appeared previous to the Publication of Profeſſor Jewett's Work in 1850. The Serapeum was commenced in 1840. It is edited by Dr. Robert Naumann, who is aſſiſted in his Duties by an Aſſociation of Librarians and literary Friends.

PART SECOND.

LIBRARIES.

"But is there to be no End to this Purchafe of Books? Oh yes; and let us fee when it is. When there have been redeemed from Time all the valuable intellectual Bequefts of former Ages; when there has been garnered up all that preceding Generations had amaffed as a facred and imperifhable Inheritance, there will then remain no Duty but to collect what the Age produces. And when literary Ambition fhall ceafe to be excited; when Genius is no longer beftowed by the Munificence of Heaven; when Induftry no longer collects new Facts refpecting Man and Nature; when the forming Hand ceafes to reproduce; when the Streams of human Intellect no longer flow; when the Springs of Intelligence and Thought are all dried up; when the Regions of Science and of Mind fleep in univerfal Lethargy,—then it will be Time to give over buying Books."

LIBRARIES.

THE following Notices of Publick Libraries make no Claims to Originality, but ſimply to ſet forth clearly and connectedly ſuch Facts in regard to their Origin, Progreſs, and preſent Condition, as may not otherwiſe be eaſily acceſſible to the Public; Compilations have therefore been made, and free Extracts taken from the following Works, in Addition to ſuch as are alluded to in the Notices themſelves, viz:

Act of Incorporation and By-Laws of the Truſtees of the Aſtor Library; with the Annual Reports of the ſame. 1850-57.

Bibliotheca Sacra, Vol. VII. January and April Numbers. 8°. Andover. 1850.

British Museum; New Reading Room and Libraries. With a Plan. pp. 16. 12°. London. 1857.

Catalogues of the New York State Library. 3 Vols. 8°. Albany. 1856.

Dibdin (T. F.). Bibliographical Antiquarian and Picturesque Tour in France and Germany. 2d Ed. 3 Vols. 8°. London. 1829.

Encyclopedia Britannica. New Edition; Article Libraries.

Jewett (Prof. C. C.). Notices of Public Libraries in the United States. 8°. Washington. 1851.

Jewett (Prof. C. C.). History of the Library of Brown University. pp. 21. 8°. Providence. 1843.

Norton's Literary Almanac, Register and Gazette. 3 Vols. 12°. New York. 1852-4.

Peirce (Benjamin). History of Harvard University. 8°. Cambridge. 1833.

Quincy (Josiah). History of Harvard University. 2 Vols. 8°. Cambridge. 1840.

Sims (Richard). Handbook to the Library of the British Museum. 12°. London. 1854.

United States Magazine. Vol. II. October Number. 4°. Philadelphia. 1855.

LIBRARY OF HARVARD UNIVERSITY.

75,500 Vols.

THE Collection of Books belonging to Harvard University, in Cambridge, Massachusetts, has long been regarded as the largest, and until within comparatively a recent Period, the moſt valuable one in the United States. It conſiſts of 116,000 Volumes, which are diſtributed in four Departments, viz: Theological, Medical, Law, and Publick. The THEOLOGICAL LIBRARY is in Divinity Hall. Perſons entitled to its Privileges muſt be connected with the Divinity School. Number of Books about 8,700. They conſiſt of ſelect Works, principally in modern Theology, with ſome of the early Fathers. The MEDICAL LIBRARY is in the Medical College in Boſton, having been placed there for the Convenience of Students attending the Medical Lectures. Number of Books about 2,000. The LAW LIBRARY, deſigned for the Officers and Students of the Law School, is in Dane Hall. Number of Books about 14,000. They conſiſt of the principal Works in Engliſh and American Law, and in the Civil Law, together with important Works by Writers in France, Germany, and Spain, conſtituting one of the largeſt and choiceſt Collections in this Department of Learning, in the Country. The PUBLICK or COLLEGE LIBRARY is in Gore Hall, and is for the common Uſe of the whole Univerſity. Number of Books 75,500, of which 1,000 belong to the Boylſton Medical Library, in immediate Connection with it. This Enumeration does not include the unbound Pamphlets, of which there are upwards of 30,000. To the foregoing ſhould be added the Society Libraries of the Students, which contain 12,000 Volumes, making a grand Total of 128,000.

This noble Collection was begun 94 Years ago. On the 24th of January, 1764, in a ſtormy winter's

Night during the College Vacation, Harvard Hall, containing the Library of about 6,000 Volumes, the philoſophical Apparatus, and all the little Collections of Objects of Intereſt belonging to the College, was deſtroyed by Fire. "Thus periſhed," ſays Elliot in his Sketch of Harvard College, "the valuable Books given by John Harvard, Sir Kenelm Digby, Sir John Maynard, Dr. Lightfoot, Dr. Gale, Biſhop Berkeley, and other diſtinguiſhed Benefactors; the Books and Pamphlets connected with the early Hiſtory of New England, the precious, though ſcanty Accumulations of a hundred and twenty-ſix Years—a Loſs which in thoſe Days muſt have ſeemed appalling, and which the Hiſtorian, the Antiquary, and the Bibliographer can never ceaſe to deplore."

The State Legiſlature was then in Seſſion. Indeed, at the Time of the Calamity, Harvard Hall was occupied by them in conſequence of the Alarm excited by the Exiſtence of the Small Pox in Boſton. At the Inſtigation of Gov. Bernard, they immediately appropriated £2,000 to erect a new Building in Place of that which had been deſtroyed. A general Subſcription was made for the ſame Purpoſe in the Towns and Counties of the State, amounting to £878. 16s. 9d. A generous Intereſt in this Object was alſo ſhown by many Perſons in the parent Country, one of whom, Thomas Hollis, ſubſcribed for the new Building £200. The Friends of the Inſtitution manifeſted not leſs Zeal and Liberality in ſupplying the new Hall with

Books. The General Aſſembly of New Hampſhire gave Books to the Value of £300 Sterling. The Society for Propagating the Goſpel in New England and adjacent Parts, gave £200 Sterling, and the Society for Propagating the Goſpel in foreign Parts £100 for the Library.

In 1790, the Library had increaſed to 12,000 Volumes; in 1830, to 30,000. It is almoſt entirely the Fruit of individual Munificence, having had to depend for its Supply even to the preſent Day, with the Exception of the Income of the Hollis and Shapleigh Fund of $6,000, upon the Liberality of private Contributors. During the Year ending July 1857, there were thus added to the Library, including the ſplendid Collection of Engravings and Works of Art bequeathed by the late Hon. F. C. Gray, and the magnificent Donation of Books in the claſſical and oriental Languages, bequeathed by the late Dr. H. W. Wales, more than 4000 Volumes. Notwithſtanding the Books in the Library are thus multiplied, the Committee in their laſt Annual Report complain of the Want of a ſuitable permanent Fund, ſtating that the true Wants of the Library can only be ſupplied by a ſteady and ſyſtematick Expenditure of Money in the Procurement of Works the moſt needed, and in which it may be moſt deficient.

Conſpicuous among the early Benefactors of the Library ſtands the Name of Thomas Hollis, a wealthy Baptiſt of London, whoſe enlarged Views of Chriſtianity, and "Deeds of Peace," entitle him to the lasting Respect and Gratitude of Mankind. The Books, which he, and his Brothers and Descendants, placed upon the Library Shelves, were very numerous, admirably well chosen, many of them, containing curious and interesting Notes in their own Hand-writing, and elegantly bound. At the Decease of Thomas Hollis 3[d], in 1774, he bequeathed to the College a Sum of Money, which now constitutes one Half of the Library Fund to which Allusion has already been made. In a Note in Giggeius's Thesaurus Linguæ Arabicæ, he says: "This is a fine Copy of a very scarce Work. T. H. has been particularly Industrious in collecting Grammars and Lexicons of the oriental *Root* Languages, to send to Harvard College, in Hopes of forming by that Means, assisted by the Energy of the Leaders, always beneficent, a few *prime Scholars*, Honours to their Country, and Lights to Mankind," &c. The Gifts to the Library and College of Thomas Hollis 1st, including those of his Brothers, John and Nathaniel, and Thomas Hollis, the Son of the latter, amounted to six thousand Pounds, Currency of Massachusetts, which, says Quincy in his History of the University, "considering the Value of Money at that Period, and the disinterested Spirit by which their Charities were prompted, constitutes one of the most remarkable Instances of continued Benevolence upon Record." Mr. Benj. Peirce, for many Years Librarian of the Institution, in his History of the Library, notices Thomas Hollis 3d, particularly, "not only on Account of his general Claims to

Reſpect and Admiration, but becauſe, from the Amount and Quality of his Benefactions, and from the Period at which they were received, he may juſtly be conſidered as the Father of Harvard College Library." Thomas Brand Hollis, and other Branches or Deſcendants of the Family, continued from Time to Time to ſend liberal Donations to the Library and College.

In the new Harvard Hall, erected immediately on the Site of the old one, the Publick Library was kept till July, 1841, when the Books were removed to Gore Hall, a ſpacious and impoſing Edifice, built for its excluſive Accommodation by Means of Funds bequeathed to the College by the Hon. Chriſtopher Gore. This Building preſents a pure and chaſte Specimen of the Gothick Style of the fourteenth Century, but the hard Sienite or Quincy Granite, uſed in its Conſtruction, made it neceſſary to omit the elaborate Ornaments with which this Style is uſually wrought. It is in the Form of a Latin Croſs; the Length of the Body being 140 Feet, and acroſs the Tranſepts 81½ Feet. The main Entrances are flanked by octagonal Towers, 83 Feet high, ſurmounted by lofty mitered Pinnacles, ſomewhat like thoſe of King's College Chapel, at Cambridge, England. The outer Walls are of rough Stone, laid in regular Courſes, with hammered ſtone Buttreſſes, Towers, Pinnacles, and Drip-ſtones. The inner Walls and Columns are of Brick, ſtuccoed. The main Floor is alſo of Brick, reſting on brick Arches, filled above to a Level, and covered with hard-pine Boards. The

Roof and Gallery are ſupported by wrought iron Rafters, and the Partitions are ſtrengthened by concealed iron Columns. The interior of the Body of the Building forms a beautiful Hall, 112 Feet long and 35 Feet high, with a vaulted and ribbed Ceiling, ſpringing from two Ranges of ribbed Columns. The Spaces between the Columns are divided by Partitions into Stalls or Alcoves for Books, having a light Gallery above, protected by an ornamented iron Baluſtrade. One of the Tranſepts is uſed as a Reading-room; the other is divided into three Apartments for Books. This Hall, in the Conſtruction of which great Caution was uſed to guard againſt Injury by Fire, is heated by Steam, which is conveyed from a Boiler in the Baſement, through iron Pipes to four Stacks of perpendicular copper Pipes, arranged like Screens at the Sides of the central Area. An ingenious ſelf-acting Contrivance regulates the Draft, ſo as to check or increaſe the Generation of the Steam. The whole Coſt, including the heating Apparatus, was little ſhort of $75,000.

The Publick Library of the Univerſity, for which alone, as before ſtated, this Hall is deſigned (the Libraries of the Theological, Medical, and Law Schools being kept in ſeparate Buildings), contains Books in all Branches of Learning. Theſe are arranged according to Subjects into the four grand Diviſions of Literature, Hiſtory, Theology, and Science, with numerous Subdiviſions. The firſt Claſſification of the Books was made in 1822, by Joſeph G. Cogſwell, Eſq., now the learned Superintendent of the Aſtor Library; and it has been continued ever ſince, upon eſſentially the ſame Plan.

The Diviſion of Theology contains the four great Polyglots, the Complutenſian, Antwerp, French and Engliſh; a very valuable Collection of the Writings of the Fathers of the Church; a complete Apparatus for the critical Study of the Scriptures and eccleſiaſtical Hiſtory, and a Body of the miſcellaneous Writings of all the beſt modern Divines. The ſcientifick Diviſion is rich in Works on the exact and natural Sciences; and the Library is well ſupplied in the Departments of Philoſophy, Ethics, ancient and modern Literature, Hiſtory, Topography, and Antiquities. Voluminous and expenſive Works, which are rarely met with, except in large publick Libraries, here have their Place. Nowhere elſe in the United States will be found ſo large a Collection of the Journals and Reports of the Engliſh Parliament; and the Department of American Hiſtory is unrivalled, at leaſt in this Country. The Collection of Maps, the Titles of which alone fill a printed Volume of two hundred and twenty-four Pages, is believed to be altogether unique. The Library contains, alſo, a few valuable and intereſting Manuſcripts; one of which, a Fragment of the Goſpels of Matthew and John, in the Greek uncial Character on Parchment, is more than one thouſand Years old, and is doubtleſs the only Specimen of this Kind and Age on this Continent.

The Benefits conferred by this Library, are rendered, by the Liberality of its Regulations, as Extenſive as is conſiſtent with the Safety of the Property. Books are borrowed and returned, in term Time, from 2 to 4 o'Clock on Mondays, Tueſdays, Wedneſdays and Thurſdays, and in Vacations from 9 to 1 o'Clock on Mondays. Admittance and Permiſſion to conſult the Books are afforded gratuitouſly to all Viſitors. Perſons having a temporary Reſidence near the Univerſity, for the Purpoſes of Study, are permitted to borrow Books without Charge; while the Library is one of the principal Attractions to an increaſing Number of Students, who reſort to this celebrated Univerſity for an Education.

John L. Sibley, *Librarian.*

YALE COLLEGE LIBRARY.

35,000 Vols.

THIS Library is designed for the Use of the several Faculties of the College, Students connected with the Theological, Law, Medical and Philosophical Departments, and the Members of the Senior and Junior Classes in the Academical Department. The whole Number of Books belonging to it, exclusive of about 5000 Pamphlets, is 35,000. Each of the professional Schools has connected with it a separate Library, making a Summary of 5000 additional Volumes. In the Library of the Linonian Society, there are

12,500 Vo'umes; of the Brothers in Unity, 12,500; making a Total of 60,000 Volumes.

The following Account of the Origin and Progreſs of the Library is taken mainly from Norton's Literary Regiſter for 1853. The neceſſary Changes and Additions have been made, bringing it down to the preſent Time.

In the Year 1700, ten of the principal Clergymen of the Colony of Connecticut met at New Haven, and formed themſelves into a Body of Truſtees for the Purpoſe of eſtabliſhing a College in the Colony. At the next Meeting, which was at Branford, each one preſented to the Body a Number of Books, and laid them on the Table with theſe Words: "*I give theſe Books for founding a College in this Colony.*" The Library thus formed, conſiſted of about 40 folio Volumes; and Rev. Samuel Ruſſell of Branford, was appointed the Keeper. This Collection, with its Additions, was kept at Branford nearly three Years, when it was removed to Killingworth, the Reſidence of Rev. Abraham Pierſon, the Rector of the College.

In October, 1701, the Collegiate School received a Charter from the Legiſlature of the Colony of Connecticut. It is probable that on the Death of Rector Pierſon, in 1707, the Library was tranſferred to Saybrook, the Seat of the College, and there remained until 1718.

About 1713, the Library was increaſed by ſeveral Donations, eſpecially by a conſiderable Collection ſent from England by Sir John Davie, previouſly of Groton, Conn. In 1714, a large Addition was made through the generous Efforts of Jeremiah Dummer, Colonial Agent at London, who ſent about 800 valuable Volumes. Of theſe, 120 were his own Gift, about 40 were given by Gov. Yale, and the Remainder were, through Mr. Dummer's Inſtrumentality, preſented by Gentlemen in England, among whom were Sir Iſaac Newton, Dr. Edmund Halley, Sir Richard Steele, Dr. Bentley and Dr. Calamy. Another Donation of about 300 Volumes was ſent by Gov. Yale, in 1717, and Mr. Dummer added in 1718, about 75 Volumes more.

In 1717-18, the College was tranſferred to New Haven, and a large College-houſe was here built, which in September, 1718, was named YALE COLLEGE, in Commemoration of the Generoſity of Elihu Yale, then a Reſident of London, but a Native of New Haven. The Name was ſoon extended to the whole Inſtitution, but was not its legal Title until 1745.

In December, 1718, the Library was removed to New Haven, not without violent Oppoſition, and about 250 Volumes were loſt in the tranſfer.

Occaſional Donations of Books were from this Time received, but none of much Magnitude until the Year 1733, when Rev. George Berkeley, Dean of Derry, in Ireland (who when in Rhode Iſland a few Years previous, had given to the Library Copies of his own Works), ſent to the College a moſt important Donation, amounting to nearly a thouſand

Volumes, and making the fineſt Collection of Books which, up to that Time, had ever come at once into America.

In 1743, a Catalogue of all the Books in the Library was prepared by Preſident Clap. It was arranged according to Subjects, and was printed in a Volume of 48 Pages, 12°. at New London, in 1743. The Number of Volumes in the Library at this Time was about 2,600. The Catalogue was accompanied with an Introduction, by Rev. Dr. Johnſon, of Stratford, afterwards Preſident of Columbia College, N. Y., exhibiting a general View of all the Arts and Sciences, with a Catalogue of ſome of the moſt valuable Authors on each Part of Philoſophy proper to be read by Students.

From this Time to the latter Part of the Century, the Library increaſed but ſlowly. The College had ſcarcely any Funds for the Purchaſe of Books, and the Number preſented was not large. During the War of the Revolution, the Library was ſent into the Interior to ſecure it from the Enemy, and many Books were probably thus loſt.

The Fund for the Increaſe of the Library was commenced in 1763, when the Sum of ten Pounds (Conn. Currency) was received by Bequeſt from Rev. Jared Eliot, of Killingworth. In 1777, a like Sum was received from Rev. Thomas Ruggles of Guilford. In 1791, a Bequeſt of $1,122 was received from Rev. Samuel Lockwood, D. D. of Andover, Conn.

In 1805, an important Addition was made by

the Purchaſe of about 2,000 Volumes by Profeſſor Silliman, during his Viſit to Europe.

In 1807, Hon. Oliver Wolcott, then reſiding in New York, gave $2,000 to the Library Fund. In 1821, a Bequeſt of $3,000 was made to the College by Noah Linſly, Eſq. of Wheeling, Va., but previouſly of Branford, Conn. By Vote of the Corporation, the Income of this Gift was aſſigned to the Library, and was ſo continued until the Year 1851.

In 1823, a Donation of ſeveral hundred Volumes was made by Rev. Jedediah Morſe and Prof. S. F. B. Morſe. The ſame Year, Eli Whitney, Eſq. of New Haven, gave to the Fund $500, the Income to be expended in the purchaſe of Books on Practical Mechanicks. Daniel Wadſworth, Eſq. of Hartford, likewiſe gave $500, the Income to be uſed for buying Books on Natural Hiſtory and Chemiſtry.

In 1833, the Sum of $5,000 was contributed to the Fund, by John T. Norton, Eſq. of Albany, N. Y., now of Farmington, Conn.

In 1836, the Library Funds were enlarged by a Bequeſt of $10,000, received from Alfred E. Perkins, M. D. of Norwich, Conn. This Legacy forms a ſeparate Fund, and the Income thereof is expended in buying Books to be kept apart, and forming a diſtinct Portion of the Library.

In 1843, a Bequeſt made in 1825, by Rev. John Elliott, of Guilford, reached the amount of $1,000. By the Terms of Gift, $50 of the annual Income of this Fund is to be applied in buying Books for the Theological Department.

In 1845, the Income of the Library Funds having accumulated to a confiderable Amount, Profeffor Kingfley, who was the Librarian for nineteen Years previous to 1825, and was every way qualified for the Undertaking, went abroad, and expended in England, Holland, France, and Germany; about $8,000 in the purchafe of Books.

In 1849, a Legacy left for the Library Fund by Mr. Addin Lewis, of New Haven (who died in 1842), reached the intended amount of $5,000, and the annual Income has fince been applied to the Library.

In 1850, a Gift of $500 to the Library Fund, refulting from a previous conditional Subfcription to another Object, was received from Profeffor Kingfley.

A Building for the Reception of the Library of the College and the Libraries of the literary Societies of the Inftitution, was commenced in 1842. The College Library was removed in 1843, into one of the fmaller Apartments, but the principal Hall was not ready for the Reception of Books until 1846. The Building is of Gothick Style, and the Material is brown Sandftone from Portland, Conn. It comprifes two Halls for the College Library, with Reading-room, Ante-room and Librarian's Room connected, and alfo feparate Halls for the Society Libraries. The fouthern Wing (neareft the Obferver, on the Sketch) is occupied by the Library of the Lionian Society, the northern by that of the Brothers' Society. The Dimenfions of the Building are as follows: whole Front, 151 Feet; Front of main Hall, 51 Feet; Length of do. 95 Feet; Front of each Wing, 30 Feet; Length of do. 67 Feet; connecting Wings, 26 Feet by 40 Feet; extreme Height of Towers, 91 Feet; interior Dimenſions of main Hall, 83 Feet by 41 Feet; Height of Nave, 51 Feet. The entire Coſt of the Structure, when ſtone Pinnacles are added, will be about $40,000.

The Library, though not ſo large as could be wiſhed, is a good one, and is gradually enlarging by the Expenditure of the Income of the Funds and by Donations. No Catalogue has been publiſhed ſince 1823. A manuſcript Catalogue on Cards is in Courſe of Preparation, but it is not propoſed to print it. The Library has no ancient Manuſcripts of Importance. Among the modern ones which it poſſeſſes are about forty Volumes left by Preſ. Styles, which are often conſulted, being ſpecially valuable in relation to the political and eccleſiaſtical Hiſtory of this Country. It has alſo a Collection of Papers relating to the Controverſy between the Mohegans and the Colony of Connecticut. Of the more valuable printed Works which it compriſes, the following may perhaps be worthy of mention, viz: A Collection of American Newſpapers of 1765-6, gathered by Dr. Stiles, with reference to the Stamp Act, 4 Vols. folio. This is a unique Collection of great hiſtorical Value, and not to be replaced in Caſe of Accident or Loſs. Purchas, his Pilgrimes, 5 Vols. folio, 1625-6 (a fine Copy);

Grævii Gronovii Thesaurus Antiquitatum, etc. 87 Vols. folio; Muratori's Scriptores Italici, 24 Vols. folio; Description de l'Egypte, Paris (an early Copy), 1809, etc. 22 Vols. folio; Kingsborough's Antiquities of Mexico, 9 Vols. folio; Silvestre's Paléographie Universelle, 4 Vols. folio; Zahn's Antiquities of Pompeii, Herculaneum and Stabia, folio; Documents Inédits sur l'Histoire de la France, 107 Vols. 4°. (in Progress); Annali dell' Instituto di Corrispondenza Archeologica, 1829-45, 16 Vols. 8°.; Bullettino do. 1829-1844; Maii Scriptorum Veterum Nova Collectio Vaticana, 10 Vols. folio; Maii Spicilegium Romanum, 10 Vols. 8°.; Piranesi's Collection of Italian Antiquities, etc. 27 Vols. folio; Pertz's Monumenta Germaniæ Historica, Vols. 1-8, folio; Fungruben des Orients, 6 Vols. folio; Milan Edition of the Italian Classics, 400 Vols. 8°.; Allgemeine Literatur Zeitung, complete, 1785-1849, 141 Vols. 4°.; Berliner Jahrbücher, complete, 1827-1845, 33 Vols. 4°.; Wiener Jahrbücher der Literatur, complete, 1818-1849; Collection of orignal Pamphlets concerning English Affairs from Charles I. to James II. Publications of the English Record Commission, 74 Vols. folio; Calvin's Opera Omnia, 9 Vols. folio; Taylor's Translations of Plato and Aristotle, 19 Vols. 4°.; Hansard's Parliamentary Debates, 137 Vols. 8°.; Ternaux-Compans's Collection of Voyages, &c. relative to the Discovery of America, 20 Vols. 8°. Paris; Ersch and Grüber's Encyclopædia, 100 Vols. 4°. (in Progress); Catesby's

Natural Hiſtory of Carolina, folio; Byzantine Hiſtorians, Venice Edition, 23 Vols. folio. A Collection of about 4,000 Vols. chiefly in eccleſiaſtical Hiſtory and patriſtick Theology, formerly belonging to Prof. J. K. Philo, of the Univerſity of Halle, who died in 1853, was added to the Library by Purchaſe in 1854.

The oldeſt printed Work in the Library is a Copy of two Tracts of St. Auguſtine (de Vita Chriſtiana, etc.), printed by Ulric Zell, of Mayence, A. D. 1467.

During Term-time, the College Library is open every ſecular Day, from 10 A. M. to 1 P. M., and from 3 to 5 P. M., and in Summer uſually an Hour or two more. The Perſons entitled to *borrow* from the Library, are the Profeſſors and Teachers of the College, Members of the profeſſional and ſcientifick Schools, and of the Junior and Senior Claſſes, and ſuch other Perſons as the Library Committee may authorize. For Conſultation, however, the Library is opened freely to every Applicant. Books are occaſionally loaned to Perſons at a Diſtance, by Permiſſion of the Committee.

EDWARD C. HERRICK, A. M., *Librarian.*

LIBRARY OF BROWN UNIVERSITY.

28,500 Vols.

THIS Library, which is in the lower Part of Manning Hall, although not ſo large, numerically ſpeaking as other Libraries which we have deſcribed, is regarded by Bibliographers as very CHOICE and VALUABLE. A large Proportion of the Books have been ſelected and purchaſed within the laſt twenty Years, with ſpecial Reference to the Wants of Students and Gentlemen engaged in literary and ſcientifick Reſearch. The Departments of Bibliography, the Claſſicks, Engliſh Hiſtory and Literature, the Fathers or Patriſticks, Mathematicks, and the Modern Languages, are quite full and comparatively complete. The Library has a large Collection of bound Pamphlets, including 278 Volumes collected and presented by the Hon. Theron Metcalf of Boston, a Graduate of the Class of 1805. Of these, 58 are Ordination Sermons, and deserve especial Notice. They contain 1300 Discourses preached at Ordinations, Installations and Inaugurations in the United States, and chiefly in New England, constituting without Doubt the largest Collection of this Kind that has ever been made. There are also in Judge Metcalf's Collection, 70 Volumes of Funeral Sermons, as follows: Ministers, 20 Volumes; Boston Ministers, 5; Ministers' Wives, 4; Women, 6; Presidents of the United States, 6, &c.; 19 Volumes of Century and Half Century Discourses; 12 Volumes of Fourth of July Orations, including all delivered before the Municipal Authorities of Boston from 1800 to 1857; Discourses on Washington, 5 Volumes; Missionary Sermons, 12 Volumes; Phi Beta Kappa Addresses, 4 Volumes, &c. &c. The Importance of such a Collection as this, in Connection with the ecclesiastical and civil History of our Country, can hardly be over estimated. The whole Number of Books in the College Library, exclusive of a large Number of unbound Pamphlets, is 28,500. In Addition to these, the Philermenian and United Brothers' Societies have about 6,000 Volumes, making a Total of 34,500.

Brown University was incorporated in the Year 1764. It was originally established in the Town of Warren, R. I., where, in the Year 1769, the firſt Commencement was celebrated. It was ſubſequently removed to Providence, where the firſt College Edifice (Univerſity Hall) was erected, in the Year 1770. The firſt Books obtained for the Library, were procured through the Agency of the Rev. Morgan Edwards of Philadelphia, who in the Years 1768-9, viſited England, Wales and Ireland to procure Funds for the College. In 1826, the Library contained 5,818 Volumes, of which 1300 were bequeathed to it by the Rev. Wm. Richards, LL. D., of Lynn, England, in the Year 1818. This Collection is in many Reſpects valuable, containing a conſiderable Number of Welſh Books, Works illuſtrating the Hiſtory and Antiquities of England and Wales, and ſeveral hundred bound Volumes of Pamphlets, many of them very ancient, rare, and curious. Mr. Richards was a Native of South Wales, and for many Years Paſtor of the Baptiſt Church in Lynn, where he died in the 69th Year of his Age.

Soon after the Acceſſion of the Rev. Dr. Wayland to the Preſidency of the College, Efforts were made to increaſe the Efficiency of the Library, by raiſing a Fund for the Purchaſe of Books, and alſo Apparatus for the philoſophical and chemical Departments of the Univerſity. Theſe Efforts were ſo far ſucceſſful, that the Sum of $19,437 was obtained, of which the Hon. Nicholas Brown, with his wonted Liberality, gave 10,000. It was put on Intereſt until 1839, when having increaſed to twenty-five thousand Dollars, it was invested in a permanent Fund, according to the Provisions of the Subscription. The annual Income of this Fund is $1,750, of which about $250 is appropriated for Apparatus, and the Remainder devoted to the Purchase of Books.

The Room used for the Library, at the Time when the Library Fund was raised, "was an Apartment in University Hall, crowded to Excess, unsightly and wholly unsuited for the Purpose to which, from Necessity it was devoted." To remedy this Defect, the Hon. Nicholas Brown erected at his own Expense a beautiful Edifice, for a Library and Chapel; to which, in Testimony of Veneration for his former Instructor, he gave the Name of Manning Hall. At the Dedication, February 4, 1835, Dr. Wayland delivered a Discourse on the "Dependence of Science upon Revealed Religion," which was published.

This Hall, the third College Building which has been erected, is of the Dorick Order, built of rubble Stone; and covered with Cement. Including the Portico, it is about 90 Feet in Length, by 42 Feet in Width. Its Height, from the Top of the Basement, is 40 Feet. The Library occupies the Whole of the first Floor, and is a beautiful Room, ornamented in the Centre with a double Row of fluted Columns, from which the Shelves extend to the Walls, forming twelve Alcoves. Its Dimensions are 64 Feet by 38, and 13 Feet high. Extra Shelves for the Accommodation of the Books have been constructed in every available Place throughout, and already they are completely filled. This, together with the Fact that the Building is not Fire-proof, points to the Neceſſity of a more capacious and ſubſtantial Edifice at a not far diſtant Day.

Soon after the Removal to this Building, the Library was newly arranged, and in 1843 a full Catalogue of its Contents was printed. This Catalogue was favourably noticed in the North American Review, and in other leading Periodicals, and drew eſpecial Attention to this important Department of the Inſtitution. It was prepared by Prof. C. C. Jewett, who was the Librarian of the Univerſity from 1841 to 1848, when he reſigned, in order to take Charge of the library Department connected with the Smithſonian Inſtitution at Waſhington. The Catalogue is alphabetical, according to the Authors' Names, and has a copious and analytical Index of Subjects. A Supplement much larger than the original Volume, and on the ſame Plan, has been prepared on Cards.

Shortly afterwards a Chair of modern Languages was eſtabliſhed at the College; and Mr. Jewett, the Profeſſor elect, was encouraged to viſit Europe, partly for the Purpoſe of profeſſional Study, and partly to enable the Friends of the Inſtitution to carry out their Wiſhes more effectually for the Increaſe of the Library. Prof. Jewett was authorized by Mr. John Carter Brown (Son of the Hon. Nicholas Brown, from whom the Inſtitution derives its Name), to Purchaſe at his Expenſe, ſuch Books in the German, French and Italian Languages, as he might think moſt uſeful for the College. The Collection thus obtained, numbering 2921 Volumes, was ſelected with great Pains and excellent Judgment; and notwithſtanding they were purchaſed *without regard to Coſt*, the average Price per Volume, including all Expenſes, was only 89 Cents. They are all well bound, moſt of them newly and elegantly, in half Calf, plain Gilt. The Collection includes a Set of the French, German and Italian Claſſicks, in the beſt and fulleſt library Editions; the Principal philoſophical, ſcientifick and hiſtorical Works of late continental Scholars; a complete Set of the Moniteur Univerſel, from its Commencement to 1826, a clean, beautiful, well bound Copy of the original Edition, in 77 Vols. folio; a Set of the Memoirs of the French Inſtitute ſince its Reorganization, 61 Vols. 4°.; the Collection of Memoirs relative to the Hiſtory of France, by Guizot and Petitot, 162 Vols. 8°.; Biographie Univerſelle, 52 Vols. full Calf, 8°.; a complete Set of the Allgemeine Literatur-Zeitung, 134 Vols. 4°.; and of the Allgemeine Deutſche Bibliothek, 133 Vols. 8°.; Il Vaticano, 8 Vols. folio, ellegantly illuſtrated; Il Campidoglio, 2 Vols. folio; the Muſeo Borbonico, 13 Vols. 4°., the original Naples Edition; the Works of Canova and Thowaldſen; the Muſée Français and Muſée Royal, in 6 Vols. folio; the Deſcription de l'Egypte; Canina's Architecture, and many more illuſtrated Works of great Beauty and Value, beſides rare and coſtly Maps and Prints.

Thefe Books were moftly purchafed at the Auctions in Paris, Rome, Leipfic, Frankfort on the Maine, and Berlin. Mr. Brown has fince continued the Moniteur, Memoirs, Mufeo Borbonico, &c., down to the prefent Time.

To fupply the Deficiencies of the Library in ftandard Englifh Works, a Subfcription was opened among the Friends of the College, amounting to about $5,000, and Mr. Jewett was appointed to felect and purchafe the Books. This Collection was received in the Library in 1845, and raifed the whole Number of Volumes to nearly 19,000.

Among the Englifh Books added to the Library at this Time is a Shakfpeariana, in 196 Volumes, bound in full Calf, gilt. It was collected by Thos. Rodd, Efq. Bookfeller in London, and contains Ireland's own Copy of his *Confeffions*, inlaid (as the Book-binders term it) with marginal Notes in his own Handwriting, and many original and curious Documents. The Collection was purchafed for the fmall Sum of $500, and was prefented to the Library by the late Mofes B. Ives, Efq. a Graduate of the College in 1812, for nearly thirty-two Years its Treafurer, and on all Occafions one of its moft zealous and active Friends.

The Clafs which graduated in 1821 held a Meeting in Providence, a Quarter of a Century from the Time of their Graduation, at which a confiderable Sum of Money was fubfcribed for the Benefit of the Library, in Token of their grateful Intereft in the Inftitution at which they were educated. The

Money thus obtained was placed in the Hands of Dr. Thomas H. Webb, of Boſton, who purchaſed, with excellent Judgment, about five hundred Volumes, moſtly from the Library of the Hon. John Pickering. Among theſe are 50 Volumes of the "Hiſtoire de l'Académie Royale des Inſcriptions et Belles-Lettres"; Fabricii Bibliotheca Græca, 14 Vols. 4°.; and a large, thick folio Volume of Plutarch's Lives, in Latin, publiſhed at Rome, in 1471.

The next Year, 1847, the Rev. Samuel Oſgood, D. D. of New York, at that Time a Clergyman in Providence, propoſed to ſeveral of the religious Societies of the City, a Subſcription for the Purpoſe of ſupplying the Deficiencies of the Library in the beſt Editions of the Fathers of the Church, and the ſtandard theological Writers of the Reformation. About $2,000 were raiſed, and a fine Collection was purchaſed of the Benedictine Editions of ſeveral of the Fathers; the Bibliotheca Maxima Veterum Patrum, 30 Vols. folio; Harduin's Collectio Conciliorum, 12 Vols. folio; beſides the choiceſt and moſt elegant Editions of many of the Fathers not edited by the Benedictines, and a large Collection of Works connected with Pariſtick Literature and the Hiſtory of the Reformation. To this Collection of the Fathers valuable Additions were made at the recent Sale in New York of the Library of the late Dr. Jarvis.

The following are ſome of the more important Works which have recently been added to the Library, moſtly by Purchaſe, viz: Dryden and

Swift's Works, edited by Sir W. Scott, 37 Vols. 8°.; Corpus Scriptorum Byzantinæ Hiſtoriæ, Venice Edition, 30 Vols. folio; Dugdale's Monaſticon, lateſt Edition, 8 Vols. Royal 4°.; Caſiri's Bibliotheca Arabico-Hiſpana, 2 Vols. folio; Brequigny's Table Cronologique des Diplomes, &c. 3 Vols. folio; Memoirs of Thomas Hollis, 2 Vols. Royal 4°.; Centuriæ Eccleſiaſticæ Hiſtoriæ, XIII, 13 Vols. ſmall folio; Groſe's Military Antiquities, and Antiquities of England, Wales, and Scotland, 12 Vols. 4o.; Holbrook's North American Herpetology, 5 Vols. 4o.; Gay's Hiſtoria de Chile, 23 Vols. 8°. of Text and 2 Vols. folio of Plates (preſented by Don Geronimo Urmeneta of Santiago); Tholuck's Lit. Anzeiger, 1830-49, 11 Vols. 4°.; Wailly's Eléments de Paléographie, 2 Vols. large Paper, royal 4°.; Nagler's Künſtler-Lexicon, 22 Vols. 8°.; Montfaucon's Antiquité Expliquée, 15 Vols. folio; Choiſeul's Voyage Pittoreſque de la Grèce, 3 Vols. folio; Harleian Miſcellany, edited by Park, 10 Vols. Royal 4°.; Lord Somers's Collection of Tracts, edited by Sir W. Scott, 13 Vols. royal 4°.; The Port Folio, 5 Vols. 4°. and 42 Vols. 8°.; Bloomfield's Critical Digeſt, 8 Vols. 8°.; Agaſſiz's Recherches ſur les Poiſſons Foſſiles, 5 Vols. 4°. and 5 Vols. folio; Winckelmann's Monumenti Antichi, 2 Vols. folio; Gregorio's Bibliotheca Scriptorum Siciliæ, 2 Vols. folio; Baronii Annales Eccleſiaſtici, Lucca Edition, 38 Vols. folio; Dodwell's Claſſical Tour, 2 Vols. 4°.; Calvin's Opera Omnia, 9 Vols. folio; Picart's Cérémonies et Coutumes, 10 Vols.

folio; Sigonii Opera Omnia, ed. Muratori, 6 Vols. folio; Suicer's Thesaurus, 2 Vols. folio; Pradus et Villapandus in Ezechielem, 3 Vols. folio; Moreri's Dictionnaire Historique, 10 Vols. folio; Spanheim's Numismata, Gibbon's Copy, 2 Vols. folio; Hesychii Lexicon Græcum, 2 Vols. folio; Duchesne's Scriptores Francorum et Normanorum, 6 Vols. folio; Schott's Scriptores Hispaniæ, 4 Vols. folio; Pistorii Rerum Germanicarum Scriptores, 4 Vols. folio; Audifredi's Specimen et Catalogus, 2 Vols. 4°.; Montfaucon's Bibliotheca Bibliothecarum Manuscriptorum, 2 Vols. folio; Cave's Historia Literaria, 2 Vols. folio; Dictionnaire des Sciences Naturelles, 72 Vols. 8°.; Revue Encyclopédique, 52 Vols. 8°.; Mabillon's Annales Ordinis S. Benedicti, 6 Vols. folio; Histoire de l'Académie Française, 1666-1762, 87 Vols. 4°.; Annales de Chimie, 120 Vols. 8°.; Acta Eruditorum, 95 Vols. 4°; Barros et Couto's Deccadas da Asiade, 7 Vols. folio; Bruyère's L'Art de Construction, folio; Ledebour's Plantæ Rossicæ et Altaicæ, 5 Vols. folio (a splendid and very costly Work); Popp et Buleau's Les Trois Ages de l'Architecture Gothique, folio; Brockedon's Passes of the Alps, 2 Vols. 4°.; Newton's Opera Omnia, ed. Horsly, 5 Vols. 4°.; Stephani Thesaurus Græcæ Linguæ, Vols. 1-7, folio; Otto's Thesaurus Juris Romani, 5 Vols. folio; Percy Society Publications, Vols. 1-30, 12°.; Fox's Acts and Monuments, 9th Ed. 3 Vols. folio; Dupin's Ecclesiastical History, 8 Vols. folio; Ebert's Bibliographical Dictionary, 4 Vols. 8°.; Annals of Ireland by the Four Masters,

4 Vols. 4°.; Hanſard's Parliamentary Hiſtory and Debates 1066-1857, 245 Vols. 8°.; Allgemeine Geographiſche Ephemeriden, 1797-1831, 82 Vols. 8°.; Ferrario's Romanzi di Cavalleria, 4 Vols. 8°.; Brevets d'Invention, 25 Vols 4°.; Giggeius's Theſaurus Linguæ Arabicæ, 4 Vols. folio; Hemprich et Ehrenberg's Icones et Deſcriptiones Inſectorum, folio; Graffenried et Stürler's Architecture Suiſſe, folio; Gorii Antiqua Numiſmata, *large Paper*, 3 Vols. folio; Pinkerton's Voyages and Travels, 17 Vols. 4°.; Sternberg's Flora der Vorwelt, 2 Vols. folio; Brotier's Tacitus, 4 Vols. 4°,; Folard's Hiſtoire de Polybe, 7 Vols. 4°.; Grævii Theſaurus Antiquitatum Romanarum, 12 Vols. folio; Grævii Theſaurus Antiquitatum et Hiſtoriarum Italiæ, Siciliæ, &c. 45 Vols. folio; Corpus Inſcriptionum Græcarum, ed. Boeckhius, Vols. 1 & 2, folio; Heeren und Ukert's Geſchichte der Europäiſchen Staaten, 62 Vols. 8°.; John's "Archiv," and "Jahrbücher" to 1857, 107 Vols. 8°.

The following are a few of the important Works which have recently been preſented to the Library by Mr. Brown, viz: Juſtiniani Inſtitutiones, folio; Venetiis, N. Jenſon, 1477, (a ſplendid Copy of one of the old illuminated Books, bound in full Ruſſia); Babylonian Talmud, 12 Vols. folio, (bound in full Goat, gilt); Barnard's Catalogus Bibliothecæ Regiæ, large Paper, 6 Vols. folio; Philoſophical Traſactions of the Royal Society of London, 1665-1857, 78 Vols. 4°.; Muratori's Rerum Italicarum Scriptores (with Continuation by Tartini), 30 Vols. folio;

Journal des Debats, 1800-36, 74 Vols. folio; Panzer's Annales Typographici, 11 Vols. 4°.; Livii Decades a Lucca Porro Recognitæ, folio, Tarvisii, J. Vercellius, 1842. (An uncommonly fine Specimen of ancient Typography); Year Books, 1596-1640, black Letter, 10 Vols. small folio; Aringhi Roma Subterranea post Bosium, &c. 2 Vols. folio, 1659.

The Library is open during Term-time, daily, from 9 till 1; during Vacations, weekly, on Saturdays, from 11 till 1. The Members of the Corporation and Faculty; all resident Graduates; all Donors to the Library Fund; all Donors to the Fund for building Rhode Island Hall; and all Donors to the Library to the Amount of $40, residing in Providence, are entitled to the Use of the Library without Expense. Undergraduates are entitled to the Use of the Library, and are charged therefore the Sum of $3 per annum.

The Privilege of *consulting* the Library is extended, under ordinary Restrictions, to all Graduates of the University; to all settled Clergymen of every Denomination, residing in the City of Providence and the Vicinity; and to all other Persons on whom, for the Purpose of advancing the Arts, Science or Literature, the Corporation or Library Committee may, from Time to Time, confer it. Books are occasionally loaned to Persons at a Distance by special Permission.

REUBEN A. GUILD, *Librarian.*

LIBRARY COMPANY OF PHILADELPHIA, AND THE LOGANIAN LIBRARY.

70,000 Vols.

I. Library Company of Philadelphia.

60,000 Vols.

THE Foundation of the Library Company of Philadelphia, was laid in 1731, when but few Reſources for literary Reſearch were acceſſible in America. A ſmall Number of Gentlemen, among whom was the celebrated Benjamin Franklin, having ſubſcribed the Sum of one hundred Pounds, a Collection was commenced,

Subſcribers being allowed to carry the Books to their Dwellings for Peruſal during their Hours of Leiſure. The firſt Purchaſe of Books was made in London, the Liſtfor the ſame having been made out, at the Requeſt of the Directors, by the Hon. James Logan, "a Gentleman of univerſal Learning, and the beſt Judge of Books in theſe Parts." By ſlow Degrees new Members were added to the Company, and the Stock of Books was annually increaſed by Purchaſes, and by Donations. Among the Donors, the then Proprietors of Pennſylvania are to be numbered, and from them a Charter of perpetual Incorporation was obtained in 1742.

The Books firſt received from London, were taken to Robert Grace's Chamber, at his Houſe in Jones's Alley, and there placed upon Shelves and catalogued. The firſt Librarian, Louis Timothee, gave Attendance from 2 to 3 on Wedneſdays, and on Saturdays from 10 till 4. Benjamin Franklin was the ſecond Librarian. Among thoſe who ſucceeded him are included Francis Hopkinſon, the Author, and Zachariah Poulſon, the well known Publiſher of Poulſon's Daily Advertiſer. In 1740, the Books were removed to the "upper Room of the weſternmoſt Office of the State Houſe," the Uſe of which had been lately granted to the Company by the Aſſembly. In 1773, the ſecond Floor of Carpenter's Hall was rented, and the Books removed thither. The Britiſh Army had Poſſeſſion of Philadelphia, from Sept. 26th, 1777, to June 18th, 1778; but it does not appear that the Company ſuſtained any Loſs from thoſe who compoſed it. The Officers, without Exception, left Depoſits and paid Hire for the Books borrowed by them. In 1777, the Library Room was occupied by the ſick Soldiers. In 1790, the Books were removed to the preſent Building, of which the foregoing wood Cut is a Repreſentation, in Fifth Street, below Cheſtnut.

The firſt Stone of this Edifice was laid on the 31ſt of Auguſt, 1789; the Minutes ſtate, "that, upon the Suggeſtion of Dr. Benjamin Franklin, a large Stone was prepared, and laid at the ſouthweſt Corner of the Building, with the following Inſcription, compoſed by the Doctor, except ſo far as relates to himſelf, which the Committee have taken the Liberty of adding to it:

Be it remembered,
In honor of the Philadelphia youth,
(Then chiefly artificers,)
That in MDCCXXXI,
They cheerfully,
At the inſtance of Benjamin Franklin,
One of their number,
Inſtituted the Philadelphia Library,
Which, though ſmall at firſt,
Is become highly valuable and extenſively uſeful,
And which the walls of this edifice
Are now deſtined to contain and preſerve;
The firſt ſtone of whoſe foundation
Was here placed
The thirty-firſt day of Auguſt, 1789.

The Style of Architecture is of courſe ſomewhat antique. A Niche immediately over the front Entrance is occupied by a Statue of Franklin, executed in Italy, by Francis Lazzarini, being the firſt

Specimen of Sculpture of ſo large a Size ever imported to this Country. The Head is from the Buſt of Houdon, and is an excellent Likeneſs. The Figure is arrayed in Roman Toga, the right Arm reſting on a Pile of Books, holding in the right Hand an inverted Sceptre, and in the left a Scroll.

It is much to be deſired that ſome publick ſpirited Individual, emulating the Liberality of a Brown, a Gore, an Aſtor, or a Peabody, ſhould endow this venerable and uſeful Inſtitution with Funds ſufficient to erect a fire-proof Building, the preſent, with its precious Contents, being liable at any Time to be conſumed by Fire. The Sum of $13,000 has already been ſubſcribed for a building Fund, on Condition that it be raiſed to $20,000.

The Number of Volumes now in the Library is 60,000, excluſive of 10,000 in the Loganian Library attached, of which a ſeparate Account is given at the Cloſe of this Sketch. They embrace all Subjects, the Object kept in View being to have both a good circulating Library of general Literature, and a Collection of the Standard Books of Reference in every Department. Leſs Attention is paid to Medicine, Natural Hiſtory and Law, than to Hiſtory, &c. inaſmuch as there are ſpecial Collections of theſe in the Pennſylvania Hoſpital, the Academy of Natural Sciences, and the Law Library.

The Catalogues of the Library Company of Philadelphia, now brought down to 1856, are contained in three Volumes, of which the firſt and ſecond, publiſhed in 1835, compriſe the Books in the Library at that Date, and the third contains the Titles of all Books added ſince that Time, together with a general Index. This is excluſive of the Loganian Library, to which the Members have Acceſs, and of which a Catalogue in 450 Pages, octavo, was publiſhed in 1837.

From the Preface to the third Volume we extract the following Account of the rareſt and moſt valuable Treaſures in the two Collections of the Inſtitution:

"Of Manuſcripts, the moſt ancient is an Exemplar of the entire Bible on Parchment, of the Date of 1016. The moſt beautiful is an illuminated Pſalter on fine Velum, and in perfect Preſervation; though written in Roman Characters, it appears to be a Specimen of German Art of the early Part of the 15th Century. Two Volumes of original Letters of King James I.; two of his official Correſpondence with the Iriſh Viceroyalty; an original Diary of the Marquis of Clanricarde (1641-1643); and the unpubliſhed Autobiography of John Fitch, are noteworthy.

Of early printed Books, there are ſeveral of the Date of 1470, and others without Date. The Loganian Library poſſeſſes a Copy of Caxton's Golden Legend; ſeveral Works from the Preſs of Wynken de Worde; a Vulgate Bible, printed at Rome by Sweynheym & Pannartz, in 1471, pronounced *fort rare* by Brunet; another from the Preſs of Koburger, at Nuremberg, in 1475; an

Englifh Verfion, printed by Grafton, in 1539, and a Nouveau Teftament, printed by Barthelemy & Buyer, at Lyons, about 1480. A noble Edition of Perceforeft—"de tous les Romans de Chevalerie le plus eftimé"—in 6 Vols. folio, Paris, 1531; an early German Verfion, with numerous wood Cuts, of Reynard the Fox—"Reynke Vofs de olde," Roftock, 1549; and Copland's Edition of Caxton's Recuile of the Hiftories of Troie, London, 1553, are rare and curious.

Of Works relating to Antiquities, the following are the moft remarkable: Lepfius's, Roffelini's, Denon's, and Vyfe's Egypt; Botta's and Layard's folio Plates of Nineveh; Kingfborough's and Lenoir's Mexico; eight folio Volumes of Plates on Herculaneum; Piranefi's Works; Il Vaticano; and Meyrick on Ancient Armour.

In the Department of Works relating to America, the two Libraries may, without Exaggeration, be faid to be very rich. The Sets of Newfpapers, from the firft Number of the firft Paper publifhed in Philadelphia continuoufly to the prefent Time, include a Set of Bradford's American Mercury, from 1719 to 1745; the Pennfylvania Gazette (publifhed fucceffively by Samuel Keimer, Dr. Benjamin Franklin, and Hall & Sellers) complete, from 1728 to 1804; the Pennfylvania Journal, from 1747 to 1793; the Pennfylvania Packet (afterwards Poulfon's Advertifer), under various Names, from 1771 to the prefent Time; the Federal and Philadelphia Gazette, from 1788 to 1843; and the United States

Gazette, now the North American, from 1791 to the prefent Time. After the Newfpapers, may be mentioned the ineftimable Collection of Books, Pamphlets, Broadfides, and Manufcripts collected by Pierre Du Simitiere, before, during, and after the Revolution, and purchafed for the Company. A Portion of thefe Pamphlets, and the larger Part of the Broadfides are believed to be quite unique. Befchreibung von Pennfylvania, Frankfort und Leipzig, 1704, by Paftorius, the perfonal Friend of William Penn, and the Founder of Germantown, is believed to be the only Copy in the United States; with it is bound up a German Tranflation of Gabriel Thomas's Pennfylvania, and Faulkner's Curieufe Nachricht von Pennfylvania, 1702. H. J. Wynkelmann's Americanifchen neuen Welt Befchreibung, Oldenburg, 1664, with Wood-cuts, is a moft curious and extremely rare Publication. Other German Works on America not often met with in this Country, are Gottfriedt's Hiftoria Antipodum, Frankfort, 1655, and Dapper's unbekannte neue Welt, Amfterdam, 1673; both have numerous fine Plates and Maps. Campanius's Kort Befkryfnnig om Provincien Nya Swerige callas Pennfylvania, Stockholm, 1702, with curious Plates and Maps, is one of the few Copies known to exift; and Ovalle's Hiftorica Relation del Reyno de Chile, with the Map and all the Plates, is of great Rarity. Jones's prefent State of Virginia, London, 1724; "one of the fcarceft Works relating to Virginia publifhed in the 18th Century"—is bound up with

"The present State of Virginia and the College," by Messieurs Hartwell, Blair, and Chilton, London, 1727, which appears to be still more scarce, as it is not mentioned either by Rich or Lowndes, nor does it appear in the British Museum Catalogue of 1819. These, and other choice Works on the American Colonies, have the Initials of Peter Collinson on their Title Pages. Plantagenet's New Albion, Leah and Rachel, and other scarce Books, were reprinted in Force's Historical Tracts, from Originals in this Library. Aikin's Bible of 1782, published under the Patronage of Congress, and Poor Richard's Almanac from 1733 to 1747, are very rare Works. The Library's Set of the Laws of Pennsylvania, is complete from the Beginning, and of the Journals of the Legislature nearly so. Indeed, but few Works relating to Pennsylvania and Philadelphia are wanting, and of the local Histories of other States the Collection is good. The Collection of the Publick Documents of the General Government is we believe unsurpassed by that of any other similar Institution. This is owing in Part to the Fact, that, as Congress met here until 1800, the original Editions of the early Congressional Documents found their Way very naturally into the Library.

Not the least interesting Portion of the Library is that consisting of Works in the Languages of Continental Europe. In the Departments of Belles-Lettres and History, the Collection of French, Spanish, and Italian Books embraces most of the ſtandard Authors. The Edition of the French Claſſicks, in 32 large quarto Volumes, entitled Collections du Dauphin—a beautiful Specimen of Typography—and Landino's "rare et recherché" Edition of Dante, Venetia, 1512, are worthy of Notice. The German Library is, by no means, ſo valuable, but it includes the "ſämmtliche Werke" of Luther (89 Vols.), Goethe, Schiller, Jean Paul, Zſchokke, Heine, &c. The Collection of Spaniſh Authors (moſtly in the Loganian Library) is the moſt complete, and was, and perhaps is, the fineſt publick Collection in the Country. Many of the Volumes are intereſting from their Rarity or intrinſick Worth. Among theſe may be mentioned El Conde Lucanor, by the Prince Don Juan Manuel (Sevilla, 1575), deſribed by Ticknor as "one of the rareſt Books in the World;" an unmutilated Edition of Celeſtina, the firſt Spaniſh dramatick Work of Note (1599); the Cronica del famoſo Cavallero del Cid (Burgos, 1593), and the Coronica de el Rey Don Alonzo (1604). It contains, alſo, the excellent Reprint of the ancient Spaniſh Chronicles (1787), and Zurita's Anales de la Corona de Aragon, with the Supplement of Argenſola. Not to mention the better known Names of Calderon, Lope de Vega, and the other early Dramatiſts, it may be ſaid that all the modern Authors of Conſequence, Feijoo, Father Iſla, Moratin, Yriarte, Melendez Valdez, and many others have been added to it. The Spaniſh Writers on America are equally well repreſented.

In the large Collection of Engliſh Works may

be found complete Sets of the Royal Philoſophical Tranſactions, the Gentleman's Magazine, the Annual Regiſter, Cobbett and Hanſard's Parliamentary Debates, Curtis's Botanical Magazine, and other Periodicals, ſome continued for more than a Century; the Publications of the Record Commiſſion in 177 Vols. folio and 177 Vols. octavo; a curious Collection of 700 Engliſh Pamphlets in 36 Vols. quarto, publiſhed during the revolutionary Period from 1620 to 1720, which with Somer's Tracts, the Harleian Miſcellany, and the Camden Society's Publications, eminently deſerve the Attention of the Student of Engliſh Hiſtory; a Series of the Engliſh Chroniclers from Bede downwards, in the original Latin, as well as in Engliſh; and Danſey's Engliſh Cruſaders."

The Loganian Library.

This Collection, numbering 10,000 Volumes of rare and valuable Works, principally in the learned and foreign Languages, owes its Origin to the Honorable James Logan, the confidential Friend and Counſellor of William Penn, and for ſome Time Preſident of the Council of the Province of Pennſylvania. Its Foundation conſiſts of a Portion of his own private Library, which, having collected at conſiderable Expenſe, he was anxious ſhould deſcend to Poſterity and continue to others the Means of proſecuting thoſe Purſuits he had himſelf ſo ſucceſſfully cultivated. With this View, he erected a ſuitable Building in Sixth Street, near Walnut, for the Reception of a Library; and by Deed, vested it (with the Books and certain Rents, for the Purpose of increasing their Number and paying a Librarian), in Trustees, for the Use of the Publick forever. This Deed he afterwards cancelled, and prepared but did not live to execute, another, in which some Alteration was made in the Funds and Regulations. After his Death, his Children, William and James Logan, John Smith and Hannah, his Wife (she being the surviving Daughter), with commendable Liberality, carried into effect the Intentions of Mr. Logan.

The Loganian Library is attached to the Philadelphia, and by the Rules of the Founder is open to the Publick without Charge, Visiters being permitted either to read the Books in the Room or to take them Home, leaving, in the latter Case a Deposit in Money to secure the Return. The Antiquity and learned Character of the Books, presents this Privilege being available to the general Reader. As a Library of Reference, however, it is invaluable. In early printed Books, the Classicks, Theology, French Literature previous to the nineteenth Century, and Spanish Works on America, it is rich and curious. It also includes a valuable Collection of Books on Natural History, late the Library of Zaccheus Collins, Esq.

In 1831, about 200 Volumes were destroyed by Fire, besides an original Bust of William Penn, and a Portrait of James Logan. Also a curious Clock, made by a French Artist, so constructed as to ring an Alarm each Day at Sun-ſet. This Clock was the only one of the Kind in the World.

The Income of the two Libraries is about $6,500, of which Amount $3,000 is expended for Books and Binding, thus adding to the Collections about 1500 Vols. per annum. Perſons entitled to the Uſe of the Library (or Libraries) are, Stockholders who pay $4 yearly; and others who take out Books on Depoſit and Hire.

LLOYD P. SMITH, *Librarian.*

BOSTON ATHENÆUM.

70,000 Vols.

THIS Inſtitution, which is the moſt Extenſive and Succeſſful of its Kind in the Country, owes its Origin to a Literary Aſſociation which was formed in Boſton in the early Part of the preſent Century, known as the "Anthology Club." A Publication was conducted by them, entitled "Monthly Anthology." That Society eſtabliſhed a Reading-Room and Library, which received ſo much Favor from various Quarters, that the Proprietors, deſirous of rendering their Efforts more widely uſeful, tranſferred their Property to Truſtees, and applied, through them, to the Legiſlature of Maſſachuſetts for an Act of Incorporation. This being granted them in 1807, under the Name of "The Proprietors of the Boſton Athenæum," one hundred and fifty Shares were immediately ſold at $300 each. This Amount, with the Addition of $1,800 obtained for 18 Life Subſcribers at $100 each, making in all $46,800, conſtituted the Capital of the Inſtitution at that Time.

The principal Endowments of the Athenæum before the Year 1847, are thus enumerated in an Inſcription under the Corner Stone of the new Building:

"The Sum of $42,000 was raiſed for the general purpoſes of the Athenæum, by voluntary Subſcriptions for Shares created in 1807."

"James Perkins, in 1821, gave his own coſtly Manſion in Pearl ſtreet, which from that time has been the ſeat of the inſtitution."

"In the ſame year the ſum of $22,000 was raiſed by voluntary ſubſcriptions for ſhares."

"Thomas Handaſyd Perkins (beſides his earlier and later valuable donations), and James Perkins the younger, ſeconded, in 1826, the liberality of the father and the brother, each giving $8,000; and the ſum of their contributions was increaſed to $45,000 by other ſubſcriptions, obtained chiefly through the efforts and influence of Nathaniel Bowditch, Francis Calley Gray, George Ticknor, and Thomas Wren Ward."

"Auguſtus Thorndike, in 1823, gave a choice collection of caſts of the moſt celebrated ancient ſtatues."

"George Watſon Brimmer, in 1838, gave a magnificent collection of books on the fine arts."

"John Bromfield, in 1846, gave $25,000 as a fund to be regularly increaſed by one quarter of the income, of which the other three quarters are to be annually applied to the purchaſe of Books forever."

"The ſum of $75,000, for the erection of the building, was raiſed by voluntary ſubſcription for ſhares created in 1844."

This Sum of $75,000 having been found inſufficient for the Completion of the Building, an additional Subſcription for 346 Shares at $300 each, was filled up in 1853. The Sum of $25,000, called the "Appleton Fund," was alſo received from the Truſtees of Samuel Appleton, Eſq. deceaſed, thus making the whole Amount $128,000. Liberality like this is ſeldom witneſſed, and deſerves honorable Mention. On the firſt of January, 1858, the Property of the Athenæum, conſiſting of Real Eſtate, Stocks, Mortgages, Bonds, Books, Paintings and Statuary, at their actual Coſt, (without including in the Eſtimate any of the numerous and very valuable Gifts of Books and Works of Art), amounted to $496,703, according to the Treaſurer's annual Statement. The Income for the Year 1857, was $13,407, Of this Amount $5,755 was expended for Books and Binding. The Number of Volumes added to the Library was 2,000.

The Inſtitution firſt occupied Rooms in Congreſs Street, whence it was removed to Scollay's Buildings, in Court Street, and in 1810 to the Building on Common (now Tremont) Street, North of King's Chapel Burial Ground. In the Year 1822, it was removed to the Houſe in Pearl Street, presented, as already stated, by James Perkins. In 1823 the King's Chapel Library and the Theological Library, containing together 13,000 Volumes of theological Works, were deposited in the Athenæum, where they still remain. In 1826 a Union was effected with the Boston Medical Library, and its Books, valued at $4,500, were added to those of the Athenæum. In the same Year, also, an Association which had been formed for the Purpose of a scientifick Library became merged in the Athenæum, and its Funds, exceeding $3,000, were transferred to the Athenæum to be expended in the Purchase of scientifick Books.

In July, 1849, the Library was removed to its new Home in Beacon Street, just above the Tremont House. The Location is central, yet free from the Noise and Dust of crowded Thoroughfares. The Corner Stone of this beautiful Building was laid April 27, 1847, when an Address appropriate to the Occasion was delivered by the Hon. Josiah Quincy. The Edifice which stands back from the Street ten Feet, is spacious and convenient. The Front is 114 Feet long, and 60 Feet high, built in the Palladian or later Style of Italian Achitecture, of the Paterson free Stone. The other Walls are of Brick. The Foundations are laid in the most substantial Manner, supporting the first Floor on groined Arches of Brick. The interior Arrangements of the Basement are most complete, both for warming and ventilating every Room in the Edifice, and for packing Purposes, Book-bindery, Accommodations for the Janitor, &c. The main Entrance opens into a pillared and panelled inner Veſtibule or Rotundo, 32 Feet by 28, from which the Staircaſes conduct above. On the firſt Floor are two large reading Rooms, a buſineſs Apartment, and a ſculpture Gallery, 80 Feet by 40. A Row of iron Columns in this and the Story above, renders additional Support to the different Floors. The ſecond Story contains the Library-rooms, two in Front, with a ſpacious Hall in the Rear, 109 Feet by 40, extending the entire Length of the Building. The latter is finiſhed in the Italian Style, with great Taſte, the Ceiling being decorated. An iron Gallery which is reached by five ſpiral Staircaſes, borders the Hall, which is divided by an Archway into two Copartments. Within the weſtern Diviſion are arranged the Encyclopædias, Tranſactions of Learned Societies, Magazines, and other continuous Works, in Caſes lining the Walls; while in the other Copartment are arranged the miſcellaneous Books in 26 Alcoves, between the Pillars. For Convenience and Beauty, this Library-room may well ſerve as a Model for all ſimilar Inſtitutions. One of the front Rooms is for the Uſe of the Librarian; the other is deſigned for the Diſplay of miſcellaneous Collections, and is furniſhed with Galleries ſimilar to thoſe in the Hall. Theſe Rooms together can be made to accommodate 80,000 Volumes. The Picture Gallery occupies the upper Story, which is divided into four Apartments, all lighted from above. The Roof affords a magnificent View of the City and ſurrounding Country. The whole Building is conſtructed in the moſt ſubſtantial and workmanlike Manner, and reflects great Credit upon the Architect, Mr. Edward C. Cabot. The Land coſt $55,000, and the Building $136,000, making a Total of $191,000

Beſides 70,000 bound Volumes, including nearly 2,000 Volumes of Pamphlets, the Library poſſeſſes 20,000 or more unbound Pamphlets, about 500 Volumes of Engravings, and the moſt valuable Collection of Coins in this Part of the Country. For an American Library it is rich in certain Departments, as for Example, in the Reports and Tranſactions of Learned Societies, in periodical Publications in the Engliſh Language, Works in the Natural Sciences, &c. It has complete Sets of the Tranſactions of the Royal Society of London, the French Inſtitute, the Royal Societies of Berlin, Copenhagen, Göttingen, Liſbon, Madrid, Stockholm, St. Peterſburg, Turin, &c. It has alſo the Encyclopédie Raiſonné, 35 Vols. folio; the Encyclopédie Méthodique, 258 Vols. 4°., including 37 of Plates; Buffon's Natural Hiſtory, by Sonnini, 127 Volumes. 8°. Its Collection of American Newſpapers is extenſive and valuable.

Among other intereſting Relicks which are worthy of continued Remembrance, is a Collection of about 450 Volumes, bound, and between 800 and 1000 Pamphlets, which formerly belonged to Waſhington. About 350 of theſe contain his Autograph, and a few of them Notes in his Handwriting. One little Book has the Autograph of Waſhington in a rude, School-boy Hand, at about the Age of 9 Years. There are ſeveral Autographs of Auguſtine Waſhington, the Father of the General; of Mary, the Mother, and of Martha, the Wife. One Book contains on the title Page the Autograph of John Cuſtis (firſt Huſband of Martha), and on the next Leaf that of George Waſhington. One Volume has the Autograph of Thomas Jefferſon, a Signer of the Declaration of Independence. There are ſeveral preſentation Copies from eminent Authors: Sir John Sinclair, Arthur Young, Eberling, Alfieri, Jefferſon, Dr. Morſe, and others. Ten Volumes contain the Name of Richard Henry Lee, in his own Handwriting. Theſe precious Memorials of the World's beſt Hero, were purchaſed by a few Gentlemen of Boſton, and preſented by them to the Athenæum.

The Reading-room is furniſhed with the beſt Literary and Scientifick Journals of Europe and America.

The Sculpture Gallery contains Caſts of the moſt celebrated ancient Statues, ſelected for this Inſtitution by Canova, at the Requeſt of the Donor, Mr. Auguſtus Thorndike. Among the Works in Marble, by American Artiſts, the Statue of Orpheus, by Crawford, and the Backwoodſman, by Dexter, deſerve eſpecial Notice.

In the Gallery of Pictures, there are ſome excellent early Copies of Works of the great Maſters; Weſt's great Picture of Lear; Trumbull's Sortie de

Gibralter; and Stewart's original Portrait of Washington, and of Mrs. Washington, Here are also the celebrated and unfinished Picture, by Allston, Belshazzar's Feast, several of his finished Works, and many of his unrivalled Sketches.

The following are some of the Regulations of the Institution:

The Proprietors meet annually on the first Monday of January. The Officers are chosen annually, consisting of a President, Vice President, Treasurer, Secretary, and nine Trustees. The Trustees appoint a Librarian and Sub-Librarian.

The Price of a Share is $300. Each Proprietor has, besides his own Share, two Rights of Admission transferable. Thus, the By-laws open the Doors of the Institution to a large Number of Persons; so that the Proprietor who bestows on others the free Use of all the Rights he can impart, renders himself thereby a publick Benefactor. A Life Subscription is $100. Annual Subscribers pay $10 for the Use of the Library and Reading-room, but are not allowed to take out Books. Certain Persons, by Virtue of their Office, viz: the Governor and Council, Lieutenant Governor, Members of the State Legislature for the Time being, &c. are entitled to free Admission to the Athenæum.

A Catalogue of the Library, similar in Plan to that of the Mercantile Library of Boston, with short Titles and Contents, is in Preparation, and will be published during the coming Year.

Wm. Fred Poole, A. M., *Librarian.*

LIBRARY OF CONGRESS.

50,000 Vols.

OF the early Hiſtory of the firſt Library, but few Facts can be obtained, although but little more than half a Century has elapſed ſince its Formation. Congreſs in the Year 1800 removed from Philadelphia to Waſhington, when an Act eſtabliſhing a Library was paſſed, April 24th. It was mainly through the Efforts of the Hon. Albert Gallatin, and Dr. Mitchell, that the firſt Collection, conſiſting of about 3,000 Volumes, was made. This, which at the Time was regarded as valuable, and which, in the early Days of the City was much reſorted to, was deſtroyed by the Britiſh Army on the 24th of Auguſt, 1814.

The total Loſs of the Library induced Ex-Preſident Jefferſon to offer to Congreſs his Collection, conſiſting of about 10,000 Volumes, which was Purchaſed for about $25,000, in accordance with a Bill that finally paſſed the Houſe by a Vote of 81 to 71, January 26, 1815. Reſpecting the Oppoſition to the Purchaſe, the Editor of Niles's Weekly Regiſter very properly remarks: "It is ſtrange that the Rancor of Party ſhould penetrate even in the Temple of Science, and that an Oppoſition was made to the Purchaſe of a Collection that any Monarch in Europe would be proud to own. For ſuch a Library the Britiſh Parliament would have given £50,000. We are not informed what this Library coſt, but venture to ſay that the Amount appropriated will not pay the Expenſe of it, by a large Sum, independent of the Value of the Time and Talent employed in the Collection." (*See Niles's Regiſter, Vol.* 7, *Page* 285.) It included what was chiefly valuable in Science and Literature generally, extending more particularly to American Hiſtory and Stateſmanſhip. In the diplomatick and parliamentary Branches it was eſpecially full. The Letter tendering it to Congreſs, and deſcribing its Condition and Extent, may be found in the 6th Volume of the recent Edition of Jefferſon's Works, Page 383.

In January, 1817, the annual Sum of $1,500 was appropriated by Congreſs for the Library. This Sum was afterwards increaſed to $3,000, and again to $6,000, Of this Sum $5,000 is for the Purchaſe of miſcellaneous Books, and $1,000 for Law Books.

On the Morning of the 24th of December, 1851, the Library was a ſecond Time deſtroyed by Fire. It then contained about 55,000 Volumes, of which 35,000 were conſumed. The Law Library, containing 8,000 Volumes, and the Books in the ante Rooms, were all that were ſaved. The Loſs was eſtimated at $150,000, to ſupply which Congreſs made large Appropriations from Time to Time. The Rooms were immediately repaired, and newly fitted throughout, in an elegant and ſubſtantial Manner, under the Direction of Dr. Walter, the Architect of the Capitol.

The principal Room appropriated to the Library is a large Hall in the Capitol, on the weſt Side fronting the Mall. Its Dimenſions are as follows, viz: 92 Feet long, 34 Feet wide, and 40 Feet high. The new Hall was reopened to the Publick in September, 1853. The Waſhington Union deſcribes it in the following Language:

"The whole Work, to the moſt minute Part, is Iron; and yet ſo ſplendidly is it painted and gilded, ſo elaborate and finiſhed are the Ornaments, that you can ſcarcely credit the Fact. The Ceiling, compoſed of immenſe iron Plates, looking like maſſive Blocks of brown marble Panel-work, is moſt artiſtically conſtructed, ſo as to combine Strength and Beauty in the moſt perfect Harmony. It is the only entire Ceiling on the Earth. Running through the Centre is the Skylight, which is elegantly ornamented with a Clufter of Stars, numbering fome hundreds—perhaps as many as we may yet number States in our Confederacy."

"Next are the two long Galleries—all Iron—the Pillars, the Lattice-work, the Baluftrades, the Truffes, the Scrolls, the Floors, the Shelves, the Alcoves, and the Steps by which you afcend. Nothing of the Kind can be more perfectly beautiful than the large ornamented Scrolls which appear to fupport the Sides of the Ceiling. They reprefent elaborate Carving, with golden Ears of Corn and golden Clufters of Grapes, interfperfed among their Niches."

The Alcoves are 9 and 8 Feet high, fo that the Books can be reached with Facility, without Ladder or Steps. On the weft Side of the Hall are five Windows, one of which leads out upon the Colonnade, from which is a fine View of the principal Parts of the City, including the Smithfonian Inftitution, the Wafhington Monument, the Prefident's Houfe, Patent Office, Poft Office, &c. In addition to the large Hall, three fmaller Rooms are appropriated to the Library; one containing large Works of Engravings, one ufed as a Committee-room, and a third as an Office for the Librarian.

The Law Library is feparate from the General Library, occupying a Room directly oppofite to that of the Supreme Court of the United States. It contains about 12,000 Volumes, many of them Works of great Value. Thefe added to the 50,000 Volumes contained in the General Library, make a

Total of 62,000. The Additions of the paſt Year to both Libraries amount to about 3,000 Volumes. No complete Catalogue has been publiſhed ſince the Fire in 1851.

The Library is open every Day during the Seſſions of Congreſs, and a Part of the Time during Receſs. Members of Congreſs, Heads of Departments, Judges of the Supreme Court, Foreign Miniſters, &c. &c. are allowed to take out Books. The Librarian is appointed by the Preſident. The preſent Incumbent, who was appointed by Preſident Jackſon in 1829, is JOHN S. MEEHAN.

SMITHSONIAN INSTITUTE.

STATE LIBRARY, AT ALBANY.

52,000 Vols.

THE New York State Library was founded by an Act of the Legiflature, paffed on the 21ft Day of April, 1818. The Governor, Lieutenant-Governor, Chancellor and Chief Juftice of the Supreme Court for the Time being, were conftituted a Board of Truftees who were directed to caufe to be fitted up fome proper Room in the Capitol for the "Purpofe of keeping therein a publick Library for the Ufe of the Government and People of the State." The Sum of three thoufand Dollars, and alfo the further annual Sum of five hundred Dollars was appropriated to carry out the Purpofes of the Act. By a fubfequent Enactment in 1824, the Secretary of State, Attorney General, and Comptroller were added to the above conftituted Board of Truftees. On the Organization of the Board the late Chancellor Kent was chofen Treafurer, and John Cook appointed State Librarian at a Salary of $350.

The firft Report of the Truftees, figned by De Witt Clinton, John Tayler and James Kent, was fubmitted on the 22d of June, 1819, in which it was ftated that a Beginning had been made in forming a Library, and that for the Sum of $2,617·20, fix hundred Volumes and nine Maps had been purchafed; a Lift of the fame was fubmitted. In 1820, the firft Catalogue was printed, forming a ſmall duodecimo Pamphlet of twenty-eight Pages, and containing the Titles of ſeven hundred and fifty-eight Volumes, three Atlaſes, eleven Maps, and one Print.

The Appropriation of $500 for the Enlargement of the Library was increaſed in 1825 to $1,000, and in Addition the Sum of $300 was appropriated from the Income of a Fund appertaining to the Court of Chancery. Alſo by an Enactment of that Year the Truſtees were required to make a Report and complete Catalogue annually of all Books, &c. belonging to the Library. The firſt *annual* Report, which was made during the next Winter, concludes with this Paragraph: "This Inſtitution, under the foſtering Care of the Legiſlature, promiſes to realize the Expectation of its Founders, and to extend its Uſefulneſs throughout the State."

Occaſional Alterations and Enlargements for the Convenience of the Library were made from Time to Time, and occaſionally extra Grants for ſuch Purpoſes. The Truſtees at an early Date had mainly in View the Collection of an extenſive Library of Law Books, and large Proportions of the Appropriations were expended in this Direction. Frequent Mention was made by the Truſtees in the annual Reports, of their Inability to maintain a Library of a miſcellaneous or general Character, and continue at the ſame Time the current Publications and new Treatiſes on Law, with the Amount of Means placed at their Diſpoſal.

For nearly thirty Years the Inſtitution continued

ſteadily to Increaſe. Its Importance was conceded, and it became apparent that its Superviſion required more Time and Attention than could conveniently be beſtowed by a Body of Men who were conſtantly oppreſſed with a Multitude of other official Duties. It appeared evident that the Intereſts of the Library required that a more permanent Board of Truſtees ſhould be conſtituted, and Officers and Committees appointed who ſhould be ſpecially charged with its Management and Care.

Senſible of the Importance of ſuch an Organization, the Legiſlature on the 4th of May, 1844, enacted that the Regents of the Univerſity of the State of New York ſhould be the Truſtees of the State Library. The Regents at once aſſumed the important Truſt, and their firſt Meeting as Truſtees was held on the 16th Day of the ſame Month. They immediately directed an Inventory to be taken of all the Books, Maps, &c. belonging to the Library, and as a Reſult it was aſcertained that three hundred and eleven Volumes were miſſing; a Part of which, on advertiſing in the State Paper, were returned. A Committee of the Board, conſiſting of ſeven Members, was alſo conſtituted and charged ſpecially with the Care of the Library. Important Alterations were made in the Rooms, deficient Sets of Books were promptly completed, and Correſpondence opened with the Secretaries of the ſeveral States requeſting them to complete, as far as poſſible the Collections of Laws, Journals and Documents then in the Library. It was decided alſo to procure and continue all Engliſh Reports in their original Editions. Under ſuitable Efforts, conducted mainly by the late Dr. T. Romeyn Beck, this Diviſion ſoon attained a decided Reputation as a valuable reference Library. A very valuable Addition of about 1,200 Volumes, conſiſting moſtly of elementary Treatiſes on Law was made under a Law paſſed in 1849, which directed that any Volumes in a publick Library, known as the "Chancellor's Library,"* which were not already in the State Library, ſhould be ſelected and placed in ſaid State Library.

Second to an unequalled Law Library, the Truſtees early declared that they eſteemed it a paramount Object to accumulate, as far as was in their Power, every Work of Intereſt or Value relating to the United States. In furtherance of this Deſign, in 1842-3, ſeveral Individuals, among whom none more than Mr. Iſaiah Townſend, intereſted themſelves with the Truſtees, in procuring for the State a moſt valuable Collection of Books, made in Paris by Mr. David Baillie Warden, himſelf an accompliſhed Scholar and enthuſiaſtick Collector. He was an American Citizen, and had been for many Years an active Member of the Geographical Society of Paris. The Library which it was propoſed to purchaſe of him, was compoſed of moſt valuable Works relating to the early Hiſtory of America, and was already the ſecond of this Character which Mr. Warden had made, the firſt having been

*The Court of Chancery was aboliſhed by the Conſtitution in 1846.

purchafed fome 20 Years previous by Mr. Elliot of Bofton, and prefented to Harvard College. The printed Catalogue of this Collection, and a fupplemental one in Manufcript, contained the Titles of 2,185 Volumes, 96 of which were in folio, 504 in quarto, 1,248 in octavo, 336 in duodecimo, befides 12 Atlafes, 121 Maps, &c. 9 Medals, and 2 Prints. Letters from Hon. Jared Sparks, George Bancroft, Augufte Devezac, Henry Ledyard, Dr. DeKay and others, ftrongly commending the Purchafe, were fubmitted to the Legiflature, and that Body, in 1845, made a grant of $4,000 for this Object.

During the next Year the Regents, in compliance with a Requirement of Law, iffued a new and complete Catalogue, the firft under their Aufpices. The late George Wood, the Affiftant in Charge of the mifcellaneous Department, laboured even to a Sacrifice of Mind and Health, in preparing this Volume, which, confidering the fmall Amount of bibliographical Affiftance at his Command, evinces much Intelligence and accurate Knowledge of Books.

The annual Appropriation for the Purchafe of Books was increafed in 1848 to $2,800, and again in 1857, to $4,000. In making the laft named Increafe the Legiflature had in View the Purchafe of important Works for the Library in the Department of Bibliography.

It was well known that Mr. Joel Munfell of Albany, had for many Years been engaged in collecting Works of this Speciality, including valuable Treatiſes on Printing and Engraving. The Magnitude of the State Library now ſeemed to demand that more enlarged Facilities ſhould be afforded to thoſe connected with it in Inveſtigations in theſe Departments. The Subject of the Purchaſe of Mr. Munſell's Collection was ſubmitted to the joint Library Committee of the Legiſlature, who were unanimous in their Judgment of the Importance and Value of the Suggeſtion, and they recommended that with this Object in View the Appropriation ſhould be increaſed to the Sum of $4,000, for at leaſt two Years. The Purchaſe was accordingly made in the Summer of 1857. As we have avoided noticing any of the ſpecially valuable Works in the Library, it will not be neceſſary here to make Mention of any of the Varieties included in this Purchaſe. A Catalogue of the entire Department is now in Courſe of Publication.

Although the Growth of the New York State Library, by Means of annual Appropriations from the publick Treaſury, has been ſteady, ſtill it has had Facilities afforded it which are ſcarcely enjoyed by any other ſimilar Inſtitution. The valuable Publications* of the State, on its civil and natural

*On the Part of the State, the following Works have been available for Exchanges: Natural Hiſtory of New York; Documents relating to the Colonial Hiſtory of New York; Documentary Hiſtory of New York; Meteorology of New York, from 1825–1830; Tranſactions of the State Agricultural Society; Tranſactions of the American Inſtitute; Tranſactions of the State Medical Society; Tranſactions of the American Ethnological Society; Stryker's American Regiſter; Laws, Journals and Documents of the Legiſlature; Catalogues of the State Library and State Cabinet.

Hiſtory bring Returns which enrich to an uncommon Extent this Depoſitory of the State's literary Treaſures. The Correſpondence and Exchange, conducted with foreign ſcientifick and literary Inſtitutions, is ſecond only in Extent to that of the Smithſonian Inſtitution. The Exchanges, which have already placed ſeveral thouſand Volumes on the Shelves of the Library, and for the Maintenance of which the State makes a ſmall annual Grant, has been conducted mainly through the Agency of M. Vattemare at Paris, and the Courteſy of foreign and American Conſuls, Gentlemen who have uniformly been found deſirous and ready to identify themſelves with Movements of this Character.*

The Library as at preſent conſtituted, is divided into two Departments, viz: the General Library, and the Law Library, the latter of which is nearly or quite the moſt Complete of its Kind in America, embracing, beſides the domeſtick and foreign Reports and elementary Treatiſes, a more extenſive Collection of the Laws, Journals and Documents of the ſeveral States of the Union than can be found elſewhere, while the former is particularly rich in American hiſtorical Works and in the Publications of the different European Governments.

*A recent valuable Reſult of this Syſtem, was an Exchange with the Government of the Netherlands of the Journals and Reſolutions of the States General of Holland and Weſt Vrieſland from 1524 to 1797; and ſecret Reſolutions of the ſame from 1651 to 1795; alſo a general Index; in all 260 folio Volumes. Very few Copies of this great Collection are now in Exiſtence; it is not to be found even in the Imperial Library at Paris, the largeſt and richeſt in the World. To complete this Series, the Government was obliged to add Manuſcript Volumes.

It is required by Law that a Catalogue of the State Library be publiſhed every five Years. The Truſtees preſent an annual Report to the Legiſlature containing the Liſt of Books added to the Library ſince the previous Report. The Catalogue for 1855 was publiſhed in 1856-7, in three octavo Volumes. Volume I. is a Catalogue of the General Library, and contains the Titles of 30,011 Volumes. They are arranged in alphabetical Order, according to the Names of Authors, the Whole, including a copious Index of Subjects, occupying 997 Pages. Volume II. is a Catalogue of the Law Library, occupying 412 Pages. Volume III. is a Catalogue of Maps, Atlaſes, Manuſcripts, Engravings, Paintings, Buſts, Medals, Coins, Seals, &c. including a Liſt of Donations made during the Year 1856, the Whole occupying 286 Pages. The Number of Volumes in the Library at the Time of the Publication of the Catalogue in 1850, was 23,274. Since then the Number has more than doubled, the average Increaſe having been 4,000 Volumes per annum.* In 1853 the Legiſlature authorized the Purchaſe of the Correſpondence and other Papers of George Clinton, the firſt Governor of the State. Theſe Manuſcripts has been ſubſtantially bound in twenty-three folio Volumes, and placed in the Library, forming an intereſting Addition to its Treaſures. The celebrated Andre Papers, conſtituting a Part of this

*The Number added in 1857 was 5,539.

Collection, have, for their better Preservation and more ready Examination, been framed and covered with Glass. The Papers of Sir William Johnson, extending from 1738 to 1774, have also been appropriately arranged and bound in twenty-two folio Volumes. These Collections contain much valuable Information in Reference to the early History of the State, and various Matters connected with the Revolutionary War.

In 1854, the Library was removed to the substantial and appropriate Building, west of the Capitol, constructed by the Direction of the Legislature of 1851. It is a fire-proof Structure, capable of accommodating 100,000 Volumes, and is finished throughout in the Perfection of modern Style. The front and rear Walls are faced with brown Free-stone, and represent a continuous Pedestal, which extends above the first Story, supporting a Row of engaged Corinthian Columns, and Niches with Pedestals. On the south Entablature are the Words STATE LIBRARY.

The Dimensions of the Building are 114 Feet by 45, besides a Connection to the Capitol by a Corridor of 16 Feet. The main Floor is constructed over heavy brick Arches, supported by stone Columns. The Lintels of the second Floor and Galleries, and also the arched Spans are of Iron, filled in and covered with broken Brick and Cement; the Roof, Rafters, Trusses, Window-frames and Shutters, are likewise of Iron.

The main Entrance is on State Street, the Rear

opening on the Capitol Park. The Afcent from the Street is by three Steps to the Veftibule, which is inclofed with ornamental ground Glafs. This opens directly into the Law Department. The Interior of both Stories is divided into Alcoves, and on the fifteen marble Pilafters of the lower Room are Brackets for Bufts. Each Alcove is furnifhed with a Table and Chairs of Oak. Stairs conftructed at either End of the Building, in Extenfions, conduct to the fecond Story, which has been appropriated to the general Department. This Room is lighted by fix Sky-lights befides fide Windows. A Row of Corinthian Pillars on either Side, which conceal iron Columns, fupports a Gallery, which is mounted by Stairs at the north End. The Galleries contain Newfpapers, Maps, Coins, Pictures, &c. Four Furnaces and one hundred and feventy Gas-burners are required to heat and light the Building. The entire Flooring is an ornamental encauftick Tile. Of Shelfroom the total Number of Feet is 7,812, of which 6,235 Feet are to accommodate Books of the octavo Size, and 1577 for the folios and quartos.

The Act of the Legiflature authorizing this Structure, directed the Commiffioners to erect it on the Ground owned by the State in the Rear of the Capitol, but allowed them, if they fhould deem it neceffary, to purchafe additional Land adjoining. The Sum of $50,000 was appropriated. Before the next Seffion, the valuable Library of Congrefs was deftroyed by Fire, and it having been pretty clearly demonftrated that moft of the Collection might have been ſaved, but for the Fact that Wood had been uſed in the Conſtruction of the Shelves, the Legiſlature of New York promptly directed that the Alcoves and Shelves of the new Building ſhould be Iron, and appropriated for that Purpoſe an additional Sum of $22,000. Further Grants were made in 1852-3-4, amounting to $19,000, making a grand Total of $91,000, of which Sum $11,640 was paid for Land, and about $8,000 for Fixtures, Fences, Walks; leaving chargeable to the Erection and Finiſhing of the Library Building, about $72,000.

The Library is open to the Publick daily, from the Hour of 9 in the Morning till 5 in the Afternoon; and during the Seſſions of the Legiſlature, till 8 in the Evening, except on Saturdays, when it is cloſed at 5. Any Citizen may read and conſult the Books, upon the Premiſes, at Pleaſure; and the Heads of the ſeveral Departments, Truſtees of the Library, Judges of the Court of Appeals, Juſtices of the Supreme Court, and Members of the Legiſlature are allowed to draw out Volumes.

ALFRED B. STREET, *Librarian.*

ASTOR LIBRARY.

100,000 Vols.

THIS noble Inſtitution owes its Exiſtence to the Liberality of John Jacob Aſtor, a wealthy Merchant of New York, who in a Codicil to his Will, dated Auguſt 22, 1839, bequeathed $400,000 for its Eſtabliſhment. The following is an Extract from the Will:

"Desiring to render a public benefit to the city of New York, and to contribute to the advancement of useful knowledge and the general good of society, I do, by this codicil, appropriate $400,000, out of my residuary estate, to the establishment of a Public Library in the city of New York; the said amount to be disposed of as follows:

"1. In the erecting of a suitable building for a public library.

"2. In furnishing and supplying the same, from time to time, with books, maps, charts, models, drawings, paintings, engravings, casts, statues, furniture, and other things appertaining to a library for general use, upon the most ample scale and liberal character.

"3. In maintaining and upholding the buildings and other property, and in defraying the necessary expenses of taking care of the property, and of the accommodation of persons consulting the library.

"The said sum shall be payable one-third in the year after my decease, one-third in the year following; and the residue in equal sums, in the fourth and fifth years after my decease.

"The said library is to be accessible, at all reasonable hours and times, for general use, free of expense to persons resorting thereto, subject only to such control and regulations as the trustees may from time to time exercise and establish for general convenience."

By a Provision of the Will, the Government of the Library was vested in eleven Trustees, in whose Keeping were placed all the Property and Effects of the Institution; in them existed all Power to invest and expend the Funds, and to manage the Affairs of the Library. The first Trustees were named by the Testator, and consisted of the following Gentlemen: Washington Irving, William B. Astor, Daniel Lord, jr., James G. King, Joseph G. Cogswell, Fitz-Greene Halleck, Henry Brevoort, Jr., Samuel B. Ruggles, and Samuel Ward, Jr.; also, the Mayor of the City of New York, and the Chancellor of the State, in respect to their Offices,

By a ſubſequent Codicil, Charles Aſtor Briſted, his Grandſon, was alſo appointed a Truſtee. A Proviſion of the Will alſo deſignated, as the Land whereon to erect a ſuitable Building for the Purpoſes of the Library, a Lot ſituated upon the eaſt Side of La Fayette Place, meaſuring 65 Feet in Front by 120 deep. In the further Proviſions of the Will, the Sum of $75,000 was appropriated to be expended, in the Erection of the Building, and $120,000 to the Purchaſe of Books and other Objects, in the Eſtabliſhment of the Library, and the Reſidue, after paying for the Site, to be inveſted as a Fund for the Maintenance and gradual Increaſe of the Library. As early as the Year 1839, Mr. Aſtor had purchaſed a Number of Volumes, aided by Dr. Joſeph G. Cogſwell, with the ultimate Intention expreſſed in his Will. In May, 1848, the Truſtees of the Library met for the firſt Time, and in accordance with the known Deſire of Mr. Aſtor, appointed Mr. Cogſwell Superintendent, a Poſition which he ſtill occupies. In the Autumn of the ſame Year, Dr. Cogſwell ſailed for Europe, authorized to purchaſe Books to the Amount of $20,000. During an Abſence of four Months, he collected 20,000 Volumes, which were temporarily placed in a Building rented for the Purpoſe. A ſecond and third Viſit by the Superintendent, increaſed the Number of Volumes to 70,000, with which the preſent Building was opened, Jan. 9, 1854.

The Aſtor Library is placed in a central and eaſily acceſſible Situation. La Fayette Place, on the eaſt

Side of which it is built, communicates with the two great Thoroughfares of the City — Broadway and the Bowery — by Great Jones Street at the South, Aſtor Place and Eighth Street at the North, and by Fourth Street near the Centre. A more appropriate Site could not be found in New York. The Street has a refined, claſſick Air, and is in a good Degree exempt from the Throng and Noiſe and Buſtle of buſineſs Streets. The Edifice is built in the Byzantine Style of Architecture, richly ornamented with brown ſtone Mouldings, and an impoſing Entablature. Its Dimenſions are in accordance with the Directions of the Will, its Height being about 70 feet. The Architect was Alexander Sältzer, from Berlin, whoſe Plan was adopted by the Truſtees on the 10th of December, 1849.

The baſement Story is faced with high ruſtick Aſhler, projecting ſix Inches, thus imparting an extremely bold Relief. The Window-frames are placed near the Inſide of the Wall, forming deep Receſſes, in order to ſecure the ſame Effect. Theſe conſiſt primarily of ſix, occupying the central Portion, and admitting Light to the Library Hall, placed three above and three below a given Point; the upper connected with the lower by Columns ſupported by Figures repreſenting the Genii of Literature. The remaining Windows are two in Number, one on each Side of the Entrance. The firſt Floor is uſed for the Depoſit of publick Documents, for the Meetings of the Truſtees, &c. It was originally intended for reading and lecture

Rooms. The Bafement contains the Keeper's Rooms, Cellars, coal Vaults, Furnaces for warming, &c. The Floors are compofed of richly wrought mofaick Work, refting on iron Beams. A fingle Flight of thirty-eight Italian marble Steps, decorated on either Side of the Entrance by a ftone Sphinx, leads nearly to the Centre of the Library Hall, which is 100 Feet in Length, by 64 in Width, and 50 in Height. This is furrounded by fourteen brick Piers, plaftered and finifhed in Imitation of Italian Marble, and fupporting iron Galleries midway between the Floor and the Ceiling. By four iron fpiral Stairways from the Corners of the Room the main Gallery is reached, and the intermediate Gallery of a lighter Defcription is connected with the main Gallery by eight Staircafes. The whole are very ingenioufly arranged, and appropriately ornamented in a Style correfponding with the general Architecture of the Building. At an Elevation of 51 Feet above is the principal Sky-light, 54 Feet long by 14 broad, and formed of thick Glafs fet in Iron. Befides this, are circular fide Sky-lights of fmaller Dimenfions. Thefe in Connection with the fide and rear Windows, furnifh all needful Light. Iron Fret-work in different Parts of the Ceiling, fecure a full Ventilation. In the extreme Rear are two Rooms for the Superintendent, which are acceffible by Means of the main Galleries. The internal Arrangement is a very convenient one, and very economical of Space. A Series of feven Alcoves or Apartments, open in Front and Rear, fills up the Space on each Side, from the ſide Walls to the Columns which ſupport the Roof, leaving Corridors two and a half Feet in Width along the Walls, by which a Communication is eſtabliſhed between the different Parts of the Library. On this Plan, the Capacity of the Room for Books is more than doubled, that is, for every fifty-one wall Shelves, there are ſeventy-two in the Alcoves. On no other could it be made to contain one hundred thouſand Volumes, its preſent Number.

The Syſtem of Claſſification adopted in the Aſtor Library, is that of Brunet, whoſe great Work on Bibliography, entitled Manuel du Libraire, is better, more complete, and more generally known than any ſimilar Publication. The following Account of the Character and Claſſification of the Library, is compiled from Dr. Cogſwell's admirable Letter publiſhed in the Home Journal, Jan. 7, 1854.

The Arrangement begins with Theology. This Department includes the beſt Editions of the Hebrew and Greek Scriptures, the Walton Polyglott, various Editions of the Vulgate, and numerous Verſions of the whole Bible, and of Parts of it, in the principal Languages of Europe and the Eaſt. The Collection of the Fathers is full, but not abſolutely complete, and contains moſt of the Benedictine Editions, the Bibliotheca Maxima of Deſpont, the Patres Apoſtolici of Cotelerius, and many others of this Claſs of leſs Note. It is equally well provided with Works on the Councils, including Colet's Edition of Labbe, in 29 Volumes, the Concilia Maxima, in 37 Volumes ſolio, Beveridge's Synodicon, Lorenzana, Concilianos Provinciales, etc. It is alſo reſpectable in ſcholaſtick, dogmatick, parenetick, and polemick Theology, including the early and more recent Engliſh Divines, in the beſt Editions.

Juriſprudence forms the ſecond Department. In this the Object has been to provide thoſe Works which are rarely found in this Country, rather than to form a complete Law Library. The Collection is good on the civil Law, embracing various Editions of the Corpus Juris, and Commentaries upon it; it contains, alſo, all the Codes of Scandinavia, and of other Parts of Europe, during the Middle Ages, the Syſtems of Juriſprudence as now practiſed in Italy, Portugal, Germany, Denmark and Sweden, the Fueroſs ſiete Partidas and Recopilaciones of Spain, together with the Digeſts and Commentaries on the Muſſulman, Hindoo, Gentoo, and Chineſe Laws. In French Law, the Library is really rich, beginning with the Ordonances des Rois, and coming down to the very lateſt Volume of the Journal du Palais. The Selection for the Engliſh common Law was made by two of the moſt eminent Juriſts in the Country; it is not large, but very choice. For American Law an entire Alcove is reſerved.

The next Department is that of Sciences and Arts, in which of courſe Medical Science is included. The Number of Volumes here is comparatively ſmall, this Department being well provided for in the Hofpital and other Medical Libraries of the City.

The Natural Sciences form another Divifion of this Department, and this is one of the richeft and beft furnifhed in the Library. It is neceffarily very coftly, as Naturalifts will readily underftand, when they know it contains fuch Works as the Genera et Species Palmarum of Martius, in a coloured copy; Plantæ Afiaticæ Rariores of Wallich, Roxburgh's Plants of the Coaft of Coromandel; a complete Set of Gould's Birds of Europe, Auftralia, Himelaya, Toucans, and Trogons; Illuftrations Conchyliologiques par Chenu; Audubon's Birds of America; Sibthorp's Floræ Græcæ; Lambert's Genus Pinus, and many other Volumes of the fame Character, comprifing in all about 7,000.

The third Divifion of Sciences and Arts is that of Chemiftry and Phyfics, to which, from the intimate Relation it bears to them, may be added that of the ufeful Arts or Polytechnics. The Tranfactions of Societies for the Promotion of Science and Arts may alfo be affigned to it. Thefe Collections contain Memoirs and Papers of great Importance to practical Men, as well as to Men of Science. The Library contains the Publications of the principal Societies in Great Britain, France, Belgium, Holland, Germany, Denmark, Sweden, Norway, Ruffia, Italy, Spain and Portugal, and alfo of the United States, amounting altogether to about 4,000 Volumes, principally quartos.

Next in Order are the Mathematical Sciences,

of which the Aſtor Library has a firſt rate Collection. It is rich not only in pure Mathematicks, but alſo in all the applied; in Aſtronomy, Mechanicks, Hydraulicks, Engineering, it is very full, and not deficient in military Tacticks. It has drawn largely upon the Libraries of ſeveral celebrated Mathematicians for Books to form it, ſuch as Halley's and Legendre's, which were greatly enriched by Mr. S. Ward, after they were bought by him; alſo, Jacobi's and the two Heiligenſtadts, of Berlin. To theſe have ſince been added the moſt important mathematical Works more recently publiſhed in Europe and America. Beſides full Collections of all the publiſhed Works of Euler and of Gauſs, it has ſeveral unpubliſhed Manuſcripts of theſe great Mathematicians: all the mathematical Journals; all the Works of Newton, Leibnitz, the Bernouillis, La Place, Delambre, La Croix, Legendre, Lagrange, Jacobi, Abel, etc.; the aſtronomical Obſervations generally, and a very large Number of mathematical Diſſertations and Papers, which are not eaſily found.

In the Fine Arts the Aſtor Library has a fine Collection of Works, among which are the following: A complete Set of Piraneſi's Antiquities, proof Plates, twenty-eight in twenty-one Volumes; Muſée Français et Royal, proof Plates before the Letter, 6 Volumes; Raphael's Loggie of the Vatican, engraved by Volpato, and exquiſitely coloured by Hand, in the exact Style of the Originals, 3 Volumes; a complete Set of the Grecian Antiquities, 13 Volumes; Gruner's Freſco Decorations of

Italy, coloured by Hand in the ſame Style as Raphael's Loggie, 1 Volume, and Lepſius's Denkmaler aus Aegypten, 6 Volumes. Theſe 50 Volumes, all large folios, fully bound in red Morocco, except ſix, coſt $2,975, or $59·50 per Volume.

In Linguiſticks, particularly Oriental, the Aſtor Library is unſurpaſſed by any in this Country. It has Grammars and Dictionaries of one hundred and four different Languages, and numerous Vocabularies of the rude unwritten ones. It has alſo Chreſtomathies and other uſeful facilities for ſtudying them. All the Families and Branches of the European Languages, and a greater Part of thoſe of Aſia and Africa, are repreſented in the Collection. It contains the beſt Works on the Egyptian Hieroglyphicks, the cuneiform Inſcriptions, and the other curious Records of the ancient Nations of the Eaſt, which recent Diſcoveries have brought to Light. It has alſo the beſt of the Vocabularies of the different Dialects of the Mexican and South American Indians, which were collected and publiſhed by the early Spaniſh miſſionary Prieſts. Books of this laſt Claſs have become exceſſively rare, and, conſequently, dear. A perfect Copy of Molina's Art de la Lengua Mexicana, cannot be had for leſs than fifty Dollars; and Rincon's Grammar of the ſame Language, a mean little duodecimo, bound, or rather done up in limp Vellum, which few would accept as a Gift, coſts much more than its Weight in Gold. In the Oriental Collection are the following two Works, which, in this Country at leaſt, are exceedingly rare, viz: The Seven Seas; a Dictionary and Grammar of the Persian Language, in 7 Volumes, folio, by the late King of Oude, which was printed in his Palace; and the Sabda Kalpa Druma of the Rajah Radhakant Deb, a Sanscrit Dictionary in 7 Volumes, folio. Neither of these Works was printed for Sale.

The Historical Department is the last in the Order of Classification. This Department is fuller perhaps than any other, with the Exception of Mathematicks, Languages and Bibliography. It constitutes a fourth Part at least of the whole Library. With a few Exceptions, it is arranged in the Series of Alcoves extending on the main Floor, from the southeast to the southwest Corner. Works on Chronology, Diplomaticks, Numismaticks, Heraldry, Inscriptions and Antiquities, are regarded as Introductions to the right Understanding of History, and are placed in the first Alcove, with general biographical Dictionaries and universal History. Biography does not form a Class by itself, but is placed either with the civil or literary History to which it belongs. Geography, for the more convenient Use of Maps and Charts, is placed on the second Floor; and Voyages and Travels, as most intimately connected with the Discovery and History of America, are placed in immediate Proximity to it, instead of preceding the historical Collection, as they usually do. Ecclesiastical History is appended to Theology. The remaining historical Divisions, it may be stated generally, are in the usual Way.

Sometimes it has been found neceſſary to bring the Hiſtory of more than one Country into the ſame Alcove, in which Caſes regard has been had to the Connection exiſting between them in the Paſt. Thus Spaniſh, Portugueſe and Italian Hiſtory are together; French occupies a whole Alcove; German, Dutch and Belgian are together in an Alcove, and with them Scandinavian and Ruſſian; Engliſh, Scotch and Iriſh Hiſtory fills another Alcove; Aſiatick and African Hiſtory, for Want of Room below, is placed on the ſecond Floor, in an Alcove with Oriental Literature.

To the American Hiſtorical Department a larger Space in the Library has been aſſigned than to any other, becauſe it is intended to make this the moſt complete. The Collection already formed contains moſt of the early Spaniſh Writers; the early Voyages, the Accounts of the firſt Coloniſts, the various Hiſtories of the War of Independence, and the older Books generally. In the more modern ones there are many Deficiencies to be ſupplied. Not in American Hiſtory only, but alſo in American Literature, it is hoped that the Library will, ſooner or later, be made complete.

The Library poſſeſſes a complete Collection of Engliſh Parliamentary Journals, Debates and Reports. Theſe amount to nearly three thouſand Volumes, chiefly folios; the long Room on the left of the main Entrance-door has been taken for them, and for other like European Documents. The correſponding Room on the Right will be appropriated to American publick Documents of the United States, and of the individual States. This Uſe of them will in no wiſe interfere with their being uſed as Reading-rooms, ſhould they be needed for that Purpoſe. The preſent Arrangement for reading is at the Tables in the main Library-room.

A ſpecial Technological Department, embracing the various Branches of practical Induſtry and the mechanick Arts, has recently been founded by Wm. B. Aſtor. Upwards of $15,000, according to the annual Report of the Truſtees for 1857, have already been expended for Books of this Character, under the Direction of the Superintendent.

In the Department of Bibliography, the Aſtor Library is far Superiour to any other in the Country. This Department, ſo indiſpenſable to the Knowledge of Books, and to the efficient and ſyſtematick Growth of every Library, has been founded at the Expenſe of Dr. Cogſwell, who continues, with characteriſtick Liberality, to provide for its Increaſe. It embraces, including General Literary Hiſtory, about ſix thouſand Volumes, many of which are very rare and coſtly. Indeed ſcarcely one important Work in this Department is wanting.

On the 31ſt of October, 1855, the preſent Building having become filled, and the Neceſſity for more Room obviouſly exiſting, Mr. William B. Aſtor, eldeſt Son of the Founder of the Library, made a Donation to the Truſtees of a Piece of Land immediately adjacent to the preſent Building, embracing an area 80 Feet wide, and 120 Feet deep. The Sum paid for this additional Lot was $30,476. Mr. Aſtor alſo announced his Intention of erecting at his own Expenſe a Building ſimilar to the preſent, and to be adapted to the ſame Purpoſes. Since that Date the Foundations have been laid, and the Building has rapidly advanced toward Completion. The Coſt, as eſtimated by the Truſtees, can fall but little ſhort of $100,000. It will correſpond to the preſent Building in Materials and external Appearance, imparting to the Whole the architectural Effect of a ſingle Edifice one hundred and thirty Feet in Front. A Space of fifteen Feet is left open on the northern Side for Light and Ventilation. The whole Edifice when completed, will be capable of containing 200,000 Volumes.

The Catalogue of the Aſtor Library, which has been in Progreſs ever ſince it was opened, has been a Labor of Difficulty, and requiring and receiving the moſt careful Attention. It will compriſe, when finiſhed, eight octavo Volumes, numbering upward of 500 Pages each, four Volumes being devoted to an Alphabetical Index of Authors' Names, and four to a carefully arranged Catalogue of Subjects. It will form, when completed, perhaps the moſt perfect printed Library Catalogue ever publiſhed. The firſt two Volumes are already printed, and the others are rapidly paſſing through the Preſs.

The Library is open every Day, except Sundays and eſtabliſhed Holydays, from 10 A. M., until half an Hour before Sunſet. Admiſſion free to all Perſons over ſixteen Years of Age. The Library, like the Britiſh Muſeum, does not lend out its Books.

DR. JOSEPH G. COGSWELL,
Superintendent.

INTERIOUR OF THE ASTOR LIBRARY.

PUBLIC LIBRARY OF BOSTON.

65,000 Volumes.

THE Idea of a free publick Library in Boſton doubtleſs ſuggeſted itſelf to many Individuals before any active Meaſures were taken to realize the Project. As long ago as the Year

1836, Lemuel Shattuck, whofe Labors as a Statiftician are generally appreciated, made fome Suggeftions in relation to preferving the Documents and other Publications of the City, and his Plan might have ripened into a publick Library had the Subject attracted more Attention. In 1843, the city Government received from Paris through the Agency of M. Vattemare, about fifty Volumes of valuable Books, and in 1847 a further Donation was received from the fame Source. Upon the Reception of the laft Collection a Committee was appointed by the City council to confider what Acknowledgment could be made for the Donation, and to provide for the fafe Keeping of the Books. This Committee, of which Hon. Jofiah Quincy, Jr., was Chairman, reported in detail, and introduced an Order that a joint Committee be formed to confider the Expediency of commencing the Formation of a publick Library under the Control and Aufpices of the City. In connection with this Project, Mr. Quincy offered, on the Part of a publick fpirited Citizen (now underftood to have been Mr. Quincy himfelf), the Sum of $5000 to the Library, whenever $10,000 fhould have been contributed to the fame by other Citizens.

The city Council not having the Power to appropriate Money for the Formation of a Library, Application was made to the Legiflature, and in March, 1848, an Act was paffed granting to the city Government the requifite Power to eftablifh, regulate and control a Library for the free Ufe of the Citizens of Boſton, with a Proviſo that no Appropriation for any one Year ſhould exceed $5000. This Act was accepted by the city Council on the 3d of April, 1848, and in accordance therewith Negotiations were opened with the Truſtees of the Boſton Athenæum for the Purpoſe of throwing its Library open to the Publick. The Propoſition was favourably received by the Truſtees of that Inſtitution, but was rejected by the Proprietors, and the Negotiations fell to the Ground.

The publick Library had been commenced, and although the Intereſt therein ſlumbered for a While, it was not entirely forgotten. On the 31ſt of October, 1849, Hon. Robert C. Winthrop gave one hundred and eighty-ſeven Volumes of bound publick Documents to the City. The Letter of Mayor Bigelow, acknowledging this Donation, which we republiſh in this Connection, is brief, but pointed, and gives to Mr. Winthrop the Credit of laying the firſt *American* Stone to the free Library.

About the ſame Time two hundred and nineteen Volumes were received from John D. W. Williams, Eſq., of Roxbury, and other ſimilar Contributions from a Number of other Perſons ſoon followed.

The next Step in the Formation of the Library was the one which gave the Project an Impulſe that completely overcame the previous Inertia. To the Hon. John P. Bigelow, then Mayor of the City, is undoubtedly due the Credit of having been the firſt to put the free publick Library upon a ſure Foundation. In the Summer of 1850, many of the Friends of Mayor Bigelow united to raiſe a Sum of Money for the Purchaſe of a Vaſe to preſent to him as a Teſtimonial of their Reſpect for his publick Character and Services. Mr. Bigelow, anticipating the Purchaſe of the Vaſe, requeſted that in Lieu thereof the Sum be contributed towards the Eſtabliſhment of a publick Library. On the 5th of Auguſt, Mr. Bigelow, with the Conſent of the Donors, tendered the Amount ($1000), to the city Government, in a Letter, from which the following is an Extract:

"The Want of ſuch an Inſtitution in our Midſt is generally acknowledged. It has an important proſpective Bearing upon the moral and intellectual Character of the People of Boſton, and I have Reaſon to know that there are many Perſons in this Community who are ready to tender valuable Offerings for the Purpoſe in View, as ſoon as it ſhall be known that the city Government is willing to receive ſuch Donations."

The generous Donation of Mr. Bigelow was gratefully accepted, and the Committee of the city Government on the Library was directed to "proceed with as little Delay as poſſible, and as far as the Means in their Hands would juſtify, to carry into Effect the Eſtabliſhment of a Free Publick Library." Two Days ſubſequently, on the 7th of Auguſt, the Hon. Edward Everett tendered to the city Government his large Collection of Publick Documents, the Contributions alluded to by Mr. Bigelow in his Letter to Mr. Winthrop in 1849. This Contribution was exceedingly valuable. It confifted of publick Documents and State Papers, in all to the Number of one thoufand bound Volumes. Mr. Everett ftated in his Letter that he had devoted a great Deal of Time, Labor and Expenfe in collecting thofe Documents. The Volumes embrace the moft important Documents from the Foundation of the Federal Government down to the Year 1840. In this Letter Mr. Everett ftrongly urged the Importance of erecting a Building for the publick Library, and faid:

" Such a Library would put the finifhing Hand to that Syftem of Education which lies at the Bafis of the Profperity of Bofton, and, with her benevolent Inftitutions, gives her fo much of her Name and Praife in the Land."

The city Council accepted this Donation, and voted to receive the Volumes whenever a fuitable Place fhould be provided in which to depofit them. On the 7th of June, 1851, Mr. Everett tranfmitted the Volumes to the city Council, accompanying them with a Catalogue, and with another Letter, in which he again urged the Erection of a fuitable Building for a publick Library. The Liberality of Mr. Everett was foon imitated by feveral other publick fpirited Citizens, who prefented many valuable Volumes to the Library.

Early in 1852, the Hon. Benjamin Seaver, Mayor of the City, in his inaugural Addrefs again called the Attention of the city Council to the Free Public Library. His Remarks were referred to the joint Standing Committee on the Library, who, in conformity with his Recommendations, reported, April 29, in favor of choosing five Citizens at large, who, with the joint Committee of the city Council, should constitute a Board of Trustees. They also recommended the immediate Appointment of a Librarian, in accordance with which Recommendation the present Librarian, Edward Capen, was elected on the 13th of May, the Board of Trustees being chosen on the 24th of the same Month.

One of the first Acts of the Board of Trustees was to report in accordance with Instructions from the Common Council, "upon the Objects to be attained by the Establishment of a publick Library, and the best Mode of effecting them." This Report was drawn up by Mr. Everett, and was an able and forcible Paper, setting forth in glowing Language the Advantages of the publick Library, discussing a Plan for its Formation, showing the several Classes of Books which ought to be comprised in such a Library, and considering some of the Details of the Plan of Organization. The Trustees did not deem it expedient to recommend, in the existing State of the Finances of the City, an Appropriation for the Erection of a Building, but conceived that there were Advantages in a more gradual Course of Measures, in the Continuance of such moderate and frugal Expenditures on the Part of the City as had been already authorized and commenced for the Purchaſe of Books and the Compenſation of the Librarian. In order, however, to put the Library into Operation with the leaſt poſſible Delay, the Truſtees propoſed to the city Government to appropriate for this Purpoſe the ground Floor of the Adams School-houſe in Maſon Street. This Recommendation was adopted, and ſoon after the Rooms ſtill occupied by the Library were opened for the Reception of Books. In September of the ſame Year Samuel Appleton, Eſq. encloſed to Mayor Seaver a Check for $1,000, to be devoted to the Purchaſe of Books for the Library.

But the Free Publick Library thus humbly, though ſucceſſfully commenced, had yet in ſtore a Donation which was at once to place it upon a liberal Foundation, and to eſtabliſh its Uſefulneſs upon a ſure Baſis. At about the Time the firſt Report of the Board of Truſtees, above alluded to, was iſſued, the city Government were engaged in negotiating a Loan with the Houſe of Baring Brothers & Co. Mayor Seaver tranſmitted among other Documents to Joſhua Bates, Eſq., a Native of Boſton and a Member of that Firm, a Copy of the Report of the Library Truſtees. On the 1ſt of October, 1852, Mr. Bates addreſſed a Letter to Mayor Seaver, ſtating that he had peruſed the Report with great Intereſt, "being impreſſed with the Importance to the Riſing and the future Generations of ſuch a Library as is recommended." In order to accelerate its Accompliſhment, and eſtabliſh the Library at once on a Scale which would do Credit to the City, Mr. Bates tendered the Sum of $50,000 for the Purchaſe of Books. This munificent Offer was promptly accepted by the city Government, and on the 10th of March, 1853, Mr. Bates wrote to Mayor Seaver, authorizing him to draw on him "for a Sum ſufficient to contribute a Fund of fifty thouſand Dollars, to be held by the City of Boſton in Truſt," upon the following Conditions:

"That its entire Income, but only its Income, ſhall in each and every Year hereafter be expended in the Purchaſe of ſuch Books of permanent Value and Authority as may be found moſt needed and moſt uſeful, and that the City will, ſo ſoon as it may conveniently be done, provide, and always hereafter maintain a ſuitable Eſtabliſhment for a Free Publick Library, in which Arrangements ſhall be made for the comfortable Accommodation at one and the ſame Time, and at all proper Hours of the Day and Evening, for at leaſt one hundred Readers."

In accordance with a Vote of the city Council, the Mayor drew upon Mr. Bates for the Sum of $50,000, which was Inveſted in the city Bonds as a permanent Fund for the Increaſe of the Library. The Fund was ſoon after increaſed by another munificent Donation from one of the moſt wealthy and diſtinguiſhed Citizens of Boſton, the Hon. Jonathan Phillips, who on the 11th of April, 1853, in a Letter to the Mayor and Aldermen, offered for the Acceptance of the City of Boſton, in Aid of their city Library, the Sum of ten thouſand Dollars—

——"to be forever held and treated as a truſt Fund; the Income of which ſhall be uſed excluſively for the Purchaſe of Books for ſaid Library, and if from any Cauſe whatever there ſhall at any Time happen a Diminution of the Capital, then the Income is to accumulate, and be added to the Capital, until its original Amount ſhall be entirely reſtored."

This Donation was inveſted in like Manner as that of Mr. Bates, and theſe two Donations, with that of Mr. Bigelow—in all $61,000—conſtitute a permanent Fund, yielding an annual Income of $3,660 for the gradual Increaſe of the Library. To this the City has added annually a liberal Sum. An Addition to the permanent Fund of the Library to the Amount of $10,000, will probably ſoon be realized from the liberal Bequeſt of the Hon. Abbot Lawrence, which is to be paid within three Years of the Probate of his Will.

The Free Publick Library has had many other liberal Benefactors beſides thoſe whoſe munificent Donations have founded the Library upon a permanent Baſis. Among theſe may be mentioned the lamented James Brown, who contributed $500, James Nightengale, $100, J. Ingerſoll Bowditch, $300, N. I. Bowditch, $200, and Mrs. S. I. K. Shepard, $1,000.

On the 24th of February, 1853, an Order was

paſſed by the city Council, authorizing the Committee on the Library, in Conference with the Board of Truſtees, to purchaſe a ſuitable Site for the Erection of a Building which ſhould be fully adapted to the Purpoſes of the Library and fulfill the Conditions of the Donation of Mr. Bates. Accordingly the Committee purchaſed an Eſtate on Somerſet Street, which, as not being ſufficiently central, was ſubſequently ſold, and four very eligible Lots were purchaſed on Boylſton Street and Van Renſſelaer Place, upon which the Edifice repreſented in the Cut, has been erected.

The Building is in the Roman Style of Architecture, the Exteriour being quite plain, with the Exception of the Front, being conſtructed of faced Brick, with Connecticut free-ſtone Dreſſing. It ſhows two Stories high in Front. The Baſement, which is quite light and airy, is nearly all below the Grade of Boylſton Street. The Building is rectangular, 82 Feet wide, by 116 Feet long, with two Towers 14½ by 18 Feet, one at each Corner. The Baſement is 11 Feet high, the firſt Story 21½ Feet, and the ſecond or principal Story 52 Feet. The firſt Floor is divided into five Apartments by brick Walls, deſignated as follows: Veſtibule, Converſation and Delivery Room, General Reading Room, Special Reading Room (for Ladies), and Circulating Library Room.

A ſpacious Entrance through three Sets of richly carved oak Doors leads to the Veſtibule, which occupies the central Portion of the Front of the

Building, and which is 22 Feet wide by 44 Feet deep, and 22 Feet high. The Veſtibule contains the main Stair-caſe, which commences in two Parts, one ſix Feet wide on each Side, both landing upon a Platform at an Elevation of ten Feet, and thence converging into one Flight, ten Feet wide, to the main Hall. The Converſation Room, which is entered from the Foot of the Veſtibule, occupies the central Portion of the eaſt Side of the Building on the firſt Story, and is 34 Feet wide, by 50 Feet deep, and 12 Feet high. This Room forms a Kind of inner Veſtibule, with delivery Counters for the Circulating Library, and Entrances to the Special and General Reading Rooms. It is finiſhed quite plain, with marble Floor, and Walls and Ceilings laid off in panel Work. The Special Reading Room, for Ladies, occupies the northeaſt front Corner of the Building, and is 27 Feet wide by 44 Feet deep, and 21½ Feet high. It is intended to accommodate one hundred Readers, having ſix circular Tables ſurrounding the elaborately ornamented iron Columns, which ſupport the Ceiling. The Walls and Ceiling are taſtefully laid off in panel Work, exquiſitely tinted and gilded. The Floor is of Marble, like nearly all the Floors throughout the Building, the iron Columns reſting upon Baſes of fine Italian Marble. The Arrangements for lighting this and all the Rooms are complete and ample, and the Gaſ-fixtures are Models of Neatneſs and Appropriateneſs. The General Reading Room is in the northweſt Corner of the Building. It is 28 Feet wide by 78 Feet deep, and of the ſame Height with the ſpecial Reading-room. It is alſo ſimilarly furniſhed, and will accommodate two hundred Readers.

The Circulating Library Room occupies the Remainder of the firſt Floor, being upon the ſouth End. It is 78 Feet wide by 34 Feet deep. It is ſhelved for forty thouſand Volumes. The Decorations are very few. It is plainly finiſhed, with iron Balconies, and circular Stairs, and connects with the Baſement and upper Parts of the Building by an iron Staircaſe in the eaſt Tower, and with the main Hall by a circular iron Staircaſe. It is alſo in Communication with the main Hall by Means of Dumb-waiters. Leading from this Room there are in the weſt Tower two Rooms for the Librarian and Aſſiſtants. There is alſo a Room belonging to this Floor, directly over the Converſation Room, an Apartment for Stowage of Books, 9 Feet high in clear, and 34 Feet ſquare.

The entire upper Story is occupied by the ſplendid main Hall and Library. This Hall has a clear Space of 38 Feet wide, by 92 Feet deep, and 58 Feet high, ſurrounded by three Stories of Alcoves, thirty arranged on each Side, 9 by 14 Feet in clear, and 12 Feet high, each with three Stories of Corridors on each End to correſpond with the Alcoves in Height, and finiſhed in the Roman-Corinthian, ornate Style. The Partitions between the Alcoves are faced with three-quarters Diameter, full, rich

Corinthian Columns, ſtanding upon Pedeſtals of the beſt Italian Marble, highly poliſhed. The Columns, Capitals, Baſes and Pedeſtals, occupy nearly the Height of the three Stories of Alcoves, and ſupport ſemi-circular Arches with rich Archivaults, Keyſtones, &c., which in turn ſupport a full, rich Corinthian Cornice, without Architrave, whereon reſts the Lantern. The Lantern is finiſhed with coved Angles, having perpendicular circle-headed Windows, with Arches interſecting the coved Angles, and ſeparated by heavy Ribs ſupporting a deep-ſunk diamond panel Ceiling, relieved with rich carved Mouldings, pendant Drops, &c. The Floor of the clear Space is of Marble, and that of the Alcoves is of ſouthern Pine, bedded in Cement, on brick Arches. The Alcoves on the main Floor are ſhelved for Books, in accordance with the decimal Syſtem propoſed by Dr. N. B. Shurtleff, having ten Shelves, in Height, divided into ten Spaces in Length, making one hundred Spaces in each Alcove. The Shelves are of Wood, covered with a fire-proof Solution of Glaſs, &c. Each Alcove, beſides being lighted from the clear Space, is alſo illuminated by a Skylight directly from the Roof, and the rear End of the Alcove being conſtructed in a V ſhape, leaves no dark Corner. The Alcoves on the firſt Floor are protected by iron Railings in Front from the Publick, and have Openings between each for the Paſſage of the Librarians, and alſo four Flights of circular iron Stairs, connecting with the two Tiers of Galleries. The grand Hall is one of the moſt beautiful in the Country, and for perfect Proportion, Neatneſs of Colour, and exquiſite Taſte of Decoration, can hardly be ſurpaſſed the World over.

The Building occupied about two and a half Years in Conſtruction, and coſt, including the Finiſhings, $247,051. The Land and Preparation coſt $116,582, making a Total of $363,633. It was conſtructed from Deſigns by, and under the Superintendence of Charles K. Kirby, whoſe Plan was ſelected from among twenty-four preſented by Boſton Architects in Anſwer to an Advertiſement by the Commiſſioners. The corner Stone of the Structure was laid by the Mayor of the City, on the 17th of September, 1855; and on the 1ſt of January, 1858, the new Building was dedicated, with appropriate Ceremonies. Addreſſes were delivered by Hon. Robert C. Winthrop, his Honour Mayor Rice, and Hon. Edward Everett.

As ſoon as Information was received by Mr. Bates, in London, that the Erection of a Library was commenced, he addreſſed a Communication to the Mayor, ſignifying his Wiſh, in order to render the Library immediately and generally uſeful to the Publick, in addition to the Sum of $50,000 originally given by him, to purchaſe a conſiderable Number of Books in the various Departments of Science and Literature, and to preſent them to the City for the publick Library. This new and moſt liberal Offer was gratefully accepted, and in accordance with the Requeſt of Mr. Bates, the Truſtees, with the ſpecial Aſſiſtance of Prof. Jewett and a Number of literary and ſcientific Gentlemen of known Eminence, prepared, with great Care, Liſts of Works in various Departments of Knowledge, which they deemed moſt important for the Library. The Number of Volumes thus indicated amounted to 35,000, and the Liſts, after having been carefully reviſed, were tranſmitted to the Agents of Mr. Bates in London, Paris, Leipſic and Florence. The Books were procured and forwarded with great Promptneſs. The firſt Arrival was in May, 1856. In leſs than a Year and a half 142 Boxes had been received, containing 21,374 Volumes, the Coſt of which, according to the Invoices, was $38,893. Others are conſtantly arriving, and it is probable that the aggregate money Value of this munificent Donation of Mr. Bates, will equal the Amount originally contributed by him as a permanent Fund for the Uſe of the Library. The city Government has very properly provided that a Buſt of Mr. Bates, in Marble or Bronze, ſhall be placed in the publick library Building, as an enduring Memorial of the city's Obligation and Gratitude.

It ſhould be mentioned in this Connection that George Ticknor, Eſq., one of the Truſtees, viſited Europe in 1856, to confer with and render ſuch Aſſiſtance as might be deſirable to Mr. Bates in carrying out his noble Purpoſe. He not only made Arrangements perſonally for the Purchaſes in the German and Italian Departments, but eſtabliſhed Agencies, ſecured the good Offices of ſome of the moſt accompliſhed Librarians and Bibliographers of Europe, and in other Ways materially ſubſerved the Intereſts of the Library. The Books received from Europe were placed in the Care of Profeſſor C. C. Jewett, formerly Librarian of the Smithſonian Inſtitute, under whoſe Superviſion they have been catalogued and arranged upon the Shelves.

The active Operations of the Library have been attended with great Succeſs. On the 20th of March, 1854, the Books then compriſing the Library, which had been temporarily placed in the lower Story of the Building of the Normal School, in Maſon Street, were offered to the Publick for Uſe in the Reading-room attached to the Library; and on the 2d of May following, the Books were firſt circulated among the Citizens for home Uſe—a Privilege which has been continued to the preſent Time, with the Exception of ſhort Periods, when the Library has been cloſed for the uſual annual Examination.

In November, 1857, when the laſt Examination of the Library was made by a Committee, in compliance with a Requiſition of the library Ordinance, the Number of Volumes appertaining to the Inſtitution (including the Books received from the laſt liberal Donation of Mr. Bates), amounted to about

56,000; to which ſhould be added 16,000 or more Pamphlets. The Number of Books at the preſent Time is about 65,000.

During the Time that the Library has been open to the Publick, the Books have been very actively circulated. In the Aggregate, about 90,000 Volumes a Year have been delivered to Borrowers for home Uſe; and on one Occaſion the large Number of 730 Volumes were lent in a ſingle Day.

Thus have been ſketched ſomewhat at Length, the leading Events in the Hiſtory of the Riſe and Progreſs of the Free Public Library of Boſton. The Inſtitution is one of which her Citizens have every Reaſon to be proud. It is the Culmination of that great educational Structure of which the primary Schools are the foundation Stones. Riſing in regular Gradation therefrom are the Grammar Schools, the Latin School, the Engliſh High School, the Normal School for Girls, and the Free Public Library. The Children of the City are received at the Portals of this Edifice, inſtructed in the very Elements of Learning, then conducted Step by Step to the higher Branches, until they become fitted for the active Duties of Life, and to become good and uſeful Citizens, when the Departments of Science, of Art and of Literature are freely thrown open to them, in the rich Stores of Learning which are treaſured upon the Shelves of the publick Library. May the Intereſt which is now felt in this excellent Inſtitution continue unabated, and may it go on indefinitely in its Work of gathering that which is better than Riches and more precious than Gold.

CHARLES C. JEWETT, A. M., *Superintendent.*
EDWARD CAPEN, *Librarian.*

NOTE.—The foregoing Account has been taken mainly from the Boſton Journal, and Boſton Courier, with ſlight Alterations and Changes.

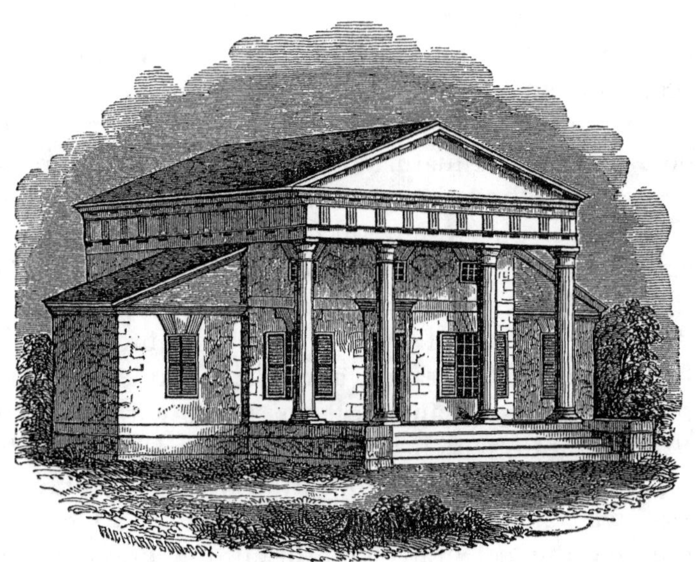

REDWOOD LIBRARY.

IMPERIAL LIBRARY AT PARIS.

825,000 Vols.

THE Imperial Library at Paris is juſtly conſidered as the fineſt in the World. It was commenced under the Reign of King John, who poſſeſſed only 20 Volumes; but the Number was ſo increaſed by his Succeſſor, Charles V., who conſtructed a Library in one of the Towers of the Louvre, that, at his Death in 1380, they amounted, according to Le Prince, to 910 Volumes, ſeveral of them ſuperbly illuminated by John of Bruges, the beſt Artiſt in Miniatures of that Time. This precious Collection was nearly deſtroyed during the Troubles in the Reign of Charles VII.; but what remained was recovered and greatly improved by Charles VIII., who added to it the choice Books, ſtill to be identified by the curious Viſitor, which he carried off to France, after the Conqueſt of Naples. Francis I. united it in 1544 with that of Fontainbleau, which had been enriched by valuable Greek Manuſcripts brought from the Eaſt. Henri IV. was alſo a munificent Benefactor. He appointed the celebrated Hiſtorian De Thou, to be Keeper; brought the Royal Library back to Paris, after an Abſence of nearly a Century (it had been removed to Blois before its Tranſfer to Fontainbleau); and added to it, the fine Collection of Manuſcripts,—more than 800 in Number, and chiefly Greek—which had been formed by Catherine de Medicis. From this Period the Royal Library continued to receive conſtant Acceſſions. In 1684 it poſſeſſed 50,547 Volumes; at the Death of Louis XIV., upwards of 70,000; in 1775 it amounted to 150,000; and by 1790 it had increaſed to about 200,000. Then came the enormous, and for a long Time the almoſt chaotick Acceſſions which accrued from the revolutionary Confiſcations. At preſent it contains about 825,000 printed Volumes, 85,000 Volumes of Manuſcripts, 300,000 Charters and Deeds, and 500,000 Pamphlets or Tracts.

In 1667, Louis XIV., having ordered all the Medals and Curioſities contained in the royal Reſidences to be collected together, cauſed them to be depoſited in this Library. Learned Antiquarians, ſent into foreign Countries, augmented this Collection; rare and precious Objects were ſucceſſively acquired; and the Library at preſent poſſeſſes the richeſt and moſt varied Collection that exiſts in Europe. The Cabinet of Engravings, alſo founded by Louis XIV., is compoſed of Paintings on Vellum, Drawings, and an immenſe Collection of Prints, from the Diſcovery of Engraving to the preſent Time. It contains more than 1,500,000, arranged in about 12,000 Volumes and Portfolios. In theſe Numbers is included a noble Series of Portraits, exceeding 60,000, arranged as far as poſſible, in chronological Order. A ſecond and ſtill larger Collection of Portraits, formed by the Debures—nearly 67,000 in Number—has been recently purchaſed, and arranged in alphabetical Order. Large Selections of Prints are conſtantly exhibited to all Comers, under Glaſs.

The Imperial Library is at prefent divided into the following Departments, viz: 1ft. Printed Books; 2d. Manufcripts, Charters and Deeds; 3d. Coins, Medals, engraved Stones, and other antique Monuments; 4th. Engravings; 5th. Maps, Charts and Plans. Thefe five Departments form five diftinct Eftablifhments, which, by their Importance and the Richnefs of their Treafures, exceed everything of the Kind that is, as yet, to be found in other Countries. A Decree of 1556, which fell, or partially fell, into Difufe during the Troubles of the Fronde, was renewed in 1689, impofed on Publifhers the Obligation of furnifhing to the Library of the King, Copies of all Works printed with Copyright; and each Copy was required to be bound. At prefent the Law prefcribes the Depofit of Copies of all Books (as well as Maps and Engravings) printed; but the Condition requiring them to be bound is difpenfed with. The yearly Increafe from this Source alone is ftated to be 12,000 Volumes.

The Additions from the Vatican Library, felected by the French Commiffioners in 1797, were particularly valuable, amounting to 501 Manufcripts. Of thefe, 20 were Hebrew; 40 Syriac; 19 Coptic; 11 Chinefe; 133 Greek, amongft which was the celebrated Codex Vaticanus of the Septuagint; 176 Latin, including the famous Virgil, Terence, Horace, Cæfar, Plautus, and other ancient claffical Manufcripts; befides many other Manufcripts illuftrative of the ninth and tenth Centuries. Numerous Manufcripts in modern Languages were alfo ſeized in virtue of the compulſory Treaty of Tolentino, particularly the Comedia of Dante, tranſcribed by Boccaccio, the Arcadia of Sannazaro, Michael Angelo's Letters, and alſo thoſe of Henry VIII. and Anne Boleyn; beſides 136 early printed Books, 13 Etruſcan Vaſes, and 737 ancient Coins. To theſe were added the Manuſcripts and early printed Books collected by the French in other Parts of Europe, to which their victorious Eagles had penetrated. But the Events of 1814 and 1815 were followed by a large Reſtitution of the literary Treaſures, as well as of the Works of Art, acquired by Right, or rather by Abuſe, of Conqueſt. Of the Contents of this magnificent Collection, it would be impoſſible, in a Sketch like this, to give anything like Details. It is rich in every Branch and Department, unique in ſome, and as a whole unrivalled. Of Books printed upon Vellum, it contains 1467, being the fineſt and moſt extenſive Collection in the World. The total Number of Books of this Sort extant does not exceed 2700. Lord Spencer's Collection, which is the richeſt in Great Britain, only contains 108. The following are a few of the literary and artiſtick Treaſures accumulated in the Library, deſcribed by Dr. Dibdin, in his Bibliographical Tour in France and Germany, Volume II.

1. *Manuſcripts.* Latin Bible of Charles the Bald. A magnificent folio Volume, depoſited in the Library by Baluze, the head Librarian to Colbert. Book of the Goſpels of the Emperor Lotharius,

executed in the Year 855, and among the moſt precious Specimens of early Art in the Collection. On the Cover are the royal Arms. Pſalterium, Latinè, 8°. The Religious Manual of St. Louis. It is in wooden Covers, wrapped in red Velvet. The Vellum is ſingularly ſoft, and of its original pure Tint. Hiſtorical Paraphraſe of the Bible. Latin and French. Folio. Containing according to Camus in his Notices et Extraits, Vol. VI, upwards of 5000 Illuminations. Such a Work could not now, in his Eſtimation, be executed under 100,000 Francs. Evangelium Sti Johannis. A ſmall oblong folio Manuſcript of the Eleventh Century, bound in red Velvet. It is executed in large coarſe Gothick and Roman Letters of Gold. Breviary of John, Duke of Bedford. "The laſt, and by much the moſt ſplendid Illumination in this Breviary, is the Aſſumption of the Virgin, for which the Artiſts of the Middle Age, and eſpecially the old Illuminators, ſeem to have reſerved all their Powers, and upon which they laviſhed all their Stock of Gold, Ultramarine and Carmine." This Breviary is one of the moſt minute, elaborate and dazzling Works of the Kind extant. Horæ Beatæ Mariæ Virginis. A ſmall Folio. One of the moſt ſuperb and beautiful Books, of its Claſs, in the Library. Hours of Anne of Brittany. "Of all the Volumes in this moſt marvellous Library, this is deemed the moſt precious." It meaſures 12 Inches by 7½. Cité de Dieu. 2 Vols. Folio. Magnificent Shew Books, ſimilar in Size and Style of Art, to the Manuſcript of Valerius Maximus, in the Britiſh Muſeum. Tite-Live. Folio. A noble Manuſcript of the 15th Century. L'Hiſtoire Romaine. 3 Vols. Folio. Among the Shew Books. The Binding is gorgeous, and in a fine State of Preſervation. Royal Biography of France. Folio. The Nonpareil of its Kind, being a Book of Portraits, with intermixed Illuminations. Lancelot du Lac, Triſtan, Le Roy Artus, Roman de la Roſe, and other Romances. A Book of Tournaments. Folio. A marvellous Volume in a perfect Blaze of Splendour.

2. *Early Printed Books.* Horæ Beatæ Virginis, Greek. Printed by Aldus. 1497. 12°. "Perhaps the rareſt Aldine Volume in the World, when found in a perfect State." There are only ten known *perfect* Copies of this Book, of which ſix are in England. The Shyppe of Fooles. Printed by Wynkyn de Worde. 1509. 8°. A far famed Volume, upon Vellum, bound in red Morocco. Pſalterium, Latinè. Printed by Fuſt and Schoiffher. 1457. Folio. Editio Princeps. Bought at the M'Carthy Sale for 12,000 Francs. Only ſeven Copies of it known in the World. Biblia Latina. (Suppoſed to have been printed in 1455.) Folio. This is the famous Edition called the Mazarine Bible, upon which Bibliographers have prepared ſo many Diſquiſitions. This Copy, which is upon Paper, is *the Copy* of all Copies. Durandi Rationale Div. Off. Printed by Fuſt and Schoiffher. 1459. Folio. Biblia Latina. Printed by Pfiſter,

at Bamberg, 1461. 3 Vols. Folio. The rareſt of all Latin Bibles, when found in a perfect State. Sts. Auguſtinus de Civitate Dei. Printed in the Soubiaco Monaſtery. 1467. Folio. "A fine Copy of this reſplendent Volume, which is truly among the Maſter-pieces of early Printing." Grammatica Rhythmica. Printed by Fuſt and Schoiffher. 1466. Folio. This very meagre little Folio, conſiſting of but eleven Leaves, was bought at the Sale of Cardinal Lomenie's Library for *three thouſand three hundred Livres*. There is but one other known Copy of it in the World. Vocabularius. Printed by Bechtermuntze. 1467. Quarto. Editio Princeps. One of the rareſt Books in the World. Virgilius. Printed by Sweynheym and Pannartz. 1469. Folio. Editio Princeps. "The enormous Worth and Rarity of this exceedingly precious Volume may be eſtimated from this very Copy having been purchaſed, at the Sale of the Duke de la Valliere's Library, in 1783, for *four thouſand one hundred and one Livres*." Virgilius. Printed by Vindelin de Spira. 1470. Upon Vellum. Plinii Hiſt. Naturalis. Printed by J. de Spira. 1469. Folio. Editio Princeps. A beautiful Book-gem upon Vellum. Livius. Printed by Vindelin de Spira. 1470. Folio. A magnificent Copy in two Volumes, upon Vellum. "I know that 500 Guineas were once offered for a Copy of this moſt extraordinary Book.—*Dibdin*. Boccaccio Il Decamerone. Printed by Valdarfer. 1471. Folio. The famous Edition of the more famous Copy ſold at the Sale of the Duke of Roxburghe's Library for £2,260. Homeri Opera. Greek. 1488. Folio. Editio Princeps. Croniques de France. Printed by Verard. 1493. 3 Vols. Folio. Upon Vellum. Coloured wood Cuts, red morocco Binding.

Hitherto there has been no complete Catalogue of the Imperial Library. That of Labbe, printed in 1653, in quarto, treats of ſome Manuſcripts, which are divided into hiſtorical and chronological, biblical and theological, epiſtolary and diplomatick, technical and philological. Anicet Melot's Catalogue of the Manuſcripts in the Royal Library was printed at Paris, 1739-44, in 4 Volumes. Folio. The firſt Volume contains the oriental Manuſcripts; the ſecond the Greek; and the third and fourth the Latin. Beſides theſe, the Collection has furniſhed the Materials for a Work, publiſhed in ſucceſſive Volumes, by the Academy of Inſcriptions, under the Title of Notices et Extraits des Manuſcrits de la Bibliothèque du Roi (or Nationale) et autres Bibliothèques. The firſt Volume, quarto, is dated 1787, the ſeventeenth, 1851. This, however, is rather a Collection of Diſſertations, and Deſcriptions of particular Manuſcripts, than a deſcriptive Catalogue. The French Manuſcripts are deſcribed with great Accuracy, by M. Paulin Paris, in his Work, Les Manuſcrits François de la Bibliothèque du Roi. 7 Vols. 8°. Paris, 1836-48.

Of the printed Books in the then Royal Library, there appeared a Catalogue compiled by the Abbés Sallier, Boudot, Capperonnier, and others, in 6 Vols.

Folio. Paris. 1739-50. It contains only the Claſſes Theology, Belles-Lettres, and a Part of Juriſprudence. After the Lapſe of a Century, the Want of a general Catalogue having been felt, the Deficiency is about to be ſupplied, by Direction of the preſent Emperor. The Taſk has been undertaken with Energy and carried on with an Amount of Succeſs worthy of the Collections which have accumulated. The new Catalogue commences with the Claſs of French Hiſtory. It is printed in large quarto, in double Columns, the Books chronologically arranged under the different Reigns or Periods of Government. The three Volumes already publiſhed, 1855-6, according to an Enumeration prefixed, include 45,729 Articles. The fourth Volume, which completes the Claſs, is in the Preſs. This will ſoon be followed by other Claſſes or Diviſions.

The Building in which this vaſt Collection is depoſited is the immenſe Hotel formerly occupied by Cardinal Mazarin, embracing the entire Space between the Rue Vivienne, Rue Richelieu, Rue Neuve des Petits Champs, and Rue Colbert. It is deſtitute of all external Ornament, and of a dark and dingy Tint. Its Length is 540 Feet, its Breadth 130 Feet; its total Surface, including the Courts, is 152,853 ſquare Feet. The Interiour is occupied by a Court, 300 Feet in Length by 90 in Breadth, ſurrounded with Buildings preſenting two Styles of Architecture, one that of the ancient Hôtel de Nevers, the other of a more modern Date. At the Extremity is a ſmall Garden, with a Statue of

Charles V. and a Fountain. The annual Sum allowed for the Support of the Imperial Library is about $80,000. Except on Sundays and Holidays, it is open daily from ten until three o'Clock. Every Book that can be found is brought to Applicants; and literary Men of known Reſpectability are permitted to take Books to their own Reſidences.

NOTE.—The above Facts are gathered from the Encyclopædia Britannica, with Additions and Changes.

VIEW OF THE FRANKFORT CITY LIBRARY.

ROYAL LIBRARY AT MUNICH.

600,000 Vols.

THIS Library, founded about 1660, by Albert V., Duke of Bavaria, is the moſt extenſive Collection in Germany, ranking in Size and Importance next to the Bibliothèque Nationale of Paris. It contains about 600,000 Volumes of printed Books, beſides upwards of 100,000 Volumes of Duplicates, which were recently on Sale, and 22,000 Volumes of Manuſcripts. From a Diſcourſe on the Origin and Increaſe of the Library, delivered in 1784, by Steigenberger, the Librarian (and tranſlated into Latin by Vitali), it appears that the Hebrew, Arabick, Syriack, Greek, and Latin Manuſcripts, which it contained, formed even then a precious Treaſure. Since that Period vaſt Additions have been made to all Departments of the Collection.

The Library, which formerly occupied a College that had belonged to the Jeſuits, is now removed to a magnificent new Building, in the Style of a mediæval Italian Palace, which was commenced in 1822 and completed in 1842. It is ſituated in Ludwig Street, and is eaſily recogniſed by four Statues of Ariſtotle, Thucydides, Hippocrates and Homer, placed upon the Steps before the principal Entrance.

From the ground Floor, where the general Archives of the Kingdom are preſerved, a magnificent Staircaſe aſcends between two marble Colonnades to the Library. The Entrance to the firſt Library-room is adorned with two Statues, one of the Founder of the Library, Duke Albert V., the other of Louis I., to whom the Building is due. This is the Hall from whence Books are loaned. After this is a large Hall, devoted to the Purpoſe of Reading and Study, and open to the Publick daily, from eight o'Clock until one, except on Fête-days and Holidays. A ſeparate Hall, aſſigned to the Reading of periodical Reviews, and of literary and ſcientifick Journals, is reſerved for Members of the Academy and for Profeſſors in the Univerſity. The loaning of Books is reſtricted to theſe Perſons juſt mentioned, to publick Officers of at leaſt the Rank of Counſellor, and Reſident in Munich, and to Perſons who obtain ſpecial Permiſſion from the Miniſter of the Interiour. Books are delivered between nine o'Clock and one. Viſitors at the

Library are not allowed to go to the Shelves where the Books are arranged, without being accompanied by one of the Librarians. For the Gratification of Strangers, however, a large Number of the rareſt and moſt curious Books and Manuſcripts are diſplayed in glaſs Caſes, where they can be conveniently ſeen.

The Library has no Collection of Coins, Medals, Statues, Paintings or Engravings, for there are extended Collections of all theſe Objects elſewhere in Munich. Printed Books and Manuſcripts are the two main Diviſions of its Property. The former of theſe are arranged upon the Shelves into twelve principal Claſſes, which are ſtill further ſubdivided into 180 Claſſes. The twelve main Diviſions are the following: 1. Encyclopædick Works, with 11 ſubordinate Claſſes; 2. Philology, with 18 ſubordinate; 3. Hiſtory, with 40 ſubordinate; 4. Mathematicks, with 8 ſubordinate; 5. Phyſicks, with 13 ſubordinate; 6. Anthropology, with 4 ſubordinate; 7. Philoſophy, with 3 ſubordinate; 8. Æſtheticks, with 15 ſubordinate; 9. Politicks, with 6 ſubordinate; 10. Medicine, with 8 ſubordinate; 11. Juriſprudence, with 16 ſubordinate; and 12. Theology, with 38 ſubordinate Diviſions.

The Manuſcripts include 580 in Greek; 268 in oriental Languages; 313 in Hebrew; 14,000 in Latin; 4,000 in German; near 600 in French; about 500 in Italian; with ſome in Swediſh, Slavick, Engliſh, and other Languages; in all, as has already been ſtated, not far from 22,000. Among theſe may be ſpecified a Greek New Teſtament, in uncial Letters, of the eighth Century; a Copy of the Latin Goſpels, of the ſame Age; a New Teſtament in gold and ſilver Letters, on purple Vellum, of the ninth Century; an Evangelarium and Miſſal, given by the Emperor Henry II. to the Cathedral of Bamberg, about the Year 1020, moſt richly decorated with Miniatures of the Byzantine School, the Binding ornamented with carved Ivory and precious Stones; a magnificent Copy of the Seven Penitential Pſalms, in four remarkable Folios, exhibiting extraordinary Proofs of the united Skill of the *Scribe*, the *Muſician*, the *Painter*, and the *Book Binder;* a Latin Manuſcript of the Goſpels, in large folio, bound in Ivory and Braſs with Borders of Portraits and precious Stones; the Romance of Sir Triſtrant, in Verſe, written in German, in the 13th Century, and containing fifteen Illuminations; an Office of the Virgin, minutely ornamented, bound in maſſive Silver waſhed with Gold, and conſtituting, according to Dibdin, a Book ſuperiour to anything of its Kind in Europe. The principal Gem, in the Department of illuminated Books of Devotion, preſerved in the Royal Library at Munich, is what is called Albert Durer's Prayer Book. This conſiſts of a Set of marginal Embelliſhments, by the Hand of Albert Durer, in a ſmall folio Volume, of which the Text, written in a very large lower-caſe Gothick Letter, forms the central Part. They are executed in Colours of biſtre, green, purple or pink, with great Beauty of Conception and Vigour of Touch, affording an additional Proof of the ſurpriſing Talents of the Author. The ancient Manuſcripts relative to the Art of Muſick, amount to a great Number, and are exceedingly curious.

Of printed Books of the fifteenth Century, the Library is ſtated to poſſeſs, beſides 50 block Books, ſome of them from the Haarlem Preſs, 3,500 without Date, and 6,000 with Dates prior to the Year 1500. Among theſe may be found the firſt printed Bible, the Work of Guttenberg and Fauſt, at Mayence, between 1450 and 1455; a Latin Pſaltery of the Year 1459, upon Vellum; Le Rational de Durand, of the ſame Year, printed by Fauſt and Schöffer; the firſt Books with Dates which were printed at Augſburg, Nuremberg and Munich; an Attempt at Stereotyping, made in 1553; the Works of Virgil, of which the entire Text is cut upon Copper, &c.

There is no printed Catalogue of the entire Library. The Catalogue in Uſe conſiſts of a Series of manuſcript Volumes, which are depoſited in Caſes, eaſy of Acceſs and convenient. Into this Catalogue new Books are entered immediately. The annual Sum allowed for the Increaſe of the Library is about $10,000. The daily Management is admirable. The Officers connected with the Library, are, a Chief Librarian, a Sub Librarian, 3 Aſſiſtants, 3 Secretaries, and a Clerk, beſides Attendants.

In addition to the Royal Library, Munich has

alſo its Univerſity Library, containing about 250,000 Volumes.

The following Account of the Sale by Auction of the Duplicates of the Royal Library at Munich, to which we have already referred, is taken from the London Athenæum. The Sale took place at Augſburg, on the 3d of May, laſt, continuing the whole Week.

The great Rarity of many of the Books for ſale attracted, as was to be expected, much Attention, and on Monday Morning, when the Sale began, there were aſſembled Bookſellers from all Quarters of Europe. From England, we noticed Meſſrs. Boone and Quaritch, of London, and Stark, of Hull; from Paris, Meſſrs. Vieweg and E. Troſs; and from Germany, there were all the principal antiquarian Bookſellers, as Aſher and Stargardt from Berlin, Baer from Frankfort, Weigel from Leipzig, and many others. We quote in Pruſſian Florins the Prices of ſome of the principal Works. A ſlightly defective Copy on Paper of the Mazarine Bible ſold for 2,336 Florins, bought for the Emperor of Ruſſia. Latin Bible, undated, but ſuppoſed 1465, by Berthold and Richel, 220 fl. A Suit of early Editions of the Bible, in German, followed: the firſt (ſee Ebert), 267 fl.; the ſecond, 360 fl.; the third, imperfect, 30 fl.; the fifth, 130 fl.; the ſixth, or firſt dated, Edition, Augſburg, 1477, 300 fl.; the ſeventh, 95 fl.; the ninth, 111 fl.; and the tenth, 115 fl. A ſecond Volume only of the firſt Low Saxon Bible brought 334 fl. Caſtilla Concionero, 1527, imperfect, 530 fl. Percival and Tyturel, 1477, 246 fl. Balbi Catholicon, by Fuſt, 1460, on Paper, 671 fl; and the ſame Edition, on Vellum, 4,410 fl. Thomaſ-à-Kempis, firſt Edition, undated, 100 fl. Ciceronis de Officiis, by Fuſt, 1465, a beautiful Copy on Vellum, 1,950 fl. Miſſale Ratiſbonienſe, 1518, on Vellum, imperfect, 710 fl. Dante a Landino, 1481, 235 fl. Block Books, Ars Memorandi, 725 fl. St. Johannis Evangeliſtæ, 1ſt Edition, 1,420 fl. The 3d Edition of the ſame curious Work, 1,255 fl. The rare Spaniſh Edition of 1529 of Marco Polo, 210 fl.

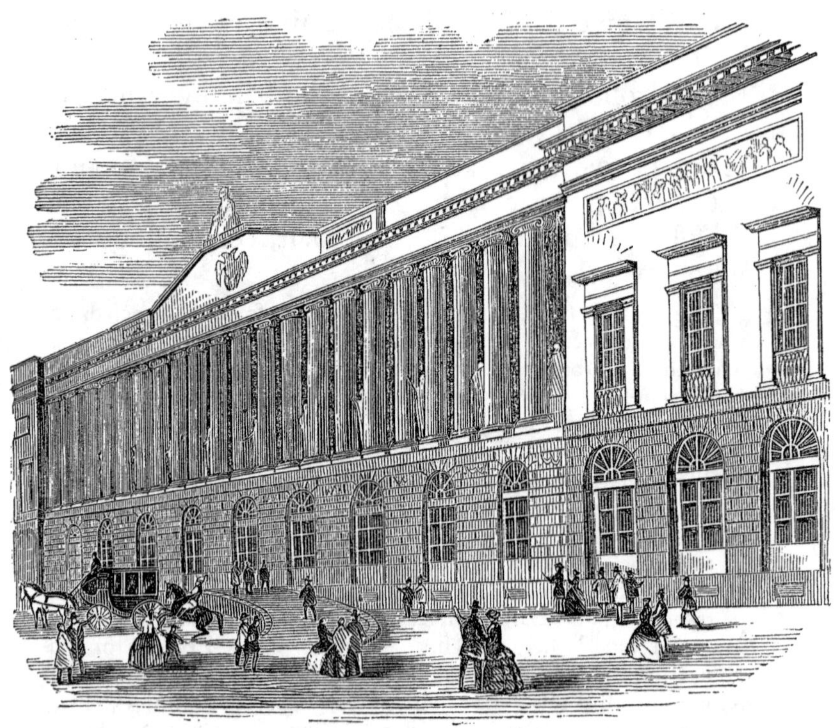

IMPERIAL LIBRARY AT ST. PETERSBURG.

525,000 Vols.

IN the Centre of the modern Capital of Ruſſia, upon one of the moſt brilliant Streets in the World, the Nevſky Perſpective, ſtands a large and beautiful Edifice, erected in the later Style of Roman Architecture, and devoted to the immenſe Collections of the Imperial Publick Library. Although this Inſtitution, like other large Libraries, is a Monument of the Development of human Intellect in all its various Phrases, yet the Officers delight to remember at the same Time that it is a remarkable Trophy of military Glory, owing the principal and most precious Part of its Treasures to the Success of Russian Arms. The Names of Suwarrow and Paskewitch are inseparably attached to the Foundation and Increase of this vast Institution, while to Field-Marshal Prince Volkhonsky, recently Minister of the Imperial Household, was reserved the Work of its definite Organization.

The History of this Collection of Books, originally located in Warsaw, is one of great Interest. The Library was commenced by Polish Counts, of the Zaluski Family, in Cracow, but in 1746 it was removed to Warsaw, where in 1747 it was opened to the Publick and formally inaugurated in Presence of the King of Poland and other high Authorities. At this Time it is said to have numbered three hundred thousand Volumes, of which fifty-two thousand were Duplicates. In 1761, one of the Counts by whose pecuniary Advances it was undoubtedly sustained, becoming embarrassed in his Affairs, transferred the Ownership to the College of the Jesuits then established in Warsaw. In 1794 occurred the Fall of Poland, and the Publick Library with the Archives of the Crown were carried off to St. Petersburg. This Transportation being made by Land, and along Roads which the late Season of the Year rendered almost impracticable, many Boxes of Books suffered from the Inclemency of the

Weather, others were broken or damaged, and the Works which they contained ſpoiled, miſplaced or ſeparated. The Collection was conveyed to the Imperial Cabinet in two Convoys, and after the Inventory had been completed on the 23d February, 1796, it was found that it ſtill amounted to 262,640 Volumes and 24,573 Prints. This Library compriſed in general all the beſt Works, up to the Middle of the ſeventeenth Century, in the Sciences, the Arts, and the Belles-Lettres. The theological, and, after it, the hiſtorical and literary Branches, were the moſt conſiderable. The former alone comprehended above 80,000 Volumes. It was alſo rich in Topography, eſpecially in the Hiſtories of Towns; and the literary Branch included a precious Collection of claſſical Books and Works on Bibliography; but the Departments of Philoſophy, Mathematicks, Phyſicks, Travels and Antiquities were very incomplete. Such was the Foundation of the Imperial Library at St. Peterſburg.

An Edifice, ordered by Catharine, having been completed in 1801, the Warſaw Library, ſtill known at that Time as the Zaluſki Collection, was removed to its preſent Accommodations. The Coſt of the Building, of which our Engraving is a good Repreſentation, was not far from 60,000 Roubles aſſignat. The Direction of the Library was at this Time confided to Count Stroganoff, at whoſe Death in 1811, it was aſſigned to the Miniſter of Publick Inſtruction. Oloueen, however, was really in charge of the Inſtitution from 1812 to 1843, and from that Time to 1849 Bourtourlin held the ſame Poſition. In October of the latter Year, the preſent chief Director was appointed, Baron Korf, a Member of the Council of the Empire, and a Secretary of State. About the ſame Time the Emperor began to take a more perſonal Cognizance of the Affairs of the Library, and accordingly in February, 1850, the Juriſdiction was tranſferred from the Miniſter of Publick Inſtruction to that of the Imperial Houſehold. In the ſame Month, the Regulations now in Force concerning the Uſe and Management of the Library, were approved and publiſhed. In addition to the eminent Names already mentioned, Count Uwaroff, afterwards Preſident of the Imperial Academy of Sciences, and the well known Writers, Kriloff, Batowſhkoff, and Gnaideech, have been at different Times in charge of Portions of the Library.

One of the moſt remarkable Departments in this noble Collection of Books, is that of the oriental Manuſcripts, which, both in Extent and Value, is perhaps unſurpaſſed. It owes its Origin to the celebrated Zaluſki Library, and many Works ſtill retain the Annotations of Count John Zaluſki. But a ſtill more important Collection of oriental Writings was received ſoon after the Eſtabliſhment of the Library at St. Peterſburg. It was that of Dubroffki, who had improved a Reſidence of twenty Years in different Capitals of Europe, as a Member of the Ruſſian Diplomatick Service, to collect a

Mafs of Documents and Books, in all Languages and of every Age. The Diforganization of fome of the moft valuable Libraries in France, near the Commencement of the prefent Century, and particularly the Deftruction of the Baftile, and of the Abbey St. Germain, and other Monafteries, furnifhed him with rare Opportunities for the Enlargement of a Colleftion which was otherwife very rich. On his Return to Ruffia, the Treafures he had accumulated were purchafed by the Emperor Alexander, and placed in the Publick Library. Between 1828 and 1830 five other important Acceffions were made. The firft was the Library of Ardebil, which had long enjoyed great Renown in Perfia, not fo much for its Size as its Value. It was brought to St. Peterfburg in 1828, and placed by Command of the Emperor, as a Trophy of War, in the Imperial Library. There were in all 166 rare Volumes, comprifing, exclufive of Duplicates, 96 different Works. Another Prize gained by the Ruffian Victories over the Crefcent, was brought to St. Peterfburg in 1829. It was a Collection of one hundred and forty-eight Volumes, chiefly in Arabick and Turkifh, which were taken by Prince Pafkevitch, at the Mofque Ahmed, in Akhaltfik. In the fame Year, forty-two other Works, a Part captured from the Turks, and a Part purchafed from them by their Conqueror, were likewife incorporated in the Imperial Library. The fourth of the Collections to which Allufion has been made, was prefented to the Emperor, in

1829, by the Perſian Shah, Feth Ali. It included only eighteen Manuſcripts, but theſe were in the moſt elaborate Style of the caligraphick Art, and were otherwiſe of high Value. The fifth Collection, numbering ſixty-ſix Volumes, was taken at the Arſenal of Eſkiſerai, in Adrianople, and received in St. Peterſburg in 1830.

Thus it will be ſeen that in two Years alone, the Wars of Ruſſia in the Eaſt enriched the publick Library of its Capital with four hundred and twenty Manuſcripts of remarkable Value. Among other Means of Increaſe, the Miſſion of the Greek Church in Pekin has done its full Share, by contributing for many Years ſuch Works in the Chineſe and Tartar Languages, as it has been able to procure. In addition, the duplicate Volumes from the Library of the Academy of Sciences in St. Peterſburg, and from the Hermitage, or Imperial Muſeum, have been tranſferred to the Publick Library. In the Year 1831, nearly 8,000 Volumes taken at Poulavy from the Library of the Princes Tchartoriſki, and the large Number of 150,000 Volumes taken at Warſaw, when the Ruſſians re-eſtabliſhed their Authority in Poland, were likewiſe brought to St. Peterſburg, as new Trophies of military Power. Since then, by Donation and Purchaſe, the Library has continued to advance, till now in point of Numbers, at leaſt, it ranks among the firſt in Europe.

The whole Collection of Books is now arranged in nineteen Departments, namely: 1. Manuſcripts;

2. Works printed in the Ruſſian Empire; 3. Bibliography and literary Hiſtory; 4. Polygraphy; 5. Philology and ancient Claſſicks; 6. Oriental Writers; 7. Hiſtory and its Auxiliaries; 8. Theology; 9. Juriſprudence; 10. Philoſophy; 11. Belles-Lettres; 12. Fine Arts; 13. Natural Sciences; 14. Medicine; 15. Mathematicks; 16. Technology and Mechanicks; 17. Incunabula; 18. Foreign Works relating to Ruſſia; 19. Engravings.

Among the many admirable Things which have been undertaken by the preſent learned Director-in-Chief, Baron Korf, is the Collection of all printed Works which have ever appeared in Ruſſia, or pertaining to Ruſſia. His Efforts have thus far been highly ſucceſſful, and through active Agents, he is conſtantly augmenting this national Department. Works of great Age and Rarity, as well as others more modern, which are prohibited by the Cenſor from general Circulation, have been thus quietly collected to the Number of many thouſands.

There is no complete printed Catalogue of the Books, although an excellent one in Manuſcript is found in the Library. There is alſo a printed Account by Adelung, of the Collection of Dubroſſki. In 1852 there was publiſhed in French, an admirable Catalogue raiſonée of the Oriental Manuſcripts and Xylographs, which forms a royal octavo Volume of more than 700 Pages. It muſt be remembered that the Study of Oriental Languages is conſidered of great Importance in Ruſſia, on account of the immenſe Extent of its eaſtern Frontier, and the

Variety of Nations with which it is there brought in contact. The Government does all in its Power to encourage this Branch of Study, and perhaps there is no City in Europe, which in Books and Instructors, furnishes so good Opportunities for the Prosecution of oriental Researches, so far, at least, as Language is concerned. The Catalogue just alluded to is understood to be principally indebted to the Labours of M. Dorn, an oriental Scholar, still attached to the Corps of Librarians. Copies of it have been sent, in America, to the Library of the American Academy of Arts and Sciences in Boston, the Smithsonian Institution in Washington, and the American Oriental Society in New Haven.

In 1849 the Library amounted to 451,532 printed Volumes, and 20,689 Volumes of Manuscripts. Of late Years, the official Reports have been annually published in the *St. Petersburger Zeitung*, and reprinted in the *Serapeum*. From these Returns the average yearly Accessions from all Sources, from 1849 to 1857, are found to have been about 8,000 Volumes. The present Total is 525,000 Volumes of printed Books; about 22,000 Volumes of Manuscripts in 41 Languages; 30,000 Autographs in 350 different Collections; 40,000 Engravings, and 60,000 Pamphlets. From an official Document lately published at St. Petersburg, it appears that whilst the Number of Readers in the Library was only 7,720, it rose to 17,897 in 1853, to 27,866 in 1856, and to 31,151 in 1857.

Note.—The foregoing Account has been compiled mainly from Norton's Literary Gazette, with Additions, and slight Alterations.

ROYAL LIBRARY AT BERLIN.

ROYAL LIBRARY AT BERLIN.

500,000 Vols.

THE Royal Library at Berlin was founded in the Year 1661. It occupies a large Edifice in the Opera Platz, erected for its Use in 1780, by the distinguished Frederick the second. It is difficult, as indeed it is in all Cases, to state the precise Number of Volumes which it contains, but there are probably not less than 500,000 printed Books, besides somewhat more than 10,000 Manuscripts. The Collection includes Works upon almost all the Sciences, and in nearly all the Languages, but is perhaps most complete in the Sciences. Its oriental Section is very rich, and comprises the entire Series of Sanscrit Manuscripts which had been formed by Sir R. Chambers, Chief Justice of Bengal. The manuscript Department includes also several Manuscripts of Veyssière de Lacroze, the celebrated Author of the Lexicon Ægyptiaco-Latinum. Liberal Appropriations have been made by the Government, during the last few Years, for the Support of this Library; and, accordingly, about nine thousand Volumes have of late Years been annually added to its Numbers. The annual Amount allowed for the Purchase of Books, is about 10,000 Thalers, and the Sum assigned for the other Expenses of the Institution is not far from 15,000 Thalers. The Building is wanting in architectural Beauty, owing its Shape, it is said, to a Whim of the King, who desired the Architect to take a Chest of Drawers for his Model.

The Library is open for Consultation on week Days, from nine o'Clock until four, and on Sundays, from nine o'Clock until one. Admission is easily obtained to use in the Library such Works as it possesses, and in addition, Books are loaned to Persons connected with the University and with the Government, and, under certain Restrictions, to other Individuals who are known to the Library Officers. It is estimated that the Number of Volumes thus loaned from the Library, is between thirty and forty thousand annually. Dr. Pertz continues to be the head Librarian.

Like other large European Institutions, this Library possesses many rare Incunabula and curious Manuscripts, as well as Books, which are Interesting from the Associations therewith connected. Among these may be mentioned, Luther's Hebrew Bible, the Copy from which he made his Translation, with marginal Notes in his own Hand; the Manuscript of Luther's Translation of the Psalms, with his Corrections in red Ink; the Bible and Prayer Book which Charles I. carried to the Scaffold, and gave before his Death to Bishop Juxon; Guttenberg's Bible, Date 1450-55, on Parchment, being the first Book on which moveable Type was used; a Consular Diptych of Ivory, with Reliefs, Date 416, one of the earliest known; the Codex Wittekindii, a Manuscript of the Gospels of the 9th or 10th Century, given, it is said, by Charlemagne to Wittekind; ſeveral Ivories, or Diptychs of the earlieſt Chriſtian Times, and of Roman Work; an Album, with ſix beautiful miniature Portraits, by Luke Cranach; ſeveral block Books; the Rationale of Durand, on Vellum; the Aldine Petrarch, &c. The Collection of Hiſtorical Portraits is very large, amounting even in 1851, to nearly 30,000.

As a *working Library*, this is generally regarded as one of the beſt, if not the beſt, in the World; certainly no large Library upon the Continent is more efficiently managed. It has no printed Catalogue, but in Place thereof there are two excellent ones in Manuſcript, both of which may be freely conſulted. One of theſe is alphabetical, extending through 650 Volumes; the other is claſſified, and extends through 250 Volumes. A new claſſified Catalogue has been for ſome Time preparing, and is now nearly ready for the Preſs. Two printed Catalogues of the Manuſcripts have recently been publiſhed, in quarto Volumes, with Illuſtrations.

THE BRITISH MUSEUM.

LIBRARY OF THE BRITISH MUSEUM.

575,000 Vols.

THE Britifh Mufeum was founded by Sir Hans Sloane, of Chelfea, an eminent Phyfician, Naturalift and Benefactor of Learning, who, dying in 1753, bequeathed to the Nation his Collection of Medals and Coins, ancient and modern Antiquities, Seals, Cameos, Drawings and Pictures, and his Library, confifting of 50,000 Volumes of Books and Manufcripts, on Condition of the Payment of £20,000 to his Heirs. The Britifh Parliament accepted this Condition, by an Act paffed in the Month of June, 1753, and by the fame Act directed that the Cottonian Library, a Collection of valuable hiftorical Manufcripts which had been made by Sir Robert Cotton, during the Reign of Elizabeth and James I., and which had been acquired by Government in the Reign of Queen Anne, fhould be added to the Sloane Collection, together with a Library of about 2,000 printed Volumes, called Major Arthur Edwards's Library, which had exifted as an Appendage to the Cottonian Library fince 1738, the Year in which it had been bequeathed to the Truftees by its Proprietor. Thus, a confiderable Addition was made to the book Department of the Sloane Collection. But this Department was ordered to be ftill further increafed by the Purchafe for £10,000, of the Harleian Library of Manufcripts, a fplendid Collection of about 7,600 Volumes of

Rolls, Charters, and other hiſtorical Documents, which had been accumulated by Robert Harley, Earl of Oxford, and his Son and Succeſſor, Edward Harley.

In 1754, Montague Houſe, one of the largeſt Manſions in the Metropolis, was appropriated for the Reception of theſe Collections, which have ſince gradually been increaſed by the Munificence of ſucceſſive Parliaments, and by Gifts, Bequeſts, and Copy-right, conſtituting at the preſent Day the great national Inſtitution of which the Engliſh Nation is ſo juſtly proud, unrivalled in the Variety, Extent and Uſefulneſs of its Treaſures, by any ſimilar Inſtitution in the World.

From the rapid Increaſe of the various Collections, and the Inſecurity of the old Montague Houſe, a new and more commodious Structure for the Britiſh Muſeum became neceſſary. Accordingly, in 1823, the preſent noble Pile of Buildings, of which our Engraving preſents the principal Front, deſigned by Sir Robert Smirke, was commenced, and in the Summer of 1850 completed, at a Coſt amounting to nearly £700,000. It is not far from the Centre of London, a little north of Oxford Street, one of the great Arteries of the City. It has Montague Place on the North, Montague Street on the Eaſt, Great Ruſſell Street on the South, and Charlotte Street and Bedford Square on the Weſt. Its Situation is thus admirable for Safety, and for Convenience of Reſort from all Parts of London.

The different Departments of the Britiſh Muſeum

are ſeven in Number, namely: Manuſcripts, printed Books, Antiquities, Prints and Drawings, Mineralogy and Geology, Zoology, and Botany. To theſe ſhould be added the new Reading-room juſt completed. All of theſe Departments are under ſeparate Keepers; to whom and their Aſſiſtant-keepers and their Aſſiſtants, Attendants and ſubordinate Officers, in ſuch Strength as the Duties of each Department may require, the Buſineſs of the Muſeum is entruſted as regards the Care and Preſervation of the Collections, and the Acceſs of the Publick for the Purpoſes of Inſpection and Study. Some Idea of the Magnitude of the Muſeum, and of its vaſt Reſources, may be formed by conſidering that the whole Expenditure for Purchaſes, and for the Maintenance of the Inſtitution ſince 1755, independently of the Amount expended on the Buildings ſince 1823, exceeds the Sum of £1,500,000, or nearly eight Millions of Dollars. The annual Receipts of the Inſtitution, from parliamentary Grants and the Intereſt of private Bequeſts, have of late Years been upwards of £50,000. The Receipts for the Year 1847, as given by Mr. R. W. Pearſon in the Minutes of Evidence before the Commiſſioners appointed to examine into the Conſtitution and Management of the Muſeum, amounted to £53,999 13s. 6d. independently of ſpecial Grants. Of this Amount £21,041, 10s. 3d., or upwards of one hundred thouſand Dollars, was expended for Salaries. The total Expenditure for the Year ending

March 31, 1858, as ſtated in Bent's Literary Advertiſer, amounted to £85,992, 2s. 9d.

Our further Account of the Britiſh Muſeum muſt be confined to the Library and Manuſcripts. In 1837, when Mr. Panizzi became Keeper of the printed Books, the Library contained about 235,000 Volumes. In December, 1849, it was found by actual Count to number 435,000 Volumes. In May, 1851, it contained 460,000 Volumes. At preſent the Library contains 575,000 Volumes of printed Books and 40,000 Volumes of Manuſcripts, excluſive of more than 20,000 original Rolls, Charters and Deeds. It has alſo a noble Collection of Pamphlets, about 200,000 in Number, including the Collections of George Thomaſon, who lived in the Time of the Commonwealth, a French Collection of 60,000, publiſhed during the French Revolution and the one hundred Days, &c. &c. The following chronological Summary of the more important Donations and Purchaſes ſince 1753, compiled from Sims's Hand-book to the Library, will ſerve to illuſtrate its Progreſs and preſent Condition:

1759. A Collection of Hebrew Books, chiefly ancient Editions of valuable Works on *Jewiſh Hiſtory*, *Theology* and *Juriſprudence*. 180 Volumes. *Preſented* by Solomon Da *Coſta*. 1762. A unique Collection of Tracts relating to Charles I. and the Commonwealth. 30,000 Articles. *Preſented* by George III. 1766. A Collection rich in Biography. Bequeathed by Rev. Dr. Birch. 1768. A fine Collection of Bibles. Bequeathed by Arthur *Onſlow*. 1780. A Collection of *Engliſh* Plays, formed by Mr. Garrick. *Purchaſed*. 1786. A fine Collection of *claſſical* Authors. 900 Volumes. Bequeathed by Mr.

Tyrwhitt. 1790. A Collection of biographical Works. 400 Volumes. Presented by S. W. Musgrave. 1799. A splendid Collection, including many rare and valuable Editions of Classicks as well as Italian Authors, amounting to 4500 Volumes. Bequeathed by Rev. C. M. Cracherode. 1799. A further Collection of biographical Works, amounting to about 1500 Volumes. Bequeathed by Sir W. Musgrave. 1813. A highly valuable Collection of law Books. Purchased from Francis Hargrave, Esq. 1815. A fine Collection of Books on Musick, forming the Collection of Dr. Burney, Author of the History of Musick. Purchased. 1815. A Collection of Books, comprising 20,000 Volumes, mostly upon Science, belonging to Baron de Moll. Purchased at Munich. 1818. A fine Collection of printed Books, forming the Library of Dr. Burney, the most remarkable of which were Greek Classicks, a Series of Newspapers, in about 700 Volumes, and Materials for a History of the Stage. The whole was valued at about 9,000 Guineas. Purchased by a special parliamentary Grant. 1818. A fine Collection, consisting of 4,391 Articles concerning the Literature of Italy, forming the Ginguené Collection. Purchased. 1820. A splendid Library, particularly Rich in scientifick Journals, Transactions of Societies, and Books on Natural History. Consisting of about 16,000 Volumes. Bequeathed by Sir Joseph Banks. 1823. The magnificent Library, amounting to about 80,000 Volumes, formed by King George III. This Monarch began to collect a Library in 1762, and laid the Foundation for it by the Purchase of a Library of a very eminent Character at Venice, belonging to Consul Smith, for £10,000. In 1768, Mr. (afterwards Sir Frederick) Barnard, the Librarian, was dispatched to the Continent by his Majesty; and as the Jesuits' Houses were then being suppressed, and their Libraries sold throughout Europe, he was enabled to purchase, upon the most advantageous Terms, a great Number of valuable Books, including some very remarkable Rarities, in France, in Italy, and in Germany. The entire Collection was formed and arranged under the judicious Direction of Mr. Barnard, assisted by Mr. George Nichol, Bookseller to his Majesty for upwards of half a Century. Its entire Cost was about £130,000. It contains Selections of the rarest Kind, especially of scarce Books which appeared in the first Ages of the Art of Printing; in particular it boasts of nearly forty Volumes printed by Caxton, a larger Number than can be found in any other Library, with the Exception of Earl Spencer's. It is alſo rich in early Editions of the Claſſicks, in Engliſh Hiſtory, and in Italian, French and Spaniſh Literature; and there is likewiſe a very extenſive Collection of Geography and Topography, and of the Tranſactions of learned Academies. Preſented to the Nation by his Majeſty George IV. 1825. A remarkable Collection of Works relating to the Topography, and to the local as well as general Hiſtory of Italy. Preſented by Sir Richard Colt Hoare. 1847. A Collection of Chineſe Books of the late Robert Morriſon, Eſq., in 11,500 Volumes. Preſented by the Secretary of State for the Foreign Department. 1847. The Library of the Right Honourable Thomas Grenville, bequeathed in 1846, and removed to the Muſeum in February, 1847. It conſiſts of 20,240 Volumes, and coſt upwards of £54,000. The Books are arranged in a ſeparate Apartment; and for Rarity, judicious Selection, and Beauty of Condition, and for the Number of Copies of Books on large Paper, it is equal to any Collection of the ſame Extent that could be named. Among the many choice Treaſures, may be mentioned the Mentz Latin Bible, uſually known as the Mazarine Bible, by Guttenberg, 2 Volumes on Vellum, printed about the Year 1455; Livy, by Sweynheim and Pannartz, printed in 1469, the unique Copy of the firſt Edition, on Vellum (purchaſed in 1815 for 860 Guineas); the firſt Edition of Ovid, by Azzoguidi; a Copy of the Aldine Virgil of 1505; a ſplendid Set of De Bry's Voyages; an uncut Copy of Purchas's Pilgrims; a firſt Shakſpeare, 1623, one of the fineſt known; and a remarkable Series of the early Editions of Orlando Furioſo. 1848. The Collection of Hebrew Literature formed by Dr. Michael, of Hamburg, conſiſting of 4420 Volumes of Bibles, Commentaries, ſcientifick Works, and Documents illuſtrative of the Hiſtory of the Jews. Purchaſed. The moſt recent Addition has been, a vaſt and ſyſtematick Selection of Books in every Department of Literature, and in all Languages, choſen with ſpecial Reference to the previous Deficiencies of the Library, as they were aſcertained on a careful Survey in 1843, and deſcribed in Mr. Panizzi's elaborate Report of January 1, 1845.

The Department of Manuſcripts in the Britiſh Muſeum is not leſs valuable and important than that of the printed Books. It embraces ſeveral diſtinct Collections, as follows: (1.) The

Royal Collection, presented to the Nation by George II., in 1757. It contains 1950 Volumes. Among these precious Manuscripts is the Codex Alexandrinus, a Present from Cyril, Patriarch of Constantinople, to King Charles I. It is in four quarto Volumes, written upon fine Vellum, in uncial Characters, probably between the fourth and sixth Centuries, and is believed to be the most ancient Manuscript of the Greek Bible now extant. (2.) The Cottonian Collection, 900 Volumes, purchased in 1700, and added to the British Museum in 1753. It is especially rich in historical Documents, from the Time of the Saxons to that of James I. (3.) The Harleian Collection, 7,639 Volumes, purchased in 1753, for £10,000. (4.) The Sloane Collection, 4,100 Volumes, obtained in 1753. This comprises the chief of Kaempfer's Manuscripts, and also 30 Volumes of Dr. Sloane's Correspondence, Drawings of Animals, &c. (5.) The Lansdowne Collection, 1245 Volumes, acquired in 1807. (6.) The Hargrave Collection, 499 Volumes, purchased in 1813, for £8,000. (7.) The Burney Collection, 524 Volumes, purchased in 1817. (8.) The King's Collection, 438 Volumes, acquired in 1823. (9.) The Egerton Collection, 1613 Volumes, acquired in 1829. (10.) The Arundel Collection, 550 Volumes, acquired in 1831; valued at £3,560. (11.) The additional Manuscripts, as they are called. These consist of smaller Collections, acquired by Purchase or Gift, and are constantly increasing. Among the more important Additions of the last few Years, may be noticed the splendid Bible, in 2 Volumes, of Charlemagne; the celebrated Bedford Missal, executed for John, Duke of Bedford, Regent of France under Henry VI.; the Correspondence and other Papers relating to the Captivity of Napoleon and St. Helena; and a remarkable Series of Papers of the Florentine Family of Gualterio, extending to about 400 Volumes, and rich in Materials for Italian History during the last Century.

The following Account, abridged from Norton's Literary Register of 1854, will enable one to comprehend at a Glance the general Character and Arrangements of the library and manuscript Departments of the British Museum:

The Library opens out of the Hall on the right

Hand or eaſt Side. On entering, we find ourſelves in a handſome Room, 73 Feet long by 33 Feet wide, devoted to the ſplendid Collection of the Right Hon. Thomas Grenville. It conſiſts chiefly of rare Editions and Copies of the Claſſicks, many of them unique, all beautifully bound, and in the fineſt Condition. To ſeveral of the Books, Notes, in Mr. Grenville's Hand-writing, are attached; ſhowing at once the great Value of the Bequeſt, and his own extenſive Learning and unwearying Energy and Liberality in the Acquirement of his bibliographical Treaſures. On the right-hand Side of the Room is a Buſt of Mr. Grenville, preſented by Sir David Dundas; and a Table where, as in the Hall, ſhort Guide-books to the Library may be purchaſed for two Pence. On the left, in handſomely carved glazed Caſes, are exhibited two Copies of the celebrated Mazarine Bible, the firſt Book, as well as the firſt Bible ever printed with moveable Types, the one on Vellum, belonging to the Grenville Collection, and having been purchaſed for little ſhort of £500; the firſt Pſalter, being the firſt Book with a Date and the earlieſt Example of Printing in Colours, and various other Rarities.

From the Grenville Room we enter the manuſcript Department, a large and heavy-looking Room, whoſe dingy Walls and blackened Ceiling—Strangers to Whitewaſh for three-and-twenty Years—give it a Sort of ſolemn, grim, literary Look, that conſiderably enhances the Effect of the beautiful and intereſting Relicks diſplayed in its Caſes. On either Side of the Door are Cafes containing Autographs of great and diftinguifhed Men. In one Divifion may be feen original Letters of all the great Reformers; in another, thofe of Englifh Kings; in a third, thofe of Newton, Locke, Bacon, Pope, &c. In one, the bold, dafhing Signature of Rupert; in another the ftubborn Hand of Oliver Cromwell. One Cafe is devoted to Charters of moft of the early Englifh Sovereigns (including one of William the Conqueror), another to the Letters of foreign Princes—Napoleon, Peter the Great, Louis XIV., and many more; and ftill another is filled with various eaftern Manufcripts, chiefly intended to illuftrate the Variety of Materials ufed for writing, viz.: Bark, Leaves, Wood, Gold, Silver, &c., and containing fome Perfian and Chinefe Paintings of extraordinary Finifh and Brightnefs. To the left of this, againft the Wall, is an upright Cafe containing an ancient Latin Manufcript of the Bible, fuppofed to have been the Property of Charlemagne; while immediately oppofite are two Rolls of the Hebrew Scripture in a fimilar Cafe. In two Table-cafes, right and left of the Door, leading out of the Room, which we now approach, are feveral Manufcripts of almoft pricelefs Value. The moft remarkable, though far from the moft beautiful of thefe, is the celebrated Codex Alexandrinus, the moft ancient Copy of the Greek Bible known to exift. Befide it is the no lefs famous Durham Book, being a Copy of the Scriptures in Latin, with a Commentary in Anglo-Saxon, illuminated in a moft wonderfully elaborate and beautiful Style, and ſuppoſed to have been written between the Years 690 and 720. But the fineſt of all theſe Treaſures is in the right-hand Table-caſe. It is a ſplendid Manuſcript of Valerius Maximus, illuminated in a Style of ſurpaſſing Beauty and Richneſs, and exciting Aſtoniſhment, no leſs by the vivid Colouring of the Scenes than by the extreme Accuracy and Finiſh of the Drawing. We need ſcarcely add, that its Value is ineſtimable. In the next Compartment are two or three of the exquiſitely illuminated Miſſals, "by monkyſſhe Labourre wroughte."

Paſſing between two lofty oak Doors, beautifully inlaid with Bronze, we next enter the Royal or King's Library. This magnificent Gallery is of conſiderable, perhaps diſproportionate Length, meaſuring from Door to Door no leſs than 300 Feet, and occupying the remaining Portion of the eaſt Wing. It is 41 Feet in Width, except in the middle Compartment, where it increaſes to 58 Feet, and is 30 Feet in Height—the uniform Elevation of the whole Suit of Rooms. The Floor is of poliſhed Oak, handſomely inlaid; and the Ceiling, eſpecially in the Centre, richly decorated. All the Preſſes on the ground Floor are protected by trellis Doors of braſs Wire, which, with the bright braſs Railing of the Galleries, add very much to the Appearance of this ſplendid Library. In each Receſs cauſed by the additional Width of the Centre are two Corinthian Columns of poliſhed Granite, valued at £1,000 each; the Shafts being ſingle Blocks nearly 20 Feet high, and 2 Feet 6 Inches in Diameter. This Room contains the Library of King George III., preſented by George IV. to the Britiſh Nation. In Table-caſes on both Sides of the Centre are ſhown various Objects of typographical and bibliographical Intereſt. On one Side is a Compartment devoted to early Hebrew Books; on the other, a ſimilar Compartment filled with Aldine Claſſicks on Vellum, and numerous other Treaſures. A Catalogue of this noble Collection, including the Maps and Charts, prepared by the Librarian, Sir F. A. Barnard, was publiſhed in 1820-29, in 6 Volumes imperial folio. Along the whole Length of the King's Library, on its eaſtern Side, but riſing no higher than the Window-ſills, is a ſupplementary Gallery, lately erected; called very appropriately the Long Room. It is devoted to the recent and daily augmenting Acceſſions to the General Library.

From the King's Library we paſs into a Veſtibule whence a Staircaſe leads up to the Natural Hiſtory Department, and a Door, which faces us, into the eaſtern or firſt Reading-room. Thither the Publick are prevented from intruding by a Barrier. Turning ſharp to the left, we enter the firſt Room of the General Library. This is in Part occupied by the Collection bequeathed by Sir Joſeph Banks. It is a Room of moderate Size, but giving, like the ſucceeding Rooms, with one Exception, an Impreſſion of unneceſſary Darkneſs as well as Loſs of Space above the gallery Book-caſes.

The next Room in which we find ourfelves, and which we enter from the Bankfian Room, at the foutheaft Corner, is called the Great or Large Room—a fufficiently obvious Appellation. It is a Saloon of coloffal Dimenfions, though much broken up by the Receffes on each Side, the Projections forming which are terminated by fquare Pillars fupporting the Roof. It meafures 80 Feet long and 90 Feet wide, and occupies the whole Depth of the north Front, fo that it is lighted with Windows on both Sides. All along the Barriers are placed glafs Cafes, containing bibliographical Rarities of greater or lefs Value. Here are to be feen Coverdale's Bible, the firft complete Edition of the Scriptures in Englifh; The Game and Play of the Cheffe, the firft Book printed in England, having been iffued from Caxton's Prefs in 1474; the firft Edition of Chaucer's Book of the Tales of Canterburye, of which only two perfect Copies are known; and many other Objects of the greateft Intereft.

At the fouthweft Corner of the Large Room, and on our left as we pafs out, is a Door leading to the Cracherode Room, which is oppofite to, and of the fame Dimenfions as the Bankfian Room above noticed. It contains principally the Library bequeathed by the Rev. Dr. Cracherode, very rich in Claffícks; and the Collection called the King's Pamphlets, a Mafs of Tracts and curious Works, printed for the moft Part about the Middle of the 17th Century, and chiefly relating to the Affairs of the Nation at that Period, presented by George II.

We next pass through two Rooms, called respectively the First and Second Supplementary Rooms, in which there are chiefly to be noticed four Cases, containing Books with the Autographs of illustrious Men, viz: Shakespeare, Ben Jonson, Bacon, Luther, Voltaire, &c., and three others filled with Specimens of ancient Binding, some of them very elaborate. A Door from the south Side of the Second Supplementary Room leads into the Egyptian Antiquity Gallery, or west Wing of the Building.

Last of all we come to the arched Room, the Termination of the Suit of Rooms forming the Library and the north Front of the Museum. The double Galleries of this handsome Apartment produce an Impression of additional Height, while their pierced iron Floors and the arching of the Piers of the Recesses give the Room an Appearance of Lightness and Elegance which show it in favourable Contrast with the others.

The chief Officers of the library and manuscript Department of the British Museum consist, *first*, of a principal Librarian or Warden, who exercises a general Superintendence over the whole Establishment, sees that the Duties of the other Officers are severally performed, grants temporary Admission to the Publick, and carries into effect the Orders of the Trustees. This Post, which was occupied for more than fifty Years by Sir Henry

Ellis, has been recently filled by Antonio Panizzi; *ſecondly*, a Keeper of the printed Books, J. Winter Jones; *thirdly*, a Keeper of the Manuſcripts, Sir Frederick Madden.

New Reading Room.—This vaſt Structure, which has been completed within the paſt three Years, at a Coſt of £150,000, occupies an Area of 48,000 ſquare Feet, its Site being the internal Quadrangle of the Muſeum. It was commenced in 1854, and firſt opened to the Publick on the 18th of May, 1857. The Building does not occupy the whole Quadrangle, there being a clear Interval of from 27 to 30 Feet all round, to give Light and Air to the ſurrounding Buildings. The Reading Room is circular, with a Dome 140 Feet in Diameter and 106 Feet high. The Building is conſtructed principally of Iron, with brick Arches between the main Ribs, ſupported by 20 iron Piers. It contains ample and comfortable Accommodations for 300 Readers, each Perſon having alloted to him a Space of 4 Feet 3 Inches long, with Deſks, folding Shelves for ſpare Books, &c. The Caſes for Books are formed of galvanized Iron, the Plates or Shelves being covered with Leather to prevent injury to the Bindings. The Building contains 3 Miles of Book-caſes, 8 Feet high, thus forming 25 Miles of Shelving, ſpaced for the average octavo Size. The Books in the Muſeum occupy already upwards of 40 Miles of Shelving. The Decorations throughout are exceedingly elegant, light Colours and the pureſt Gilding having been preferred.

The main Entrance into the New Reading Room is direct from the great Hall, and there are ſecondary Entrances for the Officers from the King's Library, and the great Northern Library Rooms, through which all Books are conveyed to the Centre of the Reading Room, whence they are diſtributed.

The Amalgamation of the ſeveral Catalogues of the printed Books, which are drawn up on various Plans, into one manuſcript Catalogue on a uniform Plan, is proceeding rapidly. One third of the Alphabet, to the Letter I, has already been completed, compriſing 623 folio Volumes. The whole will form when finiſhed, a manuſcript Catalogue of about 2000 folio Volumes. The Preparation of this Herculean Work is under the reſponſible Superintendence of Mr. J. Winter Jones, the Succeſſor of Mr. Panizzi in the Keeperſhip of the Department of printed Books.

The Truſtees of the Britiſh Muſeum, having ſucceeded in providing for the Publick a Reading-room ſuperiour in its Conſtruction and Appointments to all other Buildings of the ſame Claſs, have wiſely placed its Management in the Hands of one of the chief Officers of the Library, who, in addition to his general Duties, is charged with the ſpecial Duty of aſſiſting the Readers in their Reſearches. This Gentleman, poſſeſſing a large Store of miſcellaneous Information, an extenſive

Acquaintance with the Languages and Literature of modern Europe, and an intimate Knowledge of the Contents of the Library, is eminently qualified to difcharge the Duties confided to him to the great Advantage of the Readers.

The Preffes under the Gallery are filled with a large Library of reference Books for the Ufe of the Readers, comprifing moft of the ftandard Works on the various Branches of Learning, and an extenfive Collection of Dictionaries of all Languages, biographical Works, Encyclopedias, parliamentary Hiftories, topographical Works, &c., &c. Thefe Books, which are about 40,000 in Number, are regarded as "indifpenfably neceffary to Students of all Denominations." They can be confulted at pleafure, without the Trouble of filling up Tickets, as for other Books. A Catalogue of a Portion of them is given in Sims's Hand-book, to which reference has already been made.

The Reading Room is open, with the Exception of Holidays, &c., from 9 till 4 in the Months of November, December, January, and February; from 9 till 5 in the Months of September, October, March, and April; and from 9 till 6 in the Months of May, June, July and Auguft, except on Saturdays when it clofes at 5. The Number of Readers for the Year 1856, was 53,209, or an Average of 181 per Diem; the Number of Volumes read or confulted, was 344,358, or 1175 per Diem. The Britifh Mufeum is open to publick View on Mondays, Wednefdays, and Fridays, from 10 till 4 during January, February, November, and December; from 10 till 5 during March, April, September, and Oċtober; and from 10 till 6 during May, June, July, and Auguſt.

As a Sequel to this Account of the Library and Reading-room of the Britiſh Muſeum, the following excellent Article, giving Details of their daily Management, will be found to be exceedingly uſeful, ſuggeſting to every intelligent Librarian invaluable Arrangements, even for Libraries of the moſt limited Extent. It is taken from the May Number of the North Britiſh Review for 1851. The Buſineſs of the Library is claſſed under three Heads—Acquiſitions, Catalogues, and Arrangement; to which are added, Service of the Reading-room, Regiſtration, Binding, &c.

I. Acquisitions.

Books enter the Muſeum Library by three Channels, viz: by Copyright, by Purchaſe, and by Preſentation. By the recent copyright Aċt an Advantage is conferred upon the Britiſh Muſeum which is not enjoyed by the other four Libraries of publick Depoſit; that is to ſay, the Muſeum is not obliged to demand Works, but the London Publiſhers are bound to deliver their Books within one Month of Publication, and thoſe reſiding in the Country within three. For the Reception of Works ſo delivered, an Office is fitted up where a Perſon is in conſtant Attendance to give the neceſſary Receipts. Theſe Receipts are drawn up on a printed Form, the Particulars peculiar to each Work—ſuch as the Title, Number of the Volume, Size, Date, Place of Printing, and Publication, &c.—being filled up in Duplicate by Wedgwood's Manifold Writer. Of this Receipt the Duplicate is kept by the Muſeum, and thus forms not only a Check upon the Publiſher, but alſo upon the Receiver, and a Regiſter of the Receipts under the copyright Act.

In the Library everything is ſyſtematized as much as poſſible; the Conſequence is, that little Time is loſt in giving Directions. Every one knows his Duty, and knows at the ſame Time that he muſt perform it. There are two Peculiarities in Mr. Panizzi's Arrangements; one is, that each Part is made to depend more or leſs upon the Reſt, ſo that Derangement in one Quarter is ſure to be felt in another, and thus Neglect is at once detected. The other is, that, wherever it is poſſible, one Proceſs is made to anſwer two or three Purpoſes. The Mode of giving Receipts is one Inſtance of the latter Peculiarity, and we ſhall have Occaſion to point out others as we proceed.

Purchaſes are effected either by direct Orders, or in the Way of Selection from Books ſent in for Approval. This Duty reſts ſolely with the Keeper of the Department, who alone is authorized to decide in the firſt Inſtance what Works ſhall be added to the Collection. The Truſtees, however, poſſeſs a Veto upon the Purchaſe of even the ſmalleſt Work. All Parcels of Books are accompanied by an Invoice. The Contents of each Parcel are checked by the Invoice, and then examined by the Keeper, who makes his Selection— rejecting all ſuch as he thinks it inexpedient to purchaſe either on the Ground of Price or Condition. The Invoice is then corrected, by ſtriking out from it all ſuch as have been ſo rejected; and the Books retained are handed over to an Attendant in order that the Catalogues may be ſearched for the Purpoſe of aſcertaining that the Books propoſed to be retained are not already in the Library. When this Proceſs has been carefully gone through, and the Invoice again weeded, by ſtriking out all ſuch as are found to be already in the Collection, a Bill is made out by the Bookſeller from the Invoice as finally corrected, and the Books retained are again compared with the Bill, which is ſubmitted to the Keeper a few Days before a Meeting of the Truſtees. At the Foot of the Bill, the Keeper writes an Order for Payment, and the Bill ſo ſubſcribed is laid before the Truſtees, and, if approved by them, they make their Order authorizing Payment.

In the Caſe of Books which from their extreme Rarity, from being printed on Vellum, or from any other Cauſe, do not come within the Claſs of ordinary Acceſſions to a Library, a ſpecial Report from the Keeper of the Department, is required by the Truſtees, ſtating the Grounds upon which it is conſidered adviſable that the Article in queſtion ſhould be added to the Collection. Theſe Reports are not mere Matters of Form. A Collection of ſuch Documents would prove a moſt curious and valuable Addition to bibliographical Literature. The Truſtees, although actuated by a liberal Spirit in this Reſpect, occaſionally exerciſe their Power of Rejection. But it muſt be preſumed that the Recommendation of their Officers always has great Weight, the Truſtees being well aware that the Deſirableneſs or Non-deſirableneſs of an Object muſt be judged of in Connexion with the particular Collection to which it is propoſed that it ſhould be added, and not upon its own individual Merits. For this Reaſon it is, that no Work can be conſidered too coſtly for the Britiſh Muſeum Library, provided the Price be not exceſſive. The Art of Printing has its Hiſtory, like every other Art, and its Hiſtory requires Illuſtration, like the Hiſtory of every other Art. The Hiſtory of Printing is the Hiſtory of civil and religious Freedom. When Providence determined that mental Darkneſs ſhould be removed, Man was made the Worker-out of his own Emancipation, by the Inſpiration of the Diſcovery of Printing. This was a ſecond Creation of Light. If we give to the Hiſtory of Printing the Importance it really poſſeſſes, and regard great Libraries, like that of the Britiſh Muſeum, as the Depoſitories of the Evidences of its miraculous Progreſs and Effects—then a Fragment of a Donatus, a Caxton, an early Edition of a Bible, a firſt Edition of a Claſſick, or the firſt Productions of the Printing Preſs in the United States, Mexico,

California, Auſtralia, or the Sandwich Iſlands, ceaſe to be Curioſities, and take their deſervedly prominent Place in the Hiſtory of Civilization.

In ſelecting the Acceſſions to be made to the Library of the Britiſh Muſeum, this Illuſtration of the Paſt has been kept conſtantly in View, at the ſame Time that every Effort has been made to give the current Literature of all Countries a Place on the Shelves of the Inſtitution. It muſt not be aſſumed that every, or indeed any Claſs is perfect. For ſuch a Conſummation two Conditions are indiſpenſable—unlimited Funds, and unlimited Space. An Approximation might be made to the firſt Requiſite, for to the Honour of Parliament in general, and of Mr. Hume in particular, be it ſpoken, every Diſpoſition has been ſhown to make Grants in the moſt liberal Spirit. But Space is another Queſtion. Walls of five Feet in Thickneſs are not of rapid Growth; and if they were, Bedford Square and Upper Montague Place exerciſe a rather powerful Veto upon any very extenſive Ramification. We have, however, great Reliance upon the Reſources and Energy of the preſent Keeper of the printed Books, upon the Readineſs of the principal Librarian to ſupport, and of the Truſtees to adopt any Suggeſtion for the Improvement of the noble Inſtitution the Affairs of which they adminiſter; and we do not deſpair to ſee the Library repreſent in a complete Form, not only the ſcientifick and polite Literature of the United Kingdom, but of the whole World.

Presented Works are laid before the Trustees at the monthly Meetings, and Thanks ordered in the usual Manner in such Cases.

The next Process is to attach to each Part or Volume a Mark by which it shall be distinguished as the Property of the Museum. This is now effected by impressing at the Beginning of the Book the Museum Stamp, and at the End the Date of the Day, Month and Year, when the Bill was signed for Payment by the Keeper of the Library. We have before observed that whenever it is practicable, one Process is always made to subserve more Purposes than one—and this Stamping of the Books is another Instance of it. It is a Proof in the first Place that the Book has been paid for, and is thus in every Sense the Property of the Trustees; and, secondly, the Bills being kept in chronological Order, Reference can be immediately made to them from any Book of which it may be desired to ascertain the Price, or of whom purchased.

Books obtained by Copyright are stamped in like Manner by the Person who receives them.

Ink of three different Colours is used in stamping Books, for the three different Modes of Acquisition—red, indicating that a Book was purchased; blue, that it came by Copyright; and yellow, that it was presented.

II. Catalogues.

Having thus ſhewn how Books are acquired and ſtamped, we ſhall now proceed to the important Detail of Cataloguing. And here we muſt beg our Readers not to be alarmed by this awful Word *Cataloguing*—a Word ſuggeſtive of laborious Reſearch and mechanical Care and Preciſion to an Extent ſuſpected by few. It is far from our Intention to enter into the Subject of claſſed and alphabetical Catalogues, or to attempt to decide the Queſtion between long and ſhort Titles. Theſe are Matters which have already been productive of too many Scratches and hard Knocks to haſty Volunteers in this dangerous Field.

For the Purpoſe of forming the Catalogue, ſeveral Gentlemen poſſeſſing peculiar Qualifications are employed in the Library. All are Linguiſts to a conſiderable Extent, ſome poſſeſſing this Accompliſhment in a more than ordinary Degree. In a Library like that of the Britiſh Muſeum, where the Literature of every Country in the World, and of every Age is repreſented, it is of courſe the Duty of the Authorities to ſee that there ſhall be found in it Perſons capable of deſcribing Works of ſuch varied Character. This Duty has not been neglected. One Cataloguer attends ſolely to the Chineſe Books; another when requiſite to Oriental Works; a third to Hebrew and rabbinical Literature; a fourth devotes his Attention to the Maps; a fifth, in addition to other Duties, catalogues the

Mufick and Slavonick Works; while Books in Latin, Greek, French, Italian, Spanifh, Portuguefe, German, Dutch, Danifh, and Swedifh, find ready Hands for regiftering their Contents.

Great Efforts are made to fecure Uniformity of Plan in cataloguing, fo far as that moft defirable Object is attainable. For this Purpofe a Code of Rules has been drawn up, and revifed and fanctioned by the Truftees. Objections have been brought againft thefe Rules on the Ground of their Number and Minutenefs; but as no Objector has yet fhewn how fix Perfons can be brought to catalogue in one and the fame Manner, Books which may be catalogued fix different Ways, unlefs they are told which of the fix Ways they are to follow, we think we are at Liberty to adopt the Views fo fully explained by Mr. Panizzi in his Evidence before the Commiffioners on the Britifh Mufeum, wherein he brings his own matured Experience to bear with overwhelming Force upon the Fancies of his Opponents.

When a Book is catalogued it is paffed over to a Revifer, whofe Duty it is to fee that all the Rules laid down for cataloguing have been duly obferved. This is a Work of no flight Labour and Refponfibility, and it is intrufted to thofe only who have had great Experience, and have fhewn much Care and Skill as Cataloguers. This may be regarded as an Excefs of Caution, but it has been found advifable in Practice. It is evident that there will occur Differences of Opinion in the Interpretation of Rules, however clearly and ſtrictly worded, and that when ſeveral Perſons work independently of each other, although under the ſame Rules, Diſcrepancies will be found which muſt be reconciled. This is one of the chief Duties of the Reviſers. The Keeper of the Department is the ultimate Referee in all Caſes of Difficulty. Theſe Diſcrepancies occur moſt frequently in the Titles of anonymous Works; and we muſt here give in our Adheſion to the Opinion expreſſed by more than one Witneſs before the Commiſſioners, viz., that there ſhould be one ſimple and uniform Rule, for cataloguing anonymous Books; the firſt Word or the firſt Subſtantive of the Title is better than any other, becauſe it is more ſimple than any other; but let there be one Rule—let that Rule be one that can be uniformly adopted, and let there be plenty of Croſs-references from what are termed leading Words of the Title; as Croſs-references theſe leading Words enable us to find the Book, but they only lead us aſtray in Proportion to their Number, when one is ſelected for the main Entry of the Work.

III. Arrangement.

The Books being catalogued and reviſed, the next Care is to arrange them on the Shelves. This is a very important Proceſs, and one the Execution of which requires a vaſt amount of general Information, and a Knowledge of not leſs than twelve Languages. In the Library of the Muſeum the Objection to Classification extends no farther than to the Catalogue. The Books are arranged in six great Classes, viz: 1. Religion. 2. Jurisprudence. 3. Philosophy. 4. Arts and Trades. 5. History. 6. Literature. The Subdivisions under each of these Classes are strictly and even minutely observed. We regret that our limited Space forbids our entering more into Detail upon this Branch of our Subject, as it is one of great Interest and Utility, and is that Part of the Arrangement of the Library which is far from being the least creditable to the Gentlemen engaged in carrying it out.

The Library is divided into Presses, each of which has a Number; the Shelves of each Press are distinguished by a Letter of the Alphabet, and the Place of each Book on a Shelf is indicated by a Number; thus, 573 c 13, means the thirteenth Book on the third or c Shelf of Press 573. When the present Library was erected, the Numbers of the Presses were carried on from those of the King's Library, and when a supplementary Room to the new Library was built, the Numbers were again carried on, thus forming a regular Series from 1 to 1618. A natural Consequence of this Arrangement has been that the same Class of Books will be found in more Places than one, it being evident that when all the spare Room left between one Class and another has been filled up, a fresh Locality must be assigned to subsequent Acquisitions in the same Class. In order to avoid this Inconvenience as far as poſſible, a new Plan has been introduced into a ſupplementary Library recently erected. The Numbers of the Preſſes are no longer in immediate Sequence, thus—ſuppoſing the firſt Preſs to be numbered 2000, and that the Works under the Claſs Religion occupy two Preſſes, twenty Numbers may neverthleſs be allotted to this Claſs.

The firſt three Numbers would then be 2000, 2001, 2020. When a third Preſs was required for theological Works, inſtead of placing them in another Part of the Library, the Books in the Preſs called 2020, together with its Number, would be moved on to the next Preſs, and the Preſs occupied by 2020 would be called 2002. By this Proceſs all the Works belonging to one Claſs may be kept together for a longer Period than was practicable under the old Syſtem. This Arrangement involves two indiſpenſable Conditions, viz: plenty of Room and that all the Preſſes ſhould be exactly of the ſame Size. This is called the expanſive Syſtem.

An expanſive Syſtem, but of a different Character, has alſo been applied to the periodical Publications, and to the Maps. This Plan conſiſts in attaching a Number to the Book or Map, but not to the Locality in which it is placed; the Numbers in theſe Inſtances, alſo, not being in immediate Sequence. Thus the Periodicals may be marked 1, 5, 10, 15, 20, &c., leaving the Intervals to be filled up by future Acquiſitions; the Advantage of which is, that thoſe of a particular Character and

Country can be kept together, without interfering with the Sequence of Numbers.

The Maps, requiring more minute Claſſification alſo, demand a more complicated Syſtem of marking. The following is the Mode adopted: The Collection is arranged geographically. All the folded Maps, compriſing almoſt the entire Collection, are kept in light millboard Caſes, ſomewhat reſembling ſolander Caſes. Maps of the World, of the great Diviſions of the Globe, and of particular Countries or Localities, form what are termed Claſſes, and no two Claſſes are allowed to be placed in the ſame Caſe. Theſe Claſſes are numbered, but not in regular Sequence, Intervals being left for additional Claſſes. Maps of the ſame Claſs are arranged in the Caſes chronologically, and numbered, but not in regular Sequence, Intervals being left greater or ſmaller according to the Date to be provided for; thus, fewer Numbers are left open between 1500 and 1600 than between 1600 and 1700, it being very properly conſidered that the Acceſſion of Maps printed in the ſeventeenth Century will be much larger than of thoſe printed in the ſixteenth.

The Books, when catalogued and reviſed, are ſorted into their ſeveral Claſſes and Subdiviſions; theſe Parcels ſo ſorted are carried to their reſpective Localities, and arranged on their proper Shelves, the Titles remaining in the Books. When the Books are placed, an Attendant marks the Books and their reſpective Titles with the Preſs-mark proper to each, throwing each Title as he marks it into a box. When the Book is marked the next Proceſs is to attach the Preſs-mark to the Back of it. Theſe Preſs-marks are printed on Paper of various Tints, to match the different coloured Leathers uſed in Binding. They are printed in large Sheets and cut out with a Stamp of an oval Shape. The Number of the Preſs is attached to the upper Part of the Back of the Book, the Mark for the Shelf, and Number of the Shelf, to the lower Part of the Back. This Plan ſaves a great Deal of Time. Before its Introduction, the Place of a Book could not be aſcertained without opening it—now it is only neceſſary to look at the Back, and its proper Locality is ſeen at once. Another Advantage is, that if a Book be placed by Accident into the wrong Preſs or on the wrong Shelf, the Miſtake is ſure to be detected.

The Titles, when marked as above deſcribed, are ſent to the Superintendent of the Tranſcribers, whoſe Duty it is to ſee that all the Titles are duly entered in the Catalogues, and to reviſe the Entries ſo made, in order that there may be no Blunders in the Tranſcript. Theſe Duties of Tranſcription and Reviſion demand a conſiderable Acquaintance with Languages in the Tranſcribers, and, more eſpecially in the Reviſer. It is evident that the latter muſt be familiar with all the Languages known by the whole Body of Tranſcribers. The Proceſs of inſerting Titles in the Catalogue is ſo peculiar, that we feel ourſelves juſtified in going ſomewhat into Detail in deſcribing it. Each Maſs of Titles is, in the firſt Place, ſeparated into Engliſh and Foreign. Each of theſe Sets is then arranged in alphabetical Order, and incorporated with thoſe which may have already been accumulated for Tranſcription. When the Titles are to be copied, they are diſtributed among the Tranſcribers according to the Languages each may beſt underſtand. This Tranſcription is not made into the Catalogue, but into a Book, the Leaves of which conſiſt of the thineſt Paper, prepared for Wedgwood's Proceſs of manifold Writing. Four Tranſcripts are taken at once, carbonic Paper being placed between the firſt and ſecond Sheet, and the third and fourth. Each Tranſcriber uſes two Books, by which Arrangement the Superintendent is enabled to collate with the original Title-ſlip the Work of each Day, without ſtopping the Tranſcribers, who continue the Tranſcription in the Book not under Reviſion. Theſe Books, as they are filled and reviſed, are handed over to the Binder, who mounts each Leaf upon one of rather ſtronger Paper. Theſe Leaves when dried are ſubjected to enormous Preſſure. Each four duplicate Sheets are then pinned upon a Board and cut into Slips between each Title. We now have the Tranſcription on ſeparate Slips, the four Duplicates being kept together. The next Proceſs is to arrange them in their proper Order, and incorporate them with the Maſs of Titles (if any) already prepared and arranged for Infertion in the Catalogue. When the Infertion is to be made, the tranfcribed Titles are divided into Parcels according to the Letters contained in each Volume of the Catalogue, and then each Title is marked with a Number, and a correfponding Number marked in the Place in the Catalogue the Title is to occupy. Each Volume of the Catalogue fo fupplied with Titles is then handed over to two Binders, one of whom paftes the upper and lower Edge of each Title and hands it to his Companion, who inferts it into the Catalogue—the two Ends of each Title being left open. When it becomes neceffary to fhift one of thefe Titles, in order to preferve the ftrict alphabetical Arrangement, a Paper-knife is inferted into the open End, and the Title is removed without difficulty. The Slip upon which the Tranfcription is made being mounted upon another, any Abrafion which may occur from this Procefs affects not the Slip written upon, but only that upon which it is mounted.

Should a thicker Paper be introduced, and the Procefs of mounting be difcontinued, this Advantage will of courfe be loft. Before we quit the Subject of Tranfcribing, we will mention a ftriking Fact connected with the Expenfe of this Branch of the Management. It appears from the Evidence of Mr. Panizzi before the Mufeum Commiffioners, that at one Time the Tranfcribers were paid at the Rate of one Penny per Title. Under the prefent Syftem, this fame Item amounts to about three-fourths of one Farthing per Title, or three-fixteenths of the former Charge; in other Words, the ſame Amount of Work which formerly coſt four Pounds, is now obtained for about fifteen Shillings.

When the Title of a Work is entered in the Catalogue, the Work may be ſaid to be then at the Command of the Readers; we believe, however, that we are juſtified in ſtating, that at no Time has a Reader been denied the Uſe of a Book merely becauſe the Title had not appeared in the Catalogue.

IV. Reading Room.

The Service of the Reading-room, like every other Service in the Department, is ſyſtematized. We have already given the Hiſtory of a Book from the Shelves of the Bookſeller to thoſe of the Muſeum; we will now give the Hiſtory of a Book from the Shelves of the Muſeum to the Handsof a Reader, and back to its Shelf again.

The Readers are provided with blank Tickets, on which they write the Preſs-mark, Title, very ſhortly, Size, Place, and Date of the Book they want, the Date of the Application and Signature of the Reader being ſubſcribed. Theſe Tickets are handed to an Attendant who ſits at a Bar which ſeparates the Reading-rooms from the Library. The Tickets are paſſed by him into the Library, where they are placed on a Table in the Order in which they are delivered from the Reading-rooms. The Attendants, whoſe Duty it is to ſupply the Readers with Books, take theſe Tickets in the Order in which they are received, no one being at Liberty to ſelect a Ticket, unleſs it be for a Book which ſtands near to one he is about to fetch. To each of theſe Attendants a Number is attached, regulated originally by the Order of the initial Letter of his Name in the Alphabet, and each Attendant is alſo furniſhed with, ſay, 200 Pieces of Millboard, the Ends being covered with red roan Leather, on the Edge of which the Number of the Attendant is ſtamped, and on the Side the Number of the Board, theſe Boards being numbered in regular Sequence, from one up to as many as the Attendant has. When a Book is taken from a Shelf, the Attendant puts one of his Boards in its Place, taking Care to uſe them in their regular Order, that is, having once uſed, ſay, No. 10, he will keep that back until he has gone through all his Boards and come round to 10 again. Each Attendant is alſo provided with a Book filled with blank Leaves. When he has taken from the Shelf a Book for a Reader, he marks in Pencil on the Back of the reader's Ticket the Number of the Board he has left in its Place. He then enters in his Book, in one Line, firſt the Preſs-mark of the Book, the Name of the Reader, and his own Number, and the Number of his Board; and then in the ſame Line the Preſs-mark again, the Name of the Author or firſt Word of the Title of the Book, the Size, Place, and Date, the Name of the Reader, and the Number of his Board.

When the Work has been entered by the Attendant, it is placed on the Bar which ſeparates the Library from the Reading-room, whence it is taken by one of the Attendants in the Reading-rooms, and delivered to the Reader. The Attendant who ſo delivers it then writes on the Ticket the Letter D (meaning delivered), and hands it to the Attendant we have before mentioned as ſtationed at the Bar, who depoſits it in one of a Set of Pigeon-holes fixed beneath the Bar under the initial Letter of the Reader's Name. The Reader is reſponſible for the Book ſpecified on his Ticket ſo long as the Ticket remains in the Poſſeſſion of the Authorities of the Library. When a Reader has no longer Occaſion for a Work, he returns it to the Attendant at the Bar, who delivers to him his Ticket in exchange, having firſt compared the Work with the Ticket, in order to ſee that all is returned that is ſpecified upon it.

The Books ſo returned are placed on a Table and ſorted according to their Preſs-marks, for the Purpoſe of being reſtored to their reſpective Places on the following Morning.

It frequently occurs that a Reader is deſirous of uſing the ſame Book from Day to Day. When this is the Caſe he writes his Name on a Slip of Paper and places it with the Books, which are then depoſited in Cloſets fitted up with ſliding Shelves for this eſpecial Purpoſe. The Utility of this Plan may be appreciated from the Fact, that every Year nearly 100,000 Volumes are in this Manner laid aſide for continuous Uſe by the

Readers. The consequent saving of Time and Labour is immense. It must not be imagined, however, that through this Process a Reader can insure to himself a Monopoly of any Work. The Maxim "first come first served," is strictly adhered to. Should a Reader apply for a Work so set aside before the Person for whose Use it is kept presents himself to claim it, it is transferred, as it is termed, to the new Reader. This Process consists in entering the Work in the usual Form, but in a particular Book and in red Ink. These Entries are made by an Attendant whose Duty it is to take Charge of the Closets, and also to see that the readers' Tickets are actively and properly attended to.

Every Attendant writes in his Book the Day of the Month at the Commencement of the Entries of each Day. At the End of the Day he cuts between each Line of Entries as far as his own Number. The Books of all the Attendants are then taken away by the Bookbinder, whose Duty it is to cut off all the Entries as far as they have been cut through by the respective Attendants, to arrange them all into one Series according to their Press-marks, and paste them into a Book, heading each Day's Work with the Date, and writing at the End the Number of these Dockets. This forms a daily Register of all the Readers who have written for Books.

Every Morning the Books returned from the Reading-rooms on the previous Day are carried to the ſeveral Parts of the Library to which they reſpectively belong. Two Attendants then go round with the Regiſter of ſhort Entries or Dockets above referred to, and while one puts each Work on the Shelf, and calls out the Preſs-mark, the other calls out the Number of the Attendant he finds in the Regiſter, whoſe Board is then removed, and the Docket is ſtamped in red Ink, with the Date when the Book is returned; thus, 18 3 51, indicating that the Work was reſtored to its Place on the 18th of March, 1851.

All this will doubtleſs appear complicated and confuſed to our Readers; and it may by ſome be conſidered that Refinement and Minuteneſs of Detail had been carried too far. In the actual working of the Scheme, however, there is neither Complication nor Confuſion. Every Effort is made to economize Time and Labour, but without ſacrificing that Care or giving up thoſe Checks which are abſolutely indiſpenſable in the Management of a large publick Library. A Compariſon of the annual Returns of former Years, with thoſe of more recent Date, will ſhew with what vaſt Rapidity the Labours of the Department have been extended, and to how great a Degree of Perfection the Syſtem of ſtatiſtical Detail has been carried.

V. Registration.

The Contents of every Bill is analyzed; that is to ſay, the Number of Volumes, of Parts of Volumes, of Maps, and of Sheets of Maps, are taken out and entered in a Book in their reſpective Columns. The ſame is done with Objects preſented. At the End of the Year theſe Columns are caſt up, and it is immediately known what has been the Number of Articles procured during the Year through theſe Channels reſpectively.

The duplicate Receipts kept by the Receiver of Works under the copyright Act give the ſame Information for this Branch of the Acquiſitions.

The Regiſter ſhews the Number of Books returned to the Shelves, every Day. A Book kept by the Attendant who has Charge of the Cloſets affords ſimilar Details reſpecting the Number of Books kept for the Readers from Day to Day.

Every Cataloguer regiſters daily, in a Book kept by himſelf, the Number of Titles written by him; the Aggregate of theſe Books gives the Number of Titles written in the Department during any Period.

Reviſers and Tranſcribers keep ſimilar Accounts.

One of the Superintendents of the Reading-rooms regiſters the Number of Viſits made daily to the Reading-rooms, and reports the Total, at the End of the Year, to the Keeper of the Department of printed Works. A ſimilar Account is kept in the readers' Lobby; but as this latter Account makes no Diſtinction between thoſe who come to read and thoſe who may paſs into the Reading-rooms for other Purpoſes, Diſcrepancies may occur, and in the Returns for the Year 1850 actually did occur, between the two Accounts.

The Refult of all this is, that in the Courfe of a few Hours an exact and minute Return can be given of everything done in the Department during the Year, or any other given Period, the whole forming an Array of Numbers truly ftartling.

We have before obferved that one Procefs, whenever it is poffible, is made to fubferve feveral Objects. We have fhewn how the Receipts for Books delivered under the copyright Act anfwer not only the ordinary Purpofe of a Receipt, but alfo of a Regifter of fuch Books.

The readers' Regifter fhews at one Glance how many Books were fent to the Reading-rooms on a particular Day, the Day any Book was removed from the Shelves, for whom it was taken, by whom it was taken, the particular Board left for it, and when it was returned. Each attendant's Regifter fhews what Books he removed from the Shelves on a particular Day, for whom, and the Number of his Board; while the Board on the Shelves fhews what Attendant removed the Book, and by its Number points to the particular Entry in his Regifter. By Means of this Syftem a Book can be traced regularly through any Number of Hands for any Length of Time, and Faults in the reading-room Service can in like Manner always be traced to the guilty Party.

VI. Binding.

The Binding of Books forms a very important Item in the Economy of a publick Library. The great Deſideratum for the Maſs of Books is Strength and Durability at the leaſt poſſible Expenſe. In a Library like that of the Britiſh Muſeum, it may well be imagined, there is abundant Opportunity for teſting the various Styles of Binding and Kinds of Leather, ſo as to arrive at the moſt correct Judgment upon this Point. The general Plan now adopted is as follows: All Dictionaries to be full bound in Ruſſia. Other Works likely to be in frequent Uſe to be half-bound in Morocco, with cloth Sides. Two or more Volumes of the ſame Work are always bound together where their Bulk will permit it. Pamphlets are half-bound in Roan, with paper Sides. Experience has ſhewn that this Plan is in every Reſpect the moſt economical that could be adopted. Different Colours are uſed according to the Subject of the Book, thus, *red* for Hiſtory, *green* for Botany, *blue* for Theology, &c.

In the Library of the Britiſh Muſeum, as in other large Libraries, certain Works conſidered to be ſelect, are ſet apart from the Reſt and preſerved with greater Care. Among theſe are ſeveral remarkable for their Bindings, which are arranged ſo as to illuſtrate as far as practicable the Styles of different Schools, Engliſh, French, Italian, &c. The preſent Keeper of the Department, looking upon Bookbinding as ſomething more than the Art of ſtitching loofe Sheets neatly into a Cover, has endeavoured, in binding rare and valuable Books, to follow the grand Example fet by Grolier, Majoli, De Thou, and others, and would fain give an Individuality to the Drefs of his Protégés. In fome Inftances the Succefs has been great. A good Bookbinder ought to be a Man of great Tafte, and an Artift. All ufe Flowers and Studs and Fillets; but what Flowers were ever fo graceful as the Flowers of Roger Payne? who has ever fprinkled his Studs as he fprinkled them? who can not immediately recognize Lewis's fimple Fillet, fo beautifully true? The German Style of Tooling at the End of the 15th Century was heavy, but it was blind, and the Effect, confequently, was maffive and grand. German Tooling at the prefent Day is no lefs heavy, but it is no longer blind, but in Gold; and the Effect is no longer maffive and grand, but vulgar. The Materials are there, but the artiftic Tafte is wanting.

But we are diverging into a Differtation upon Bookbinding. By the Statutes of the Britifh Mufeum, no Object is allowed to be removed from the Premifes. This Regulation involves the Neceffity of having a Bookbinder attached to the Eftablifhment. When Books are removed from the Shelves for the Purpofe of being bound or repaired, a Board fimilar to thofe above defcribed as ufed by the Attendants is left in its Place. On this Board the letter B is ftamped, indicating that the Book is in the Hands of the Binder. The Books fo fent are entered by an Aſſiſtant in what is termed the binder's Book, a Margin being left on both Sides. In that on the left the Binder writes the Preſs-mark of the Book, in that on the right Mr. Panizzi writes Directions as to the Manner in which the Book is to be bound or repaired. The Entry of each Batch of Books is dated and ſigned by the Binder, and when returned each Entry is ſtamped with the Date. The Signature makes the Binder reſponſible for the Books, the Stamp is his Diſcharge. The Date at the Head and the Stamp on the Entry ſhew how long he has kept each Book. The Entries alſo are made in the Form to be obſerved for the lettering Piece on the Back of the Book, and this is again an Inſtance of one Proceſs ſerving a double Purpoſe.

We will only mention one Point more; all the Shelves upon which large and heavy or handſomely bound Books are placed are lined with hard and ſmooth Leather. This ſimple Proceſs tends greatly to preſerve the Binding.

INDEX.

PART FIRST.

BIBLIOGRAPHY.

NOTE.—The Figures refer to the Pages of the Manual.

Nn

PART SECOND.

LIBRARIES.

NOTE.—The Index to this Part conſiſts chiefly of Names, the Titles of Books being omitted.

Printed by J. Munſell, 78 State Street, Albany, N. Y.

www.ingramcontent.com/pod-product-compliance
Lightning Source LLC
LaVergne TN
LVHW020230110826
845151LV00003B/882